Library of
Davidson College

The Experience of Modernity

The Experience of Modernity

*Chinese Autobiography of the
Early Twentieth Century*

Janet Ng

THE UNIVERSITY OF MICHIGAN PRESS   Ann Arbor

Copyright © by the University of Michigan 2003
All rights reserved
Published in the United States of America by
The University of Michigan Press
Manufactured in the United States of America
∞ Printed on acid-free paper

2006   2005   2004   2003   4   3   2   1

No part of this publication may be reproduced,
stored in a retrieval system, or transmitted in any form
or by any means, electronic, mechanical, or otherwise,
without the written permission of the publisher.

*A CIP catalog record for this book is available
from the British Library.*

Library of Congress Cataloging-in-Publication Data applied for
ISBN 0-472-09821-7

Contents

Preface vii
Acknowledgments xiii

Introduction *1*

Chapter One
A New Strategy for Autobiographical Narratives
Chen Hengzhe's Writing of Aurality 21

Chapter Two
Fragmented Subjectivities
A Reconsideration of Women's Literary Mirrors 41

Chapter Three
Nationalism and the Gestural System of Self-Expression
69

Chapter Four
Names and Destiny
*Hu Shi's and Lu Xun's Self-Nomination
through Autobiography 91*

Chapter Five
A Moral Landscape
*Reading Shen Congwen's Autobiography
and Travelogues 119*

Conclusion *145*

Notes 151
Bibliography 175
Index 189

Preface

Autobiography as a literary form is both distinct in its characteristics and undefined as a genre. The many paradoxical elements in autobiography, its simultaneous claims to facticity and subjectivity, honesty and pretense, history and fiction, are precisely what make autobiography attractive to writers and intriguing to readers. It was one of the most widely used literary forms in China in the few decades following World War I. During the cultural, linguistic, and political reform movement known as May Fourth, almost all writers, well known and less known, wrote some form of autobiography.

The autobiographic impulse in the literature of this period has been variously explained as the discovery of psychology, the new recognition of individualism, or the result of stylistic influence from Western literary schools, especially expressionism and romanticism. Emphasis has always been placed on the influence of the West in the development of modern Chinese autobiography. Without doubt, May Fourth intellectuals were extremely curious and enthusiastic about learning from the West (that is, England, France, and Germany), but also Japan, Russia, and eastern Europe. However, discussions of influence may tell us little about the political and social conditions of the "reception sites" that make certain trends congenial. It also does not explain to what ends foreign materials are used once transported to these sites. While I do not belittle the importance of foreign influence on May Fourth literature, my discussion is focused on the question of why certain methods of writing became predominant and how they functioned in the political and social context of twentieth-century China. Why did the first-person monologue, which was the basis of autobiographical writing, become such a predominant style of writing at the time? Why did the highly sentimental and melodramatic confessions that we often associate with expressionism become a preferred style in the story of the individual and the nation? Why did some writers give up the conventional teleological program of storytelling in narrating modern experience? In this study, autobiography as a formal, textual strategy is sociological and political, even if the content is personal.

Formal changes in literature are related to the semiotics of the times, which are, in turn, conditioned by historical and political events. For this reason, my discussion of autobiography starts with the May Fourth language reform that began in 1917. Simply put, the movement was about promoting the use of the vernacular in writing. May Fourth reformers believed that through literature, new ideas could be conveyed to the common people. They considered the *wenyan* (classical, written language) that had dominated literary writing elitist and backward, since it could only be read by the small number of educated people, all of whom were trained in the classical curriculum that upheld, to the new reformers, old-fashioned ideals. But May Fourth changed more than the basis of writing. Language reform was more than simply a matter of semantics. It caused a shift in perception and with it, a shift in the concept of realness. This necessitated new strategies of representation. Interest in autobiographical strategies is a direct result of these new developments of perception and language.

May Fourth is now a general designation for a period defined by literary experimentation, social reforms, and patriotism. All of these developments were responses to China's political turmoil. Internally, China was plagued by warlords. Externally, it was in a semicolonial relationship with Europe, America, and Japan. This chaos culminated in 1937 when Japan launched an all-out war against China. May Fourth—a name that derives from anticolonial demonstrations on that date in 1919—is very much the intellectuals' response to China's political problems, for writing was an important way to participate in the political life of the society and nation. In fact the literary reform propagated by the May Fourth movement reinvigorates the late-nineteenth-century notion that the root of China's weakness is the ignorance of the masses, and that literature has a moral function, to educate them and lift them out of their ignorance. This didactic view of the function of literature influences our expectations and reading of the writings from this period even today. Because of this lingering predisposition to view May Fourth literature as political and didactic, autobiography, conventionally regarded as self-indulgent and egoistic, is often ignored despite its connection to the language reform advocated and practiced by May Fourth writers.

In the patriotic fervor of the 1920s and the wartime and revolutionary austerities of the 1930s and 1940s, the grand rhetoric of nationalism, personal stories and individual expressions seem to have no place. For this reason, autobiography's popularity during this era is an odd phenomenon. Nevertheless, we should not proceed as if the phenomenon did not exist. Because of the popularity of autobiography as a form, its consistent neglect in the literary studies of May Fourth, based on facile assumptions about the genre, impoverish our understanding of the era. To understand the practice of autobiography and the autobiographical impulse of this period, one needs to examine the notion of the individual as a sociological and political category and not a psychological one. With this perspective, we can understand that the personal and the political are not mutually contradictory.

Writers who emphasize their own stories have been accused of egotism, sentimentalism, or, euphemistically, "romanticism." Rather than dismiss their voices as stylistic peculiarities, however, it is more productive to examine them as politically motivated strategies. Autobiography not only is an efficient way to narrate the nation, as an allegory of the nation, but also a sensitive measure of social changes. It is often only through the personal, even physical, accounts of the individual that the health of the nation is revealed. Autobiography is a form that articulates the case of the individual as well as the nation. It fulfills an intellectual's sense of engagement and mission while providing an outlet for creativity and expression.

In the title of this book is the ever-contentious word *modernity*, of which there can be no straightforward definition. I use this term primarily as a temporal marker to bracket a particular era in which literature undergoes a significant transformation. At the same time, there is no doubt that modern autobiographies are uniquely descriptive of the modern sensibility and modern concerns.

Premodern autobiographies have been habitually read as a form of history. But autobiography can be more revealing of the time and place in which it is written than accurate about the events and times it narrates. The autobiographical impulse arises from the response to one's immediate society, even if that response is nostalgia for, or justification or legitimization of, the past. The mistake of looking for historical information in autobiography has frustrated generations of scholars in their attempts to define the "autobiographical truth."

The subject matter of autobiography is not necessarily a specific historical past or even the actual life of the author. However, these elements are crucial in the allegorical construction of modern life. Autobiography reflects an attitude or political position toward one's society. The May Fourth autobiographers all believed that they were in some ways representative of their contemporaries. Their concerns, sentiments, and experiences reflected those of the entire generation. Even those who professed unique achievements in their own lives attempted to use their successes to inspire others along the same proven paths. No matter how personal the individual stories were, many wrote from a didactic impulse to fulfill their sense of social duty through literature. However, the reverse is also true: no matter now consuming the narration of the nation is, through autobiography the uniqueness of personal stories and the peculiarities of individual voices are always evident. Autobiography is an especially important kind of writing in this era because it is singular in its capacity to demonstrate both the modern condition and individual experience.

The political and social concerns of women and ethnic minorities differ from those of mainstream, male intellectuals. The feminist consciousness, newly uncovered in the early years of May Fourth, became increasingly vulnerable to the continuing demand to put literature in the service of nationalism. Many scholars have pointed out that the early efflorescence of women's voices did not survive the nationalist and then the revolutionary projects of the late 1930s, 1940s, and 1950s. Even more crucial in terms of literary production is women's access to literary tools that a male writer may take for granted. I argue that the realist perspective, for example, so crucial to modern writing, was not available to early women writers. However, the effort to overcome a certain "lack of perspective" among women writers created the modern autobiographical strategy. It is this strategy that, in the end, preserved women's voices. Autobiography is thus strongly connected to women's writings.

Women not only have to confront social constraints *in* writing, but also the very idea *of* writing. Women have always been the objects of description. This position-as-object has been the topic of much feminist scholarship since the 1980s. In autobiography, this issue assumes a special complexity. A woman autobiographer simultaneously provides the subjectivity of her work and is the object of description. In her self-writing, how does she avoid the perspectival and representational positions that for centuries froze her into a lifeless object-state in masculine writings?

Women's issues of representation are not dissimilar to those of ethnic minorities in China. Literary portrayals of these groups are processes of objectification, similar to women's objectification. In the context of China's administrative policies of control and occasional extermination of ethnic groups beginning in the eighteenth century, this objectification is a form of imperialist violence. As in the case of woman's autobiography, self-representation by a minority writer could very well fall into self-cannibalism. Paradoxically, autobiography, the ultimate form of self-writing, becomes a way out of such narrative entrapment. The reflexivity of autobiography, as a form of self-representation, offers an opportunity to scrutinize the politics of representation. As a form of self-reading, it also investigates the morality of reading. Through both processes, autobiography offers a way out of the conventional literary entrapment.

Autobiography in the first half of the twentieth century was used variously by different writers to interrogate, to negotiate, and even to program the social and political progress of modern China. Despite the popularity and success of the genre, it is also the most frequently overlooked in literary and historical discussions of modern China. This has much to do with the difficulty and instability of this group of writings as a genre. However, it is precisely because of its ambiguities that it became a ubiquitous means of self-narration in volatile times.

The story of the Chinese modern experience is not an easy one to tell; it is made up of many competing narratives. Autobiography, renewed and reinvigorated during the May Fourth period, became the most widely used literary form because it embraces both the creative and national needs of the time. The neglect of autobiography in the studies of this period, the result of prejudices in reading assumptions and the difficulty of the genre, has diminished our understanding of the literature and the society of modern China. It is my hope that the present study will help locate autobiography in its rightful place in twentieth-century Chinese literature.

Acknowledgments

Many colleagues have read parts of this manuscript or the whole in its various stages of readiness, and have been generous with their comments. I am particularly grateful to Alyson Bardsley, Kate Crehan, Ellen Goldner, and Samira Haj. Our exchanges as a group have benefited my thinking in many ways. I also benefited greatly from Leo Chan's and Robert E. Hegel's careful readings and criticisms of two chapters that were subsequently published in the *Journal of Modern Literature in Chinese* and *Chinese Literature, Essays, and Articles*. Eva Hung and Janice Wickeri's encouragement and interest in my work in women's autobiography played an important role in the completion of this book. To my professors at Columbia University, Paul Anderer, Paul Rouzer, and especially David Der-Wei Wang, I owe a debt of gratitude. This book was developed from my Ph.D. dissertation, written under their care and guidance. I also thank anonymous readers of my manuscript whose criticisms and insights have been of great benefit. For her sense of humor, encouragement, patience, and hard work on my behalf, I am deeply appreciative of my former editor at the University of Michigan Press, Ingrid Erikson. To Anne Marie Schultz and Mary Erwin, who took over from Ms. Erikson to guide this book through the publishing process, I am equally grateful. Thanks also to the staff at the press unknown to me who brought the publication of this book to fruition.

I thank my students, who have constantly reminded me of the importance of clear articulation and the ultimate function of scholarship. Friends and family offered encouragement and inspiration through conversations and discussions, provided physical nourishment, intellectual sustenance, and mental consolation. I am grateful for their presence in my life, but I have chosen to keep this list private and to thank them in private. As for institutions, I am grateful for the financial help and administrative encouragement of the Professional Staff Congress of the

City University of New York (PSC-CUNY) Research Foundation and the College of Staten Island, the City University of New York.

An earlier version of chapter 1 was published in the *Journal of Modern Literature in Chinese* (January 2001). An earlier version of chapter 5 was published in *Chinese Literature, Essays and Articles* (2001). Both have been revised for publication here.

Introduction

The Study of Autobiography

The study of literary forms or genres is notoriously hazardous and unproductive, for as long as there are identifiable conventions, there will be deviations, innovations, and defiance. In 1968 Stephen Shapiro termed autobiography the "dark continent" of literature, because it was unexplored and unyielding to theorization.[1] Certainly, autobiography is no longer uncharted territory. In recent decades its study has become a veritable industry. Yet we are as far as ever from a conclusive articulation of this genre. Why does this seemingly futile endeavor continue to engage our critical efforts?

Georg Lukács long ago pointed out the importance of the study of literary forms: "But in literature, what is truly social is form. . . . Form is social reality; it participates vicariously in the life of the spirit. It therefore does not operate only as a factor acting upon life and molding experiences, but also as a factor which is in turn molded by life."[2] In other words, as the formal postulate of the material world, a literary form is always a worldview and an ideology. Particular literary forms are results of particular social conditions, and as such, they are sociological. Franco Moretti points out that precisely because form is an ideological product, it is conservative and limiting. He terms it a "petrification of life."[3] When form becomes convention, it is more effective in its organization, he argues, but it also loses its ability to change, and the pursuit of purity of form becomes a limit to creativity.

Genre studies that aim at grouping a variety of writings under a general rubric are perhaps hard to justify. Moretti argues that behind such an effort to organize is a presupposition that "literary production takes place in obedience to a prevailing system of laws and that the task of criticism is precisely to show the extent of their coercive, regulating power."[4] Paradoxically, it is also through identifying the coercion of forms and critical ideologies that the process of defiance can be distinguished. Through writers' attempts to break out of them, we can understand the operative constraints and all the coterminous issues, formal, social, or political, against which individual writers work. In other words the study of form is a study of antiform and, by extension, a study of resistance to the tyranny of ideological presumptions.

The Modern Period

This volume is a study of modern Chinese autobiography. The idea of modernity is, needless to say, a highly contested one. Historians variously identify Chinese modernity as occurring in the urban centers of the Ming dynasty, or push it back to the Southern Song, or more commonly, to the late nineteenth and early twentieth centuries. Literary scholars also more and more frequently look to the late Qing for the real stirrings of modern literature. However, in this discussion I adhere to the convention of the year 1917 as the beginning of a new era in literature.

In 1917, Hu Shi published the all-important "Preliminary Proposal for the Reform of Literature" (Wenxue gailiang cuiyi), in *New Youth* magazine, which not only advocated the use of vernacular Chinese as the new literary medium for the masses, but also the rejection of a cultural past represented by the elitist literature in the classical language and form *(wenyen wen)*. In 1917, the first vernacular short story, "One Day" (Yiri), was published, written by a young, little-known woman, Chen Hengzhe. The literary reform then gained momentum with Lu Xun's "The Madman's Diary" (Kuangren riji), published in 1918.

The May Fourth Incident of 1919 is the political side of the new consciousness and infused the literary reform with social and nationalist urgency. The incident began as a student protest in Tiananmen Square against Western and Japanese imperial ambitions in China. These ambitions were manifest in the Treaty of Versailles, which proposed to award the former German concession of Shandong Peninsula to Japan. This was further aggravated by Japan's Twenty-One Demands, which the Chinese president, Yuan Shikai, was on the verge of accepting. Together, these would have essentially turned China into a Japanese protectorate. The anticolonial demonstration on May 4, 1919, ended in violence. Hundreds of protesters were seized. Beijing University was effectively turned into a detention center. However, when male students were placed behind bars, female students, in a defining moment of Chinese feminism, took to the streets in place of their male compatriots. The years before and after May 4, 1919, became generally known as the May Fourth era, now used to designate the rise of both a new literature and a nationalistic consciousness among young intellectuals. As is obvious in this abbreviated description, May Fourth is a complicated movement that shuffled the cultural, political, and social alignments of Chinese society.

My discussion unavoidably refers to "traditional society" or "the past" or "patriarchy," in contrast to the sense of newness in the May Fourth zeitgeist. Without question, it is arbitrary to make a clear temporal divide between old and new. However, just as the literary language *(wenyan)* became an identifiable target of attack for the May Fourth generation, all the marks of the existing dominant society became symbols of the old and outmoded. In other words, in the May Fourth context, terms such as *tradition* and *modernity* are used as dialectical moments, and are not necessarily descriptive of material conditions.

The definition of the historical past in the dialectics of social power was different for different social groups. Women's oppression was not the same as men's. Men suffered from certain expectations from the patriarchal society from which women were exempted. Ethnic minorities had their own "dominators" against which they struggled. Urban pressures were different from rural oppressions. Intellectuals suffered differently from peasants and manual laborers. This is why there are as many autobiographical strategies as there are writers.

In terms of literature, "traditional" and "modern" are also not discrete categories. Clearly, there is no line that divides tradition and modern into two unrelated realms. There are tremendous continuities, revocations, and derivations throughout the history of Chinese literature, with each period proclaiming itself different and new.

In truth, reevaluations of existing social structures are not unique to the May Fourth generation. However, the self-perception of a wholesale refutation of the past is. Frederic Jameson has argued that "emblematic breaks" are historiographic decisions.[5] It is this self-perception of being distinguished from any existing social convention and institutional power that makes this generation call itself "new."

What Came Before

In order to understand the defiance and innovations of the May Fourth generation, it is worth a detour to an examination of the assumed tradition in autobiographical writing against which the May Fourth generation contended. Chinese biographies *(zhuan)* originally existed as an important section of both the dynastic histories *(zhengshi)* and local histories *(difangzhi)*.[6] Recognized as part of the biographical form in pre-twentieth-century Chinese letters, autobiography is manifested in short necrologies, self-prefaces, and personal annals *(nianpu)*. It is small wonder that pre-twentieth-century Chinese autobiographies are to this day read more for their historical than for their literary value. Thus, in 1933, Mao Dun complained that "there are people who say that the Chinese are a nation with five thousand years of genealogies *(jiapu)*. However, I have to say that the Chinese are a nation that has never developed a biographical literature *(zhuanji wenxue)*." He added that "although we have more than a few biographies among ancient classical works, they are only a part of the Standard Histories. The aim of such writings is to provide matter for historical investigation. They did not become an independent literature."[7] It is in agreement with this opinion that Hu Shi laments the dearth of Chinese biographical literature in 1937.[8]

The origin of the Chinese biographical form[9] has been traced to Sima Qian's (145–85 B.C.) biographies in his *Records of the Historian* (Shiji), the first of the twenty-five Standard Histories.[10] Though Sima Qian did not write an "autobiography," several self-reflective pieces extant in the *Shiji* are paradigmatic.[11] These include autobiographical references embedded in a postface and the "Letter to Ren An." These fragmented self-revelations have been referred to as "additive autobiographies."[12]

In "historical biography" of imperial times, an implicit teleology often organizes the compilation of the multifarious events of a life.[13] In the terminology of James Olney, traditional autobiographies place emphasis on the "bios" of the individuals rather than the "aute," the sense of self; or the "graphe," the individual writing style.[14] In all the twenty-five Histories, biographies are sorted in categories, such as loyal officials, virtuous wives, filial sons, and villains. These standard categorizations indicate thematic structures already in place in the narrative of a person's life. These biographies entail an organization of material and events that contributes to the culminating achievement of "virtue" or "talent." In a sense, these autobiographies or biographies are not about the particular details of one's life but about how one arrives at a certain title or becomes an exemplary stock type.[15]

The historical biographical form of the Histories serves as the paradigm in the writing of both "independent biographies" and autobiographies. This biographical convention is highly efficient. By enumerating lineage, family history, career position, and so on, a biography is an immediate reflection of the subject's social status. So strong is this convention of anchoring a narrative within the framework of one's filiations and affiliations in society that Stephen Durrant is led to call Chinese biographies "relation-centered" or "tradition-centered": the individual is legitimized by family tradition, and "genealogy is identity."[16]

The pre–May Fourth biographical form uses stringent rhetorical effects such as tabulations, figures, and enumerations of dates and facts (as in chronologies and annals) to establish veracity and authority and to avoid any suggestion of subjective intervention. These practices were even employed by Hu Shi in *Self-Narration at Forty* (Sishi zishu) in 1937. By his own admission, *Self-Narration* is mainly an aggregate of facts and data, usually at the expense of character and plot development.[17] The material proofs used to support his claims are acquired, as Hu insists, by "seeing with his own eyes and listening with his own ears *(qinjian qinwen)*."[18] In this pared-down style, Hu adheres to a traditional emphasis on facticity in a text that he imagines will contribute to the study of modern Chinese history.

Following Liu Zhiji (661–721) in *Generalities on History* (Shitong), tradition has placed Qu Yuan's (555–67) *Encountering Sorrow* (Li Sao) as the first autobiographical work. Recent scholarship, however, tends to regard Tao Qian (365–427), with his various self-conscious writings, as the first true autobiographer.[19] Regardless of where we place the "true" beginning, it is in Tao Qian's "Biography of Master Five Willows" (Wuliu xiansheng zhuan) that we see the appearance of an autobiographical paradigm—a self-conscious writing of oneself in a biography. Pei-yi Wu points out that early autobiographies "slavishly imitate" the biographical form, and Tao Qian's work is no exception. Wu argues that, inspired by the *Biography of Lofty Recluses* (Gaoshi zhuan), attributed to Huang Fumi (third century), Tao's work reflects the influence of the historical biography in both form and style.[20] However, it is obvious that Tao's spirit of imitation is ironic at best. He adheres to the conventional beginning of establishing one's social position, but only to parody it: "The origins of the Master are not known, nor are his family and given names. There were five willow trees by his house, hence he acquired this appellation."[21]

Tao's work imitates the historical *zhuan* in form. However, in effect, it is antifactual, antihistorical, and, ultimately, antibiographical. By elimination of referentiality, Tao not only rejects the historical, utilitarian attitude toward biographies, but also the literary and social institutions and the "relation-centered" ideology on which such works are commonly based. Relating the written form with the individual politics of the writer, Wendy Larson points out that Tao's work is an example of an "impressionistic autobiography," a text that reveals the writer's indifference and withdrawal from mainstream society.[22] Tao's suppression of his biographical data is a gesture of social renunciation. In this way, though confined by social conventions, Tao is able to elude social as well as literary ideological coercions. His work is about neither a loyal minister nor a virtuous scholar, but a hermit who rejects such roles and values. As such, it is counterpoised with the more common "circumstantial autobiography," which, as Larson explains, is a form that affirms one's familial and societal lineage, implicitly recognizing one's participation and belonging in society.[23] Extrapolating from Larson's discussion, the autobiographical form is an ideological and political statement, reflecting one's relationship with mainstream society.

The development of the diary form also has important implications in the rise of modern autobiography. In fact, the diary became an important autobiographical form with the May Fourth literary movement. Since the late nineteenth century (the late Qing), writers had been enthusiastically experimenting with literary forms, attempting to incorporate into fiction writing strategies of traditional genres such as travelogues, anecdotes of famous people, historical places, and jokes *(youji, yishi, zhanggu, xiaohua)*. According to Chen Pingyuan, the use of diary in narratives was introduced through Lin Shu's (1852–1924) translation of *La Dame Aux Camélias*, by Dumas *fils*, in 1901. It was not till 1912 that Xu Chenya (b. ca. 1876) in *The Spirit of the Jade Pear* (Yuli hun) first incorporated the diary into narratives as a Chinese fictional strategy. In 1914, Xu wrote another version of the *Jade Pear* by telling the story of He Mengxia, the heroine, completely through her diary entries, renaming the work *Xuehong leishi* (The sorrowful history of the snow swan). This became the first Chinese novel in diary form. However, Chen stresses, despite these first attempts, and despite the occasional diary-essays by late Qing writers, it was the May Fourth generation that self-consciously employed diary as a literary device of self-expression.[24]

So far, my discussion has addressed some fairly standard formal issues concerning the biographical genre in pre-twentieth-century literature. It is the identification of these general principles that allows scholars to group a large body of work into a single genre. It is true that when one places an individual work against the inertia of a convention, one will always find exceptions, as we have seen in Tao Qian's case. It is of course uncertain how long in literary history particular conventions hold sway, or whether one should speak of a literary institution. One should not rely on ahistorical rules of genre, yet to see in every piece of writing a radical innovation is to be oblivious of the material conditions behind a cultural form. In the case of Tao Qian, for example, to understand the peculiarity of his work, we must also understand the cultural or political conventions against which he wrote.

Modern Chinese Autobiography

The May Fourth revolution is both a distinct historical incident and an empirical decision with which we have to reckon in the study of modern Chinese literature. This movement, as I discuss in chapter 1, results in an epistemological disjunction and provides a discrete point in time and space where one can locate a real change. The May Fourth period is defined by a collective and concerted effort at producing a "spirit of the age" through a new writing and a new attitude—the so-called May Fourth spirit *(Wusi jingshen)*. Certain political and social issues that the May Fourth generation faced were unprecedented in China's past. Politically, China was slowly extricating itself from the grip of colonialism after World War I, having contributed to the victorious side of the war. However, the betrayal at Versailles, the increasing Japanese threat, and internal political turmoil hampered China's efforts at modernization. The relationship between Chinese intellectuals and the modern world, represented by the West and Japan, was ambivalent—desiring to be part of it, yet at the same time understanding that its greatness was built upon China's weakness. This tortured negotiation between the national self and foreign others is the basis of the particular kind of nationalism among modern Chinese intellectuals.[25] The "I" of the May Fourth youth was identified by an intense consciousness of the self in the world and, as such, a deep awareness of the self as a political entity. The autobiography became a unique literary tool of this period to express this new sense of self.

Tremendous changes in social values also have great effects on ideas of language and representation. With the use of the vernacular language in writing, representation is no longer fixed on the level of phenomenal reality and outward expression. In his essay on diary as literature *(riji wenxue)*, Yu Dafu proclaims: "Human life is a dangerous thing—a struggle. Heaven and hell are separated only by a piece of paper. The devil and the divine exist together within the heart of the individual."[26] It is this interest in "the interior," commonly explained as the rise of individualism, a psychological phenomenon, or as subjectivity in literary terms, that marks the modern autobiography.[27] Though this awareness of a complex internal dimension of human life might not be a uniquely modern or Chinese idea, it nevertheless complicated the convention of representation and required a new strategy. Perception no longer constituted the only method of attaining knowledge. "Seeing" could not account for the occult reality in one's interiority. May Fourth writers traversed a new realm in which the distinctions between true and false and between authenticity and mendaciousness based on appearance and perception are destabilized. Indeed, facticity, so long the standard for biographical *(zhuan)* literature, was of little use to modern writers, as

Hu Shi, who experimented on the chronological form *(nianpu)*, discovered. He discovered that the world of facts and data allows no expression of the interior reality of the individual. To modern writers, truth is no longer captured through a repetition of visible reality. It is in the method of figuration.

There are direct effects of this transformed epistemology in writing. As surfaces and structural resemblances are de-emphasized in modern self-writing, the chronicity (so-called real time or historical time) of conventional biographical practice also becomes irrelevant. The disintegration of the authority of real phenomena makes it possible for such diverse writers as Chen Hengzhe, Lu Xun, and Eileen Chang to transcend the notions of plot or teleology in their writings. Many modern works seem to be series of essays put together in collections that lack obvious causal or logical continuity. This is in part a result of the exigencies of publishing—many writers put out their works in installments in newspaper serializations or in literary journals. However, since the compilation of these collections involves selecting, editing, and arranging the different pieces of one's story from different periods of one's life, it is not far-fetched to regard it as a sort of autobiographical activity. The dissolution of traditional forms necessitates a broadening of the definition of autobiography.

Admittedly, I define autobiography rather liberally. However, one of the points I try to demonstrate is that part of the modernization of autobiography is a challenge to the existing conventions of writing and the idea of reality upon which these conventions are based. The change in the apprehension of reality is the particular "emblematic" and semiotic disjuncture from which many of the issues in modern Chinese autobiography can be worked out.

Very simply, the self-consciousness of a break with the past is what creates the experience of the modern. In a sense, I am not interested here in defining modernity, but in identifying how modernity as a consciousness affects the way one formulates oneself and one's perception of reality. The notion of newness and the self-appointment as a new person in the May Fourth period are important coordinates for the birth of twentieth-century autobiography. The reverse is also true—autobiography as a form provides an expressive venue for the self-creation and fulfillment of the modern individual.

A Theoretical Discussion of Autobiography

Despite the proliferation of writings in the first person and various forms of self-narrative in the literature of the period, no prevailing critical attitude toward the reading of modern Chinese autobiography has been established. In terms of the form itself, it is convenient to regard autobiography as part of the romanticism of the period—an angst-driven, solipsistic, albeit fashionable ideal of young intellectuals and writers. It is often assumed that romantic writers "mature" into social accountability and adopt a form that underscores this change, such as social realism. (According to a common critical perspective, only in the late 1930s, when China and Japan were moving toward all-out war, did Creation Society writers, associated with high romanticism and sentimentalism in modern literature, shed their egoism and adopt "responsible" patriotic voices.)[28] As for content, autobiographies are either read for historical interest, used as resources in psychobiographical studies of writers, or subsumed under social themes such as the relationship between self and society.[29]

There are problems with readings that confuse the narrated with the actual, or the work with the writer. Without recapitulating recent theoretical developments in autobiographical studies in their entirety, suffice it to say that the equation between the textual subject and its external referent, the author, has been fully critiqued and the subject destabilized. With his classic study "The Autobiographical Contract" (1980), Philippe Lejeune was among the first scholars to question the assumed truth content in autobiography.[30] He argues that the differentiation between autobiography and fiction cannot be based on the criterion of veracity or falsity of the events represented in the work. This is because readers of autobiography will always try to discover where the author deviates from the truth, whereas readers of fiction will always be tempted to identify "underlying motives" or elements that coincide with the author's life. In an effort to bypass the mire of truth and falsity in which the reading of autobiography was caught,[31] Lejeune approaches autobiography as a contract between readers and writers: "the contractual name of the author is a signifier/signature of his/her ontological reality."[32] Thus, autobiography is a speech act just like any other form of articulation, to be examined according to its linguistic effect. In this way, emphasis moves away from a "realist" reading that seeks referential reality or veridical proof.

Paul de Man, who analyzes the specular moment in autobiography in which the author confronts his or her textual reflection as an essential self-reading, problematizes the notion of Lejeune's "autobiographical contract." In this instance, the self divides into two parts—a historical self and a textual spectacle. The latter is a figure of speech or a trope. According to de Man, such a tropological structure underlies all cognition, including the knowledge of the self. The autobiographical moment is the alignment between the two subjects, historical and tropical, each involved in the process of reading and determining the other in a reflexive substitution. This specular structure is interiorized in the autobiography.[33]

Autobiography is a double displacement of the author, or, as de Man puts it, a "defacement" of the author.[34] The subject that is projected to the readers is not even a representation of the original, but a re-presentation of this reflection. The figure of the author in an autobiography is, to use a cliché, always "already read." In other words, meaning is no longer located in and limited to the person of the author. The subject of autobiography is not the center of meaning but is discursively created in a speech act. He or she is a textual effect inscribed in the writing. In perceiving autobiography as a linguistic structure, we release the autobiographer as well as the subject from the world of referential immediacy. The emphasis in the reading of autobiography is not on discovering *what* is represented, but *how* and *why*. What becomes exposed in this examination is the method of figuration.

However, Judith Butler returns our attention to the historic or, in her words, the psychic self. She locates two aspects of textual power in the writing—the power of the author as the autobiographical subject's agency, and the power of the author as the effect of the subject.[35] Like de Man, Butler differentiates between the author and the textual subject. However, while de Man deflates the authority of the author and places emphasis on the textually constructed being, Butler is concerned with the psychic circularity in the relationship between the author and the subject of his or her text, and their power to generate each other:

> On the one hand, the subject can refer to its own genesis only by taking a third-person perspective on itself, that is, by dispossessing

its own perspective in the act of narrating its genesis. On the other hand, the narration of how the subject is constituted presupposes that the constitution has already taken place, and thus arrives after the fact. The subject loses itself to tell the story of itself, but in telling the story of itself seeks to give an account of what the narrative function has already made plain. What does it mean, then, that the subject, defended by some as a presupposition of agency, is also understood to be an *effect* of subjection? Such a formulation suggests that in the act of opposing subordination, the subject reiterates its subjection (a notion shared by both psychoanalysis and Foucauldian accounts). How, then, is subject to be thought and how can it become a site of alteration? A power exerted on a subject, subjection is nevertheless a power *assumed by* the subject, an assumption that constitutes the instrument of that subject's becoming.[36]

The recognition of the circularity between a subject and "subjection" is an interesting analogy of autobiographical reflexivity—of the self generating the self. The relationship between these two selves can be seen as a contest of power, or in Butler's words, "opposing subordination." I will deal with some of these issues of reflexivity in chapter 2 of this volume.

The reading of autobiography should be focused on the discursive level, or how the subject is discursively related to us. It is on this level that we can understand the contest between external social powers and internal sublimation of such powers. Subject and subjection both rely on the dominant social ideology as the source of their procreation. It is precisely under this assumption of the constructedness and manipulability of the self that writers as diverse as Hu Shi and Yu Dafu design their negotiations with society. However, Butler reminds us that this constructedness is paradoxically reliant on a self-consciousness. This self-consciousness is predicated on the antagonism of an individual toward the society that is also part of his or her formation. These contradictions are the property of the textuality of autobiography.

Autobiography is the site on which the process of self-making or remaking takes place. The subject thus created has historicity and specificity as a product of a political activity—writing. Writing is political because it seeks to state the case of the self and, in May Fourth, the case of the nation as well. However, insofar as this political act is manifested in writing, its efficacy is passive—having effect only if it is read. Herein lies the limitation of the subject as a discursive product as opposed to the individual as a political being. On a textual level, it is the subject that occupies me as a topic of direct investigation. However, inhabiting this subject is the individual as a political actor who produces the discourse and invents him- or herself as a political or social act. In reading autobiography, one is constantly dealing with the negotiation between the political actor and the text as a reflexive creation, either as a political assertion or a reflection of his or her ideological capitulation.

Reading autobiographies is not about discovering whether the details relayed in the work are fact or fiction, true or false. It is not about verisimilitude. It is, however, about iterability and its sincerity. It is not what appears to be true, but what is narrated *as true*. Truth, one can safely say in this case, is a linguistic condition—what is or can be spoken. The modern experience of truth is an issue I will explore in some depth.

The Question of Western Influence

Because of the immediately related issues of individualism and interiority, the study of modern Chinese autobiography often leads to discussions of foreign influence on early May Fourth intellectuals. British romanticism, German expressionism, and Japanese naturalism and I-novels are often associated with the highly sentimental tone of early May Fourth productions. The attention on the "internal self" *(neixin)*, in the struggle between personal desire and social obligations, is often attributed to Freud's theory of the id versus the ego. Despite the proximity of my subject matter to these phenomena, I will not discuss autobiography in terms of foreign influence. Foreign influence is one way of looking at modern Chinese literature, of course, and one that has been fully explored in the scholarship of the last few decades. Labels of romanticism and expressionism have been applied liberally to writers like Yu Dafu, Guo Moro, and Lu Yin, who demonstrate an autobiographical bent in their works or exalt subjective feelings, physical desires, and behavior that pushes the limits of social propriety.[37] However, such labeling only diverts our attention from the writings themselves to formal conventions, and the only feasible conclusion in this kind of "influence study" is that modern Chinese literature, compared to the original Western forms, is inaccurate, derivative, and reductionist.[38]

Traditional "influence studies" that only examine the product of cultural transfers but do not trace the process of the transfer are problematic for other reasons. Scholars such as Mary Layoun and Alan Wolfe question the real impact of certain schools of Western literature, most prominently realism and naturalism, that seem to be particularly influential on non-Western writings. Layoun and Wolfe argue that these kinds of writings contain narrative imperatives (such as linearity and teleology) that are not just formal stylistics, but also reflect particular ideological inclinations.[39] A more significant consideration than the formal influences of the transfer of literary modes from one place to another is their ideological impact on the countries of reception.

Zheng Boqi, a founding member of the Creation Society, argued in the *Great Compendium of New Chinese Literature* (*Zhongguo xin wenxue daxi*, 1935) that the works of Creation writers actually demonstrate a complex and ambivalent relationship with the West:

> First, [the Creation members] had all been abroad for a long time, and had a rather clear perception of the flaws of other countries (capitalism) and the diseases of China (colonization): They felt a double disillusionment and a double pain. They became fed up and disgusted with contemporary society. The different kinds of oppression they suffered inside and outside their country only increased their rebelliousness. Second, since they had been abroad for a long time, they were often homesick for their motherland. However, when they returned home, the various disappointments they experienced made them bitter. This is the reason why prior to their return, they were sad and yearned to come back; but after their return, they became filled with indignation and disgust. Third, since they had been abroad for a long time, they were naturally influenced by trends in other countries. The bankruptcy of rationalism in philosophy and the failure of naturalism in literature resulted in their tendency toward antirationalistic romanticism.[40]

Many of the European values reflected in western European literary forms, as Zheng argues, were antipathetic to Chinese intellectuals and their humanistic concerns. How, for example, was the rhetoric of racism and imperialism embedded in the European novel processed, once it was commuted to the reception sites outside of Europe?[41] The reception of a particular literary form from one polity that has aggressive designs on one's own culture requires tremendous reprocessing and filtering, a procedure so complex and so elusive that traditional comparative or influence studies cannot fully encompass it.[42]

Europe's predatory behavior toward China was understood as part of its intellectual program. The Creationists' adoption of the romantic writing style is not evidence of their admiration of Western romanticism. Rather, it is a desire to adopt a kind of writing that is by nature the absolute ideological and aesthetic opposite to the prevailing realist and naturalist perspectives of the imperialistic West. The so-called romantic inclination of the Creationists, according to Zheng, does not demonstrate admiration for the West, but an emotional rejection of the Western intellectual trends at the time. The flamboyant rhetoric that we see in the works of these Chinese writers is not romanticism per se, but antirationalism. Modern Chinese literature's adoption of Western trends, illustrated by the example of the Creationists, is ambivalent at best. This is especially the case after the carnage of World War I and the signing of the Treaty of Versailles, when the imperialistic designs of the West and Japan were fully exposed.[43]

In Lydia Liu's study, the issue of influence or borrowing is recast in precise historical grounds, especially at the reception site. She addresses the issues, not only of what was transmitted, but how the transmission took place and how ideas were adapted and transformed according to the changing historical and cultural needs and tastes at their point of destination. Liu introduces into the equation the dynamics of the relationship between China and Japan and the western European imperialist powers, and the condition of China's internal struggle with modernity—in short, the social and political situation of the reception site. By her "translingual practice" of close examination of an individual term and its ideological career within Chinese letters under specific social and political contexts, Liu advances beyond the traditional idea of translation as a mere substitution of a foreign term for a local one.[44]

The exploration of "translingual practices" debunks any notion of a stable or "authentic" center of meaning, which is usually the trajectory of "influence studies." Concepts such as interiority *(neixin)* or individuality *(geren)*, which are the particular focus during the early twentieth century, have sociopolitical importance in tune with the specific values propagated by intellectual leaders. The numerous transformations each of these terms underwent after their introduction into China point to constant negotiations between China and the imperialist powers, between modernity and tradition and among the different social groups. This idea of "translingual practice" well illustrates the ideological as well as sociopolitical conditions of cultural borrowings. Especially important to my own understanding of autobiographical writing, Liu demonstrates how the notion or the invention of *geren* (the individual) is complicit with nationalism.[45] Just as the assertion of the linguistic/epistemological category of the *individual* is a political and social act, autobiography must also be seen as part of this political and social program. The new modern autobiographical form, then, is a method of discursive management of contemporary political and social ideology and, as such, requires careful scrutiny.

I regard Chinese autobiography as first autobiography, then Chinese. It shares the major generic and formal properties of autobiographies: first-person narrative, self-reference, and temporal distance between the autobiographical subject and the author. What makes this group of works Chinese are not any intrinsic or ethnic differences that condition one to think or feel a certain way. What make them Chinese are the specific historical conditions and the necessary responses by individuals to these conditions. For this reason, concerns about the suitability of "Western theories" to Chinese literature, and the nationalistic idea of using "Chinese" theories for Chinese studies, are misplaced. Should we consider the designations "Western" or "Chinese" political, racial, cultural, or disciplinary categories? At a time when there are so many crosscurrents in the international academic community, can one even differentiate between "Western" and "Chinese" theory?

I use the works of Peter Brooks, James Olney, Judith Butler, Philippe Lejeune, or for that matter, Lydia Liu, David Der-Wei Wang, and Wendy Larson—albeit with certain adaptations and adjustments—not to apply the "Western gaze" to ethnic studies, but in recognition of the universal ideas of writing and human expression, conditioned by historical circumstances. I believe that nonethnic Chinese can "truly understand" the "authentic" feelings in Chinese literature, just as North American, West African, eastern European, and South Asian literary works are not beyond the power of Chinese readers to appreciate. This is a lesson from the late Qing and May Fourth intellectuals.

In literary studies, we have emerged from an era of theoretical factionalism. One no longer calls oneself a semiotician, a poststructuralist, a deconstructionist, a Foucauldian, a New Critic. In general, one can perceive a renewed interest in historical-materialist specificity in readings and a reconsideration of psychological investigations. However, among all these various inclinations, there can be synthesis. A historicist basis does not detract from the validity of a nominalist one and vice versa. If the latter teaches a rigorous questioning of language as a discursive tool, it is the former that provides explanations of how and why meanings in language shift.

In reading autobiographies I align myself with the poststructuralist position in problematizing the notion of an a priori subject. At the same time, I identify with the cultural materialists who attend to the historical weight and nationalist principles in these writings, attempting what Edward Said would call a "contrapuntal analysis."[46] Of course, a historicist reading of modern Chinese literature is hardly exceptional. If anything, emphasis on historicist, realist, and utilitarian readings has been disproportionate, and scholars are beginning to argue for the necessity of an aesthetic discussion.[47] This study of autobiography examines the idea of a historical epoch articulated through an intense self-consciousness of its cultural and literary production. In essence, then, I am wedding historicist with literary considerations. The political nature of the form, the subjectivity of the content, as well as the historical moment of their emergence all constitute the autobiography as a system of signification. The selection of certain theorists' works to assist the reading reflects more of my intellectual milieu than the particular efficacy of specific approaches to modern Chinese autobiography. In a way, this book is a form of intellectual autobiography as well.

Conclusion

The primary trajectory of my discussions of modern Chinese autobiography is the May Fourth language reform. However, there is no necessary teleology to this book, nor can there be one. The unifying factor in the narrative is the fact that all of these writers deal with a particular process of creating, defining, and articulating the self in dialectic with the greater historical forces that envelop one's self, despite one's self. The variety in the forms of self-definition discussed in this volume represents only a portion of the problems confronting the May Fourth generation. However, despite the limited focus, this study illustrates the magnitude of the changes and challenges in the experience of twentieth-century China. What this discussion also illustrates is that the self is very much a mutable cultural product, responsive to and inflected by political and social conditions. Even the most solipsistic self-examination has a much more public objective of understanding and addressing the society in which one is embroiled. Autobiography is a varied discourse enabled by, though not solely restricted to, political and nationalistic impulses in which we find tensions between private and public as well as issues of gender and morality. Autobiography is a paradigm of the reciprocal relationship between political and textual practices.

I do not attempt to define a modern Chinese subjectivity or individuality. The location of the "I" shifts and changes. It ranges from the socially oppressed and vulnerable May Fourth youth articulated by Yu Dafu or Lu Xun to the historical oppressor or dominator, as in Shen Congwen and Hu Shi. Between these two poles are the struggles between women and men, subjects and nations, the colonized and the colonizers. This modern "I" is socially, culturally, politically, and ethnically varied.

In early-twentieth-century China's semicolonized state, the fate of the self is measured against the fate of China itself. The concept of the great "I" and the small "I" *(dawo, xiaowo)* current at the time illustrates a new bond, not between self and tradition, but between self-existence and national survival. Have the young intellectuals of the time struggled so hard to be heard against the commands of family and tradition just to be subsumed under an even larger and more powerful narrative—the nation? How does one find one's voice within the overarching rhetoric of nationalism? Indeed, the primary objective in writing an autobiography is rescuing the self from obscurity. This is most obvious in women's writings. But even in the works of prominent men such as Lu Xun and Hu Shi, the desire to assert a voice, presence, and thought against social and political arbitration is unmistakable. Many studies have told us that the individual, especially the individual woman, did not survive the story of the nation.[48] But the writers discussed here prove otherwise. This, I believe, is the important contribution of autobiographical writings to the study of literature.

The reflexive self-gazing in autobiography opens up an opportunity of rearranging the reality of one's representation. This is a point illustrated most rigorously by women writers who are confronted with historical portraits of themselves that are entirely out of date and unsuitable. They have the most to change. Self-writing is then a redesigning of the self and, even more, the world. The writing of autobiography means a self-consciousness of the significance of one's existence, role, and responsibility in society. This autobiographical impulse of the young intellectuals of May Fourth arises from the need to reexamine the values that have been passed down to them over generations. The fundamental overhauling of society and the world starts with the investigation of individual consciousness. For better or for worse, their society did change and, most would argue, for the better. Most intellectuals understood at the time that while political power shifts from one locus to another, the eradication of an external political structure means little if there is no fundamental change on the individual level.

In 1937, Hu Shi made a public call to the "famous people" of society to record their life stories in order to inspire the new generation toward greatness. Thus the writing of autobiography is equated with the great work of nation building. There is surely a proliferation of autobiographies during that period, though not really as a result of Hu Shi's plea. Many writers, major or minor, start writing autobiographically, producing the interminable monologues of the era (a serious challenge to Philippe Lejeune's *autobiographical space*—the concept that only famous people can write truly autobiographically, because the text is about a recognized name). What this generation achieved through tireless telling of their stories was the importance of a personal spoken voice—not merely narratives, not merely plots or stories, not merely descriptions. Even if we put aside the romantic notions of sincerity, true feelings, and so forth associated with first-person narration, ultimately the spoken voice asserts the individual more potently than anything else. Even under the strictest conformist atmosphere of the late 1930s and 1940s, when China was gearing up for war, this emphasis on the spoken voice provides the surest form of subversion. This voice is the greatest legacy of the vernacularization of literature. Autobiography, a form intricately associated with the use of the voice, is a fundamental development of the vernacular movement. This obvious connection has too long been overlooked.

Chapter One

A New Strategy for Autobiographical Narratives

Chen Hengzhe's Writing of Aurality

Published in 1918 in *New Youth* magazine, Lu Xun's "Diary of a Madman" (Kuangren riji) has been often recognized as the first modern Chinese vernacular short story, heralding the May Fourth literary revolution. However, a year earlier, another short story, "One Day" (Yiri), by a woman writer, Chen Hengzhe (1890–1976), appeared in the journal *Students Abroad in America Quarterly* (Liumei xuesheng jikan), edited by Hu Shi and published in the United States. Although this fact is generally known, Chen's connection to the beginning of modern Chinese literature seems to have impressed few literary historians. At most, her work is considered a minor experiment that preceded, but had little to do with, the great reforms that swept through the Chinese literary scene in the second decade of the century. Often she is relegated, perhaps derogatorily, to the category of "woman writers."[1] Her achievement is quickly dismissed as an immature experimentation, or an anomaly in the general development of literature of the period.

I begin my discussion with Chen's work not because there is any intrinsic value in the fact of her being the first Chinese writer to produce a modern vernacular story. It is because Chen's "One Day" marks an important moment in modern Chinese literature, representing a beginning of an alternative to an early-twentieth-century realist perspective that had dominated thinking about fiction writing since the late Qing.[2]

Her work, in the form of direct speech, is a crucial indicator of the direction that May Fourth fiction was to travel. This autobiographical voice was an especially significant fictional strategy for women writers at the time. It is in this context that I study Chen's first story, "One Day," as a kind of prototext of May Fourth autobiography and women's writing.

Early May Fourth women writers were often deemed unable to write "realistically" by critics of their own times. Even today, such residual attitude influences our reading.[3] In truth, it is not that women do not write realistically; they apprehend reality differently and thus record it differently, as I will show in my discussion. Having suggested that, I must stress that I am not arguing that women are essentially different, but that realism as defined at the time was a perspective and form inaccessible to women for social reasons. Thus they had to devise a different way of perceiving things and writing about them. The vernacular language reform that began in 1917 opened up a venue of expression women capitalized on, as I will show. The reform not only changed writing on the level of language usage, but destabilized a certain traditional notion of representation as well. This new method of representation is demonstrated in Chen's first work, "One Day." Seen in this light, Chen's writing is both an originating text in the development of a modern form, the autobiography, and a strategy to overcome obstacles to women's writing.

My discussion in this chapter focuses on formal literary changes. There has been an enormous amount of effort to study the new interest in the first-person narrative style in terms of foreign influence. Often, the importation of Freud's writings, the I-novels from Japan, or literary romanticism and expressionism from Europe, especially via the translations of the Creation Society writers, are used to account for this rise of new "subjective writing."[4] Many of the problems in the traditional "influence study" were mentioned in the introduction. My discussion here is not designed to challenge these studies or to deny the enormous presence of traditional literary culture in the development of modern Chinese literature.[5] Similarly, I avoid individual psychobiography, personality, or talent as explanations of a writer's creative affinities, issues that seem strangely persistent in the study of women's writings. My emphasis here is on how social and intellectual situations facilitate the development of a particular form of writing.

I begin by discussing the peculiarities of Chen's "One Day" and then account for them by examining the legacy of literary realism, especially Liang Qichao's innovations in fiction in the late Qing, which Chen inherited.[6] I then explore how Chen's work reflects the implications of the language reform of 1917 and the resultant change in epistemology that is significant in modern autobiography.

The Otographic Text

"One Day" is about a day in the life of a few first-year women students at an American college, and presumably based on Chen's own experience at Vassar College, where she studied on a Boxer Indemnity scholarship. The story is composed of transcriptions of dialogues among students in the course of one day without obvious coherent narrative structure. Events unfold "inadvertently" through the students' seemingly random and spontaneous conversations.

A striking characteristic of Chen's story is its entirely speech-motivated development. There is description of neither characters nor scene. The narration starts from the morning bells at seven, when students wake up, and ends with the bedtime bells at ten at night, when they retire. The development of Chen's story is dependent on the availability of the characters, literally on the page, to talk to each other. When the characters retire, it necessitates the end of the writing. The major extradialogic element in the work is the periodic announcement of time. Rather than any natural transition or necessity in the plot, the striking of clocks indicates the switching of scenes in the story and signals an end to a particular temporal period.

> Dong! Dong! Dong! Dong! Seven O'clock.
> In bed Anna stretches and asks, "Bertha, what time is it?"
> Bertha replies sleepily, "huh, do you hear the bell ringing?"
> Anna falls back asleep without answering.
> Bertha falls asleep again too.
> Dong! Half past seven.
> Bertha and Anna are still not awake.

The clock reads seven-fifty.
Anna suddenly wakes up. (Looking at the clock) "Oh, I've only got ten minutes."

In Class
The clock reads twenty minutes past eight and the students are arriving one after another.
At eight-thirty the teacher enters.

Noon
Bertha walks to the school store, buys a bag of candies, and eats it on her way to the library.

The Afternoon (1)
The clock points to four-fifty. Margie walks into the room and throws her books on the bed, saying, "Thank heavens, another day is over."
There is a knock on the door.
Margie: "Come in."
Bertha walks in.

Evening (1)
The clock reads six-thirty. The students leave the cafeteria one after another.[7]

As far as the "story" is concerned, changes in scenes are completely arbitrary. The periodic announcements of time occur outside the activities of the story and function as an external skeleton to the otherwise desultory writing. The artificial teleology and temporal boundary imposed from without enframe the dialogues among the students and propel the writing forward. As a result, although there is very little plot in "One Day," there is a clear notion of beginning and closure. As such, the announcement of time is a feature for the benefit of the readers rather than a plot necessity.

By conventional measures, Chen's work has little resemblance to a story. Its format looks like a play. However, it lacks an obvious plot or sustained central characters. The fluidity of subject-positions as voices relaying each other in a chain of speeches suggests a lack of coherence or focus. Some critics find it difficult to accept "One Day" as a successful specimen of the modern short story. As a result, Chen's position in the development of modern Chinese literature is often denied. Zhao Xiaqiu and Ceng Qingrui, for example, argue that her work is an accidental phenomenon that does not represent a particular presence in the literary revolution. They conclude that "although there have been some individuals who might have written individual pieces of fiction in the vernacular, these were ultimately unable to change the situation of modern Chinese fiction." Referring to the title of her collection, *A Little Raindrop* (*Xiao yudian*, 1928), they consider her work as a mere "raindrop" in the gathering storm of the May Fourth literary revolution. Similarly, Kang Yongqiu argues against the importance of this story because it was published outside of China and is thus disconnected from the general development of the May Fourth literary reform: "Since ["One Day"] was not well known among readers in China, it cannot be considered the real beginning of the new literature."[8]

Realism as a Privileged Perspective

Chen's work is neither accidental nor an anomaly. To understand its oddities, we need to place it within the situation of its production. To write a story as a woman in 1917, Chen had to overcome a number of literary obstacles created by the prevalent realist literary ideal. It is worth a brief excursion here into the development and literary ideals of late Qing fiction. In 1902, Liang Qichao's (1873–1929) pivotal essay "The Relationship between Fiction and the Governing of the Masses" (Xiaoshuo yu qunzhi zhi guanxi) was published in the inaugural issue of the journal *New Fiction* (Xinxiaoshuo). This work is part of the discussion on the reform of fiction *(xiaoshuojie geming)*. Liang's notion of fiction is largely defined by the aesthetic and ideological criteria of realism. While acknowledging the variety in traditional fiction, he divides fictional works into two main categories: idealistic *(lixiangpa)* and realistic *(xieshipai)*.[9] It is realist fiction, he asserts, that can best fulfill the mission of literature as a vehicle for civic education and reform because of its ability to expose social ills. Liang's essay raises fiction, a traditionally vitiated genre, to a newly respectable status by ascribing to it an important political and social mission. As a result, reading and interpretation of fiction became exercises in the political program of Chinese nationalism.

In the extensive discussions among intellectuals and writers of fiction at the time, the realist school was insistently championed as the most important genre of Chinese fiction writing.[10] With this late Qing precept promulgated by Liang and his supporters, realism remained unchallenged as the dominant form of May Fourth writing despite the immense innovation and experimentation in literary styles and strategies at the time.[11]

The claims of realist writers, especially of objectivity and veracity, have always been suspect. In the past decade or two, the ideological implications of realism have become the target of scrutiny, primarily among feminist scholars in the late eighties, such as Nancy Miller and Teresa De Lauretis, and more recently, by scholars of imperialism, from Mary Louise Pratt to Firdous Azim. Despite their different political trajectories, the object of their critique is primarily patriarchal structures of power, whether expressed in terms of gender oppression or in terms of imperialism. This expression of power can be seen especially in realist literature because, as these scholars point out, the perspective of realism is inherently oppressive, revealing the differential positions of power between the observing subject and the narrated object.[12] Miller and De Lauretis argue that, described through this patriarchal gaze, women are reflections of the desire and ideal of the dominant (male or masculine) society.[13] Similarly, in the context of the relationship between the colonizer and the colonized, Pratt's and Azim's studies argue that depictions of colonized people are diminished or distorted by the colonizer to fit into an imperialist ideology. In both cases, these writings reflect *what the object should be* according to the dominant standard of propriety rather than *how she or he really is*. Colonized natives should be backward and inferior to justify the effort of the imperialists to forcefully "enlighten" them. Women should be weak and irrational to justify their being taken care of by men. In other words, so-called realistic depictions are related to issues of desire, power, and control.[14] Perception is politically and socially determined and is, thus, ideological.[15]

Seen through this perspective, realism as a literary mode is implicated within a highly complex structure of ideology and control. Based on a simple principle of mimesis, to copy the real as it is, or to create verisimilitude by simulating real-life situations, realism is nevertheless predicated on what the observer views as real, which in turn depends on how the observer is related to the dominant ideology. Extending from this argument, true representation is impossible because there can be no real copy and no objective writing because there can be no unmediated perspective. Realism as a mode of writing is dependent on having social power to make things visible and credible, because they are acceptable. As Jonathan Crary writes, "the problem of mimesis is not one of aesthetic, but of social power."[16]

Similarly, in his study of Chinese realism, Marston Anderson points out that despite the claim to objectivity among realist writers, the representation of the world is necessarily staged from a "determinate perspective." Moreover, the object of description is often fixed in a particular relationship with the observing subject, which is bound by strict historical limitations. This is exacerbated in traditional Chinese literary aesthetics that emphasize didactic capacities of art.[17]

This is obvious in Liang's theory of fiction. Continuing his discussion of the social function of fiction in another essay, "A Brief Discussion of Fiction" ("Xiaoshuo xiaohua," 1906), Liang describes fiction as a mirror of truth: "Descriptions of people in fiction are like reflections in a mirror—handsome or ugly, good or bad, the person is completely revealed." He asserts the inherent veracity of fiction, claiming its description is "as true as when one is confronted by the mirror and cannot escape from his form," and that "the mirror is without subjectivity" [hujing wu wo zheye]. Surely, Liang's mirror analogy advances the notion of fiction beyond pure objective representation. Even beyond surface factuality, Liang seems to imply fiction's ability to penetrate moral truth. Through this mirror of fiction, one is able to differentiate between good and evil, beautiful and ugly, in the object perceived. The object of reflection is the ignorant masses that need guidance. They need to be judged and taught to see their own ugliness in order that they may be shamed into reforming themselves. Because of the simplicity of the use of this tool of fiction, Liang believes that even "women and children," the unsophisticated and the unschooled, are capable of benefiting from it.

Liang's mirror is moral in nature, as his notion of truth is moral. One can say that the truth function of realistic literature lies in its moral imperative. The mirror of fiction not only reflects, but also evaluates, the quality of the objects apprehended. The writer, the moral authority who holds up a mirror to the world, upholds the standard of goodness in that society. Fiction thus teaches us how to see or what to see and relentlessly imposes value judgments upon its objects according to a specific idea of morality. Things that do not fit in with this program become negligible and invisible. Perception is thus equated with epistemology—what is seen as real is equated with what is known as true. Truth is incontrovertible, objective, and monolithic. It is obvious and readily accessible through the use of the right instrument of reflection, fiction. As such, the content of truth in fiction is inevitable and inadvertent.[18]

In this view, Liang's realistic writings, which demonstrate credulity, plausibility, and verisimilitude, are actually writings in conformity with societal proprieties. The corollary, that writings that present a likeness of social organization are inadvertently moral, is also true. Anderson concludes that "objectivity" and realism in writing are often influenced by an urgent sense of moral introspection.[19] In the logic of Miller, Pratt, and others, so-called realist writings are ideological writings. The ones who own the gaze are agents of ideology.

Being a "serious" writer is premised upon being able to see "realistically," which means being able to see "morally." And for this purpose, one needs to occupy a position of authority in society, so that one can hold up the mirror and expound on truth. This is a position unavailable to the historically powerless, including women. In the same vein, feminist scholars assert that the viewer and the object have traditionally been separated along gender lines, with men occupying the position of power, and women being the objects of their gaze. Because of such a bifurcation, realism as a literary mode is specifically genderized as a masculine mode of writing, inaccessible to "feminine" or "feminized" groups. Liang's notion of the moral function of fiction held tremendous sway, not only among writers of his times, but also in the first generation of May Fourth writers. It is not surprising that many early May Fourth women writers were deemed incapable of writing realistically and unable to reflect social values in their works. As long as fiction writing is circumscribed by realist criteria, women's expression is greatly compromised.

As the habitual object in the scopic dialectic of the masculine gaze, women had to overcome a major obstacle in order to write "realistically." This obstacle was their lack of a privileged perspective. How do women construct a subject and literary subjectivity when female presence is caught in the production of the "other"?

In order to answer this question and explore how Chen eludes women's scopic bind, we need to consider the opportunities made available to her by the new standards in language and literature of the May Fourth period. I will review some of the important points of the reform debates here, especially from a perspective that is relevant to Chen's writing.

Language Reform and the Challenge to Realism

Despite a strong sense of social mission in much of May Fourth fiction and hence the preponderance of a realist perspective, language reform offers an important opening for women's expression. Liang's theory of fiction reflects a traditional epistemology and ideal of literature, which interprets truth as directly connected to worldly materiality and claims that sight is coterminous with knowledge. However, this notion of truth and the system of expression relaying it is challenged by the May Fourth generation.

In his inaugural essay for the vernacular movement, "Preliminary Proposals for the Reform of Literature (1917)," Hu Shi (1891–1962) puts forth his famous "eight don't-isms" *(babuzhuyi)* as the fundamental steps for modernizing the Chinese written language. Hu Shi's issue with *wenyan,* the classical literary language, is in part a continuation of Liang's idea of reaching the masses through a more universal and vernacular language. Where he differs from Liang is his notion of truth and the vehicle of its expression. Truth, to Hu, is no longer a material likeness or human morality, but immediacy of emotions in response to present situations. He believes that classical language, often reliant on preexisting allegories and idioms to establish meaning, is burdened by sediments from the past and saddled with a surplus of referentiality. Writing in classical Chinese continually signifies another reality and conjures up a past world. In this way, one's thoughts are mediated by the articulation and, hence, perception and sensibilities of the past. As a result, the present will be infected by the past; it will lack representational precision, or worse, have its representation suppressed. Writings will be divorced from the spontaneous and immediate thoughts and emotions of the individual author. Therefore, Hu asserts, one should use the language of the present to express oneself, instead of the idioms and allegories of the classical language. In the essay "On Constructive Literary Revolution" ("Jianshe de wenxue geminglun," 1917), Hu's point that "people today should speak today's language" is an appeal to writers to repossess their present and their individuality and to liberate themselves from the burden of the past, not merely in terms of their material condition, but also their thought, their language, and their reality.[20]

The way to channel the present, Hu implies, is through one's voice. In essence, he argues that writing is merely a tool to record speech. As such, it should imitate speech, not usurp it. However, classical writing is so belabored and ornate that it becomes separated from ordinary speech. The vernacular voice, by contrast, is directly channeled from one's heart and is thus authentic and sincere. A major aspect of the vernacular movement thus concerns the fluency of one's voice.

Hu Shi's idea of a speech-oriented writing was greatly amplified by his supporters. In an essay entitled "How to Write in the Vernacular?" (Zenyangzuo baihuawen) Fu Sinian (1896–1950) argues, "First-class writing is unadulterated speech, without any impurity. It should evoke the same feelings whether we read it with our eyes or hear it being read. If the effects of what we read and what we hear are different, then it cannot even be considered second-rate literature."[21] Fu points out that great writers of the past, the philosophers Xun Zi, Mencius, Zhuang Zi, and Han Fei, were also great orators. He urges writers to pay more attention to the way they speak, listen to how others speak, and imitate conversations in their writing. He believes that when speech is pure, it flows directly from one's heart without barriers:

> When speaking . . . the heart is open, free, and fully stimulated. [Feelings] can come rushing through the mouth. . . . From this, we can see that we are easily moved when we talk. However, it is difficult when it comes to writing. In order to fully express ourselves in writing, we must prepare ourselves by practicing and developing our speech.[22]

Speech is directly connected to the root of emotions and thoughts and is in resonance with one's heart. In other words, speech is closer to the source of the self, and thus truth. In contrast, traditional writing is derivative. It is a convention of copying exterior phenomena or repeating past writings and thus is twice removed from the source. Fu asserts that "the spirit of literature is completely dependent on the quality of speech." Only the kind of writing that directly reflects the speech of real people can be considered "living literature."[23]

Writings that directly record the voice are considered superior because more authentic. As a result, instead of what is visible, the new standard of reality becomes what can be aurally received. Mimesis as a method of writing gives way to diagesis. Writing is then released from its scopic conditions and, concurrently, its gendered ideology.

Chen was at the epicenter of the language debates instigated by Hu Shi and his associates in the United States, where they were studying. Her work obviously reflects this new view of language and reality. In the preface to Chen's short-story collection *A Little Raindrop*, Hu Shi argues,

> When we were still discussing the issues of new literature, Shafei [Chen Hengzhe] had already started to use the vernacular in her writing. "One Day" is the earliest product of the initial stages of the discussions of the literary revolution. *A Little Raindrop* is also the earliest work in the early stages of the *New Youth* magazine. Let us consider the situation of the new literary revolution at the time. Let us consider Mr. Lu Xun's first piece of fiction—"The Diary of a Madman"—and when it was published. Let us think about how few people used the vernacular in their writing at that time. After having weighed all of these, we will then be able to evaluate the position of Shafei's writings in the history of the literary revolution.[24]

As we shall see in the following, it is the reform of language that offered Chen a way to free herself from the constraints of writing as a woman.

The Phonocentric Text

Through her recording of voices and sound, Chen prefaced "One Day" by claiming to create representations that are "sincere and faithful"

(*zhongcheng*) to the real. This is a common claim among late Qing writers of social fiction *(shehui xiaoshuo)* and exposé fiction *(qianze xiaoshuo)*.[25] These writers assume the role of an eyewitness to create authority for the claimed veracity of their writing. An obvious example is Wu Woyao's (1866–1910) *Bizarre Happenings Eyewitnessed in Two Decades* (*Ershinian mudu de guai xianxiang,* completed in 1910), in which the reality effect lies in the claim of ocular accuracy *(mudu de)* as a rhetorical device.

Often mentioned in conjunction with *mudu* is *erwen* (heard by one's ears). Sight and sound together form the compound of empirical experience—*jianwen* ("general knowledge," literally, "the seen and the heard"). While Wu Woyao uses sight as a synecdoche for experience, a generation later Chen recalls reality through what she hears. In "One Day," voice and speech constitute truth. She duplicates the diagetical and phonic texture of the original moment, reflecting her authorial role as an ear instead of an eyewitness. It is aural, rather than visual, resemblance that she attempts to capture, thus creating for us a reading experience that imitates the "other" reality. In other words, Chen's is an "otographic" text in which the ear registers movement: the striking of clocks announces a new scene; a knock on the door indicates a change in dialogical situation with the introduction of new conversation partners and topics. Every description in the writing is aurally directed, while visual representation is minimized.

The second vernacular short story that jump-started the entire modern literary movement is Lu Xun's "Diary of a Madman," published in *New Youth* in 1918. Lu Xun's first story displays an affinity to Chen's diagetic approach. Lu Xun's narrative is composed of a collection of diary entries in which a "madman" tells his perception of reality and feelings in the first person. In this short story, too, the plot movement hinges upon temporal devices exterior to the narrative, such as the dates of the diary entries, inserted artificially into the text. There is neither plot nor mimetic descriptions of characters.

It is not hard to see how this new ideal of writing that simulates direct speech or interior dialogue gradually gave rise to the proliferation of first-person writings, such as diaries, epistles, confessions, which are described as expressing interiority or psychological depth. These kinds of writings typify the works of Yu Dafu, Guo Moruo, Zheng Boqi—in other words, the "romantic generation" of May Fourth.[26] These writers' works are often seen as antithetical to the realist movement at the time. Chen's favoring of diagesis over mimesis in the representation of the real becomes a significant strategy among early May Fourth writings in general.

"One Day" breaks with the traditional realistic devices that characterize short-story writing. Judging from a narrowly defined perspective of stylistics, critics have so far failed to notice its function as a critique of traditional realism. In view of the May Fourth literary reform as a whole, the story is an illustration of the privileging of the voice as the new term of reality. In the following section, we shall see that Chen's work not only challenges literary ideology, but the social as well, and as such, it is an important beginning for the writing of the new generation of women.

Without Subjectivity

I mentioned before that "One Day" is a narration based on a strategy of direct speech. There is no stable subject position or perspective because the speaker to which these are attached in the story keeps shifting. The characters of the story are composed of several recurrent proper names. Familiarity with certain characters is an effect of the frequency with which their names appear in the writing. However, these names are not intrinsically associated with particular attributes, nor distinguished by any physical or psychological simulation. The association between a voice and a name or that between the speaker and her speech is arbitrary because there is no substantiation other than a colon to mark a proper name and its ownership of the proceeding speech. Names have significance only within a discourse in the very moment of exchange among characters and do not stand independently as references to real actors. For example, Anna is Anna only because within a discourse, she is not Eunice. In other words, these names do not have the metonymic, much less metaphoric, property of proper names found in traditional fiction.

> Anna: "Did the new student know about this?"
> Eunice: "She knew. She should take care or she'll receive quite a punishment."

Anna: "What time is it now?"
Margie (looking at her watch): "eight-ten."
Anna: "Will you please excuse me. I still have an essay to write during these ten minutes."

Noon
Bertha walks to the school library....
Mary: "Bertha, are you coming here to study without having lunch again?"
Bertha: "Lunch? I haven't even eaten breakfast."[27]

Names function purely as nominals with a one-dimensional referent. They are ciphers with no fixed referentiality to a subject. Loosely attached to a speaking party, they divulge little of the speaker's intrinsic character and identity. In this way, Chen destroys the viability of the subject in her text.

I have said that the relationship between the narrator/subject and the object of gaze is best described as a hierarchy in which the narrator/subject evaluates the object based on a prescribed notion of propriety. The condition of "reality as witnessed" in Liang Qichao's concept of fiction produces a distinct and powerful perceiving subject whose omnipotent gaze imposes moral evaluation on all his objects. In this way, there is an obvious equation between the subjectivity of the writing and the dominant ideology.

By obliterating the perennially present storyteller or witness one finds in late Qing fiction, Chen dissolves the notion of a subjective center in her story. Moreover, her "aural" strategy challenges the kind of reading that depends on a stable authorial subjectivity as the originating source of information, perspective, and thus, judgment. The interweaving of voices in her work precludes the possibility of a stable voice or authority through which a dominant ideological stance can be articulated. The author exists entirely outside of the world of the text and is not privy to any internal aspects of the characters. Chen thus negates the opposition between subject and object and the traditional power structure that defines realism. In this way, she also eludes the necessity of authorial alignment with the dominant social ideology in narratives that had inhibited women and other marginal groups and had rendered them without stories. In other words, Chen circumvents the fundamentally oppressive and elitist tendency of realist writing by removing the subject-center.

Chen's diegetic work is very clearly a kind of prototext of modern women's literature. In her use of an aural strategy, she defies the realist writing's requirement of an omnipotent visual field, a perspective inaccessible to women. The strategy that Chen demonstrates in "One Day" is especially favored by the first generation of May Fourth women writers. Lu Yin (1898–1934), for example, frequently uses direct speech in her narratives, designing stories with plots that unfold through letters within letters, dialogues within dialogues in which one individual voice follows another in a string of I-narrations. Like Chen's "One Day," the subject position in Lu Yin's stories changes continuously, deflecting a unified perspective. "After Victory" ("Shengli yihou," 1925) is a short story exploring the struggles of a few modern young women trying to justify the different choices they have made for their future, whether settling into a traditional marriage, pursuing romantic love, or struggling against social expectations to achieve a fulfilling career. The main narrative is provided by one character who reads a letter from a friend in which there are long quotations of letters from other friends. The narrating subject fluidly flows from one voice to another. Similarly, in her novel *Ivory Rings* (*Xiangya jiezhi*, 1934), based on the life of the writer Shi Pingmei (1902–1928), the entire narrative is unfolded through the conversations between two characters, the alter egos of Lu Yin herself and Lu Jingqing (1907–1993).[28] Many of Lu Yin's works exhibit this characteristic of narration conveyed in direct speech to both a targeted textual audience as well as the implied one that is the reader.

"Separation" (Gejue, 1923), an early work of another female writer, Feng Yuanjun (1900–1974), also demonstrates a similar diagetic strategy. The "story" is composed of a collection of letters intended for the narrator's lover, from whom she was forcefully separated. In them she confesses her thoughts and feelings. Bai Wei (1894–1988), in her touching autobiographical piece "The Reason I Joined the Literary Circle" (Wo toudao wenxuequan li de chuzhong), creates a sense of closeness with the reader through her confessional tone.[29] Even the title of this piece reveals her desire to establish a dialogue with the reader.

These are only a few examples among a large body of literature that uses or simulates direct speech as a main narrative device.[30] The feeling of intimacy and subjectivity in these writings is an effect created by simulation of speech. This is the absolute opposite of the stated realist pursuit of objective distance.

Unaffiliated Writing
◇

Chen Pingyuan points out that fiction produced during the late Qing often falls into the categories of exposé fiction, stories of ghosts and spirits, stories of crime and judgment, detective stories, mandarin ducks and butterfly (love) stories, and so on.[31] Chen Hengzhe's short story pointedly breaks away from her late Qing predecessors in terms of subject matter. She invents a writing that textualizes experiences and sensibilities that are new, dispensing with elements that are the norm in late Qing fiction. Set in a campus of an American college, Chen's story displaces her subjects from traditional literary landscapes, thus denying any spatial association with the traditional literary imagination. This is a significant move when one considers how much a writer relies on the allegorical associations of certain images of land and places in literary antecedents. A later writer, Shen Congwen (1902–1988), depicts "Peach Blossom Spring" (Tao Yuan) in his travelogue (discussed in chapter 5), immediately evoking the Jin dynasty poet Tao Qian (365–427) and his imaginary utopia.[32] Situated in a rich metaphorical landscape, Shen's text is multivalent, evoking in one stroke a whole tradition of meaning long established by a classic motif.[33] "Peach Blossom Spring" participates in a spatial context that is imbued with subliminal and intertextual associations within Chinese literature. Shen's writing typifies contemporary writers' continuous memory, engagement, and dialogue with the past.

Chen, however, refuses such inadvertent or deliberate connection in her writing. Most of the stories in *A Little Raindrop*, such as "The Dilemma of Louise" (Luo Qisi de wenti) and "Bo-er," are situated in unspecified, vaguely non-Chinese locations, with protagonists of ambiguous ethnicity or nationality. Others, for example "A Little Raindrop" and "Westerly Wind" (Xifeng), are fables in which nature is animated with human sentiments and set in mythical times or places. Even those with specified locations, such as "The Woman in the Wu Gorges" (Wuxia li de yige nuzi) and "The Canal and the Yangzi River" (Yunhe yu Yangzijiang), are often read as fables because their unearthliness distances them from the actuality of their named locations.[34] Chen is perhaps more interested in creating stories and myths for the new China than in continuing the psychic legacy of traditional Chinese literature.

Tendencies to dissociate herself from her literary and geographical lineages and social conditions are clearly reflected in "One Day." Her protagonists are separated from all possible connections with traditional society, spatially and socially, by the unusual quarantine of a foreign campus. Their anonymity is also a peculiarity in the story. In a foreign location, away from conventional society, her character's identity can no longer be defined according to traditional filiative and affiliative connections—family, class, ethnicity, and so on. Surnames, which indicate familial designations and mark one's identity, status, and participation in society, are dispensed with. Chen's characters are referred only to by their first names, and often European names. This is perhaps a small gesture; however, this lack of nominal ties with traditional society has great significance from the point of view of women's writing. Fictional depictions of women have traditionally confined them to particular, well-defined social types such as wives, daughters, mothers, or maids. However, women's modern experiences exceed such prescriptive roles and categories. Chen herself became China's first female professor at Beijing University and a formidable historian whose textbook on world history became a standard and influenced a whole generation of students. In her stories, the assertion of this modern reality is indismissible. Stripped of traditional ontology and social expectations, her modern characters' sole identification is *what they say*, not their lineage, family position, status, or significance in society. Thus, Chen's literary strategy is also a feminist one.[35]

The day depicted by Chen through the conversations of her characters is a prototype of what any normal day or conversation might be among any group of university students. With these most typical experiences and most mundane conversations, Chen creates a quintessentially *normal* day. The absence of motivating agents, such as a main protagonist, narrator, or event, and the lack of a conventional plot development, upset many traditional expectations. In dispensing with plot, Chen's writing duplicates the way we experience reality, unmindful of particular teleologies that drive our actions and reactions. We will see in the later chapters that this dispensing of conventional fictional teleology also became an aspect of the modern strategy of self-writing. Representation of the minuteness and typicality of life and ordinary people with little social and political significance is of course the very quality in writing often deplored as women's narrowness and lack of political consciousness and social realism.

However, it is through the absence of contextual ties, combined with the absolute present-centeredness of the conversations and the anonymity and randomness of the day-to-day, that Chen articulates the reality of the modern experience. In this way, she eliminates any cross-signification from traditional writing, going perhaps even farther than Hu Shi's notion of a new literary language for a new era. Chen attempts to represent a true present—writing from "degree zero," to use Roland Barthes's term.

Conclusion

Because of her strategy of "aurality," Chen's work drastically differs from the kind of realist writing advocated by her predecessor, Liang Qichao. Liang's strategy of verisimilitude emphasizes the objective reflection of phenomenal realness in the belief that truth is imbued with, or implied in, physical forms. He asserts fiction's mimetic power to capture the materiality of the world, and by extension, its moral and didactic capacity. The aspect of reality that Chen purports to capture in her writing is what she calls "human sentiment" *(renqing)*, an interior truth that arises through the course of human interactions. Her diagetic text transcribes speech as an alternative to the idea of truth as bound to the material world that is perceivable through sight. Voice is directly connected to one's interiority, the *neixin*, where a more elusive inner truth is found. The voice is thus superior to sight in articulating this new truth. Chen was the first to put into practice this precept of the vernacular language reform and the proposal to reconnect written language with speech. She uses this strategy to textualize a new modern experience that evades traditional literary expectations. Chen's writing marks the new terms of reality of the time. Her diagetic writing also marks the new methods to represent this new reality.

Chen is a minor writer in the sense that her literary output is extremely small. However, her experimentation with the short story in "One Day" illustrates an important alternative to the realist perspective. In this way, her work not only points the direction out of inherited constraints on women writers, but is also the first example of the new emphasis on the personal voice. The natural outcome of this new writing is the rise of the autobiography.

Chapter Two

Fragmented Subjectivities

*A Reconsideration of
Women's Literary Mirrors*

There is much discussion about women as objects of undisguised male erotic desire in pre-twentieth-century literature. It can be argued that in the new political and literary discourses of women's condition in early-twentieth-century China, women instead became objects of the intellectual gaze. What remained constant was women's object position. As I discussed in the previous chapter, women's position of powerlessness in patriarchal society is often expressed in a scopic relationship between a woman as an object of perception seeking approval and her male observer. This representation of women's situation explains why it has traditionally been difficult for women to write a certain way or express a viable subjectivity. In the previous chapter, I argue that the championing of the voice in the May Fourth vernacular movement released women from their scopic bind and afforded them a literary space. Not only did the language reform affect the way women wrote in the early years of May Fourth, it was also directly responsible for the flourishing of first-person narratives. As a result, diaries, letters, confessions, testimonials, and autobiographies become particularly associated with "women's writings," especially of the first generation of May Fourth writers. In these works, the unceasing disquisitions among women wove a tight female network, creating a kind of literary sanctuary for women who found themselves suddenly adrift from familiar social environments.

The second generation of women writers of the 1930s and 1940s, a few of whom I discuss in this chapter, turned away from efforts of self-affirmation through personal testimony to contend directly with the state of their perpetual object position of passivity as receivers of the male gaze. They maneuvered to gain their textual self-determination by manipulating the gaze.

In the last two decades many scholars, challenging the pervasive notion of women as innocent and passive victims of patriarchal societies, have pointed out the complicity of women in their own objectivization. The failure of these revisionist arguments, as I will show, is the result of a tendency to reduce the relationship between the subject and the object, the gazer and the gazed, to a simple gender dyad. Reviewing this equation, I explore women's own agency in self-articulation and the power of their self-invention in spite of, and even because of, their particular position as the traditional objects of the gaze. In order to accomplish this, I reexamine the gesture of mirroring, the most common trope in women's writing, and revisit some of the discussions on women's objectification in the scopic convention.

For obvious reasons, autobiography is an important place to study the issue of the self. The writing of autobiography is a familiar task for women because autobiography is a textual form of self-gazing. Looking into mirrors is women's perennial preoccupation. Through their mirrors, they measure their beauty and acceptability, often according to standards established by their society. Mirrors thus have particular symbolic importance in women's writings.

Women's Traditional Object Position

Women, *funu*, as a social and political category are a modern construction. This process in China began at the turn of the twentieth century when political thinkers such as Liang Qichao and Kang Yuwei realized that a strong female population meant a strong nation in general.[1] Women as an aspect of humanity came into consideration during the early 1920s. Zhou Zuoren's essay "On Humane Literature" ("Rende wenxue," 1918), which advocates the writing of, and writing for, the common people, also argues for the need to eradicate the traditional misogynistic social and literary treatments of women, and for their inclusion into the category of full-fledged individuals.[2] The appearance of professional women writers early in the May Fourth era is obviously an important factor in bringing into focus "women's issues" in literary discussions. First-generation May Fourth women writers such as Yuan Changying (1894–1973) and Lu Yin (1898–1934), through their numerous essays, are instrumental in raising consciousness about the conditions of modern women.[3] The new topic of women in the general intellectual discussion of the time was formally established when the influential *New Youth* magazine called for submissions to a special issue on women.[4]

In her study of Mao Dun and Ba Jin, Rey Chow argues that merely speaking about women's condition, no matter how sympathetically, does not change women's situation of voicelessness. Despite the genuine concern these two writers display toward women's situation, their women characters are still spoken for in male language and are represented through male feelings toward them. In the end, Ba Jin and Mao Dun reveal great sensibilities as male observers, but the female objects are as faceless and voiceless as ever. In this way, according to Chow, a woman's articulation of self and her sense of reality are usurped by a literary language dominated by the overarching rhetoric of humanism.[5]

This questionable advancement in women's situation in literature is also reflected in women's social condition. In "Invention and Intervention: The Female Tradition in Modern Chinese Literature," Lydia Liu discusses how Ding Ling, in the *Diary of Miss Sophie*, attempts to invert the traditional heterosexual hierarchy by allowing Sophie control of the specular situation during a sexualized confrontation between Sophie and her lover. Ding Ling not only gives Sophie a voice in the I-narrative, but also ownership of the subjectivity of the gaze, exchanging her position with her male counterpart, making him the object of her desire. However, as women became increasingly empowered in this kind of role reversal, usurping the originally male position, women merely became male impersonators. Their feminine subjectivity was ultimately sacrificed. Liu points out that the feminist movement that flourished during May Fourth was in the end co-opted by the political rubric of the state.[6]

In her more recent essay, "Women's Body and Nationalist Discourse," Liu examines Xiao Hong's work in this trajectory and argues that women's bodies and real sufferings of the body have been sacrificed and turned into a trope of the nation. In Xiao Hong's attempt to reinstate discursive ownership of women's bodies, she has been accused of being apolitical, apathetic, if not unpatriotic. Liu's argument is that Xiao Hong's contemporary reading ideology blocks the feminist reading of her works. The influence of this ideology still reverberates today, and Liu thus calls for revisionism.[7] Similarly, Wendy Larson's *Women and Writing in Modern China*, on the historical development of women's literature, demonstrates that women's suffrage was surrendered in the name of a greater humanistic or patriotic interest of the state during and after the 1930s. She thus claims that the rise of nationalism is responsible for the ultimate end of the woman's movement.[8] The failure of women's discourse in modern China leads Tani Barlow to conclude that "women" have been co-opted by the discourse of the state: "What had begun as a daring use of the European discourse on sexual difference in the May Fourth revolution against the Confucianized received tradition had, through decades of use and appropriation, became a wholly political category of mobilization to national development. The category 'women' was a part of the Maoist renaming of social order."[9] By these accounts, despite the efforts to liberate women from their traditional position of silence, women's actual individuation was subsumed under the hegemonic rubric of the nation. Woman, *funu*, became a social and political category.

Much recent feminist theory can be used to explain the seeming failure of Chinese feminism in the early twentieth century. One problem, as Barlow suggests, is the construction of a binary differential of power between men and women: women are what men aren't, and the obvious deduction is that to end victimization, women have to become men. Many argue that women are so circumscribed within the world of men that their articulation incorporates this negation. In chapter 1, I mention Nancy Miller's Hegelian understanding of the relationship between men and women as a "heterosexual contract." This is a relationship of erotic power sealed by "the gaze and the interpretation of the gaze" that "occurs in a context organized by an economy of radical otherness."[10] The conventional heterosexual contract is established in a dialectics of power that differentiates between the subject and the object, the viewer and the object of *his* desire. A woman's resistance to being "mapped within the precinct of the male gaze" and "her very awareness of such a scrutiny becomes an integral part of woman's identity: of woman's sense of herself as sighted and sited in a dialectics of power."[11] As traditional objects of scopophilia, women are only hallucinatory effects of male power, desire, and pleasure. They are the objects of reading pleasure and are aesthetic commodities. This notion is explored tirelessly in women's writings. Eileen Chang, for example, writes abundantly about the female observed as a kind of art object. In the short story "Jasmine Tea" (Molihua xiangpian), her image of the female protagonist as an embroidered bird, beautiful, yet lifelessly trapped in opulence, is unforgettable:

> Biluo's life after marriage Chuanqing did not dare imagine. She was not a bird in a cage. A caged bird can still fly away when the trap is released. She was a bird sewn onto a screen—a white bird in clouds of golden thread, sewn on a satin screen of a depressing purple. After months and years, its feathers would start to fade, become moldy and rot. Even when it died, it would only die on the screen.[12]

Chang describes women as aesthetic objects of the male gaze, beautiful ornaments, framed and hung to adorn men's dwellings.

Since women are desirable commodities within the social economy of power, the value of Chang's protagonists is calculated according to their marketability (marriageability). In the story "Withering Flower" (Huadiao), Chuanchang is continuously picked over and then passed over by different men in their quest for the perfect wife. She dies at the end from a prolonged illness, exhaustion, and disappointment in her marriage prospects. Chuanchang's life is unremarkable and pathetic. Ironically, it is in death, when enshrined in a beautiful marble tomb, that her real value to her family and in society is most evident. Dead or alive (the difference is insignificant), women's true value is as trophies of the male world:

> When her parents came into some money, they restored her tomb. They added a white marble angel in front of her tombstone. Bowing her head and holding her palms together, she was surrounded by a group of cherubs who gazed, with dozens of pairs of white,

marble eyes upon her bosom. Her petrified hair tossed in the stony breeze. The white drapes of her dress covered a strong fleshy body of milky white flesh, icy cold. It was a beautiful tombstone, like those seen in the movies. Amid the fragrant grass and setting sun, anyone offering flowers in front of this tomb would surely feel the melancholic beauty.[13]

If the figure of Pygmalion has been a Western metaphor of the creative and life-giving force of male attention, through which an object of art comes into being, in Chang's story, the male gaze is petrifying. In these stories, Biluo became a bird pinned to a tableau; Chuanchang became a stone angle. Not only are they art objects, these objects are placed in a world designed according to male aesthetics.

Feminists have argued that men's eyes systematically and cannibalistically break up and consume the body of women. A woman's subjectivity becomes an abstract fantasy created from a montage of such fragments. In Laura Mulvey's words, women are illusions "cut to the measure of desire."[14] Susan Sontag thus argues that woman see themselves as a sum of body parts. To evaluate oneself is to inventory oneself.[15] In this constant position as the object of social gaze, women in their self-regard see not their own selves, it is argued, but a "male-formulated image of femininity."[16] Virginia Woolf is one of the first in a long line of feminists who have commented upon the implications of women's confrontation with themselves: "Women have served all these centuries as a looking-glass possessing the magic and delicious power of reflecting the figure of man at twice its natural size."[17] This point is driven home poignantly in Ling Shuhua's autobiography written in English, *Ancient Melody*.[18] In this work, Ling describes a childhood incident in which she was being groomed for the celebration of her father's receiving a new concubine. Ling describes examining herself in front of a mirror, trying to compare herself to a picture of a girl in a New Year's poster. She wondered if she was as picture-perfect: "I was delighted to hear [my nanny's] praise. As soon as she had finished, I climbed up on a chair to look at myself in the mirror, which hung on the wall. The girl in the mirror smiled at me shyly. She was in a shiny dress, rather like those little dolls sold at the fair on New Year's day."[19] It was not herself that Ling saw in the mirror, but her father's perfect little girl. Whether as a poster girl, an embroidered bird, or a marble angel, women and girls function in the patriarchy to reflect and celebrate its prosperity. The mirror in Ling's work, as in her autobiography, reflects values of the male world according to which women negotiate their acceptance.[20]

A woman's individuality has been inaccessible to herself because it is constantly deflected from her. Women are not just the object of the direct male gaze, but also the object of the implicit male gaze in their own mental mirrors. Jenni Joy Labelle thus remarks, "What the mirror stands in place of (men, society, the world) does impose on the woman the various faces she exhibits. The medium of reflection *does* have enormous power, the power of the world to determine self."[21] Similarly, Brian Finney claims that "[w]hile the traditional male artist uses the mirror for self-portraiture, women find themselves painting their faces in the looking-glass to conform to a male-formulated image of femininity which deprives them of their own sense of identity."[22] John Berger puts it more succinctly, "The surveyor of woman in herself is male: the surveyed female."[23] There is a chorus of consensus among critics that within female autocontemplation, the implicit male presence is a given.

As an act of textual mirroring, women writing autobiography is a complicated process. Their relationship with their text is much like their relationship with their mirrors. The writing is both highly reflexive and self-conscious. While attempting to fulfill ambitions of self-expression, they constantly, anxiously examine the impression they create at the same time. Thus in these writings a woman often seeks to conform to or rebel against an imagined public norm or implied interrogator. Either way, women's writings are often responsive to well-defined boundaries of public propriety; and either way, women are bound by the "heterosexual contract."

What complicates the relationship between the objectified women and the ideological gazer is that the objectification of women is not a result of passive acceptance by women. Women are fully complicit in their own subjugation, suggests De Lauretis, who long ago established that "[t]he construction of gender is both the product and the process of its representation."[24] Spectatorship is "a site of productive relationships" between the hegemonic ideology and the individuals that continue to pro-create images and consciousness that further foster and stabilize the existing imbalanced relationship. The receiver of the gaze is thus entrenched within the process of its own objectification. In the moment of self-viewing through a mirror, the object also becomes, if temporarily, the spectator. Whatever subjugation the object receives, it is also generated by itself in collaboration with the ideological gazer.[25]

Using De Lauretis's theory of women's complicity in creating the unequal relationship between the gazer and the object, Rey Chow also explains this process in terms of self-fetishism. While stressing the predatory and aggressive condition of the gaze, she also highlights the self-fulfillment of the object.[26] The signification process depends on the viewer who produces the fantasy according to his desire. However, it also relies on the object to motivate the production through her will to self-fetishize as a compensation for her own powerlessness (or lack, in psychoanalytical terms). Simply put, reception of the specular is not passive, nor is the production single-mindedly male directed. Hence, a woman occupies an uneasy and ambivalent position in this scopic economy. She is both the spectator and the object, the subjugated and the originator of the scopic self-violence.

According to these theories, the image of a woman is a fantasy that is socially constructed and mapped within the subjectivity of a woman. A woman affirms the fantasy while she is concomitantly affirmed by it. It is only through this fantasy-object that a woman can be represented or can represent herself and generate meaning. Woman's self-meaning is, in the end, encoded within patriarchal discourse, and the voice of an individual subjectivity is drowned out. Thus, De Lauretis adds that the woman viewer who occupies the position between the look of the camera and the image on the movie screen is outside of the mimetic order and has neither self-representation nor self-meaning, because she occupies a space unrepresented.[27]

For my purpose, the above discussions regarding the position of women can be summarized in three points. First, women's speech is described as completely circumscribed by the articulation of the patriarchy or the nation. Second, this phenomenon can be theoretically explained by the fact that women have two ways of expression, either adopting male speech directly or becoming complicit in the male production of the fantasy female. Finally, the concept of female is manufactured by society, albeit with female consent. As a result, women can only participate in a "virtuous transaction," to use Chow's terms, with the primary culture.

Their "true subjectivity" can only be revealed in such a cryptic manner that female voices have to be rescued through our revisionist efforts today.[28]

I am not in complete disagreement with this way of looking at women's writing. However, if it is true that the individual is totally subsumed within her social ideology, then why bother writing at all? Despite the seeming futility, women show an obvious urge to produce individual testimonies in the May Fourth era. It is a mistake to over-problematize female writing to the point where we erase its actual impact. I wonder if scholars, in their earnest feminist agenda to speak on behalf of women, overcompensate for their so-called voicelessness that they actually overlook the important individual strategies of women writers. My point is that women's writings are not and cannot be totally circumscribed or defensive as they have been described, though they might have been reactive. Vindication of the feminine subjectivity and female writing should not be focused on a recovery of "authentic" feminine self from which true desires of the real being emanate. The very self-lessness that cannot be affixed, like Eileen Chang's embroidered bird on a tapestry of the male landscape, can itself be a factor of feminine textual assertion.

It is true that in a large sense, the mirror's power reflects a society's enforcement of individual conformity. Eileen Chang would be the first to admit to the ubiquitous male presence as the undergrid of women's identity and women's general consciousness: "All women talk about all their lives are men. All they think about are men; all they complain about are men, always, always."[29]

Indeed, to speak from a subject position for themselves, women have to achieve more than simply reversing the traditional object-subject assignment and putting themselves in the position of men. This is because, as I will demonstrate, the relationship between a subject and an object is not a simple binary. Writing as a woman involves more than a female body or feminine dress. It requires the ability to manipulate a whole tangle of gender relations often expressed through the multivalent dimensions of sight. The feminine mirror does not simply reflect the woman transcribed within social norms. In other words, the mirror is not only a space of passive reflection of social definitions. The act of mirroring is an intensely private event of active self-creation.

The Process of Self-Reflection

In her early autobiographical work *Market Street* (*Shangsji jie*, 1936), written under the nom de plume Qiaoyin ("secret murmur"), Xiao Hong records her feeling of suffocation when she waited anxiously in her lonely apartment for her lover to come home from work to give her daily food and emotional sustenance. She bewails the fact that in the apartment where she lived with her insensitive lover, there was no window to look out of and no mirror to look into. Lacking these reflective surfaces, she had neither accreditation from without nor reflective affirmation from within. In her writings Xiao Hong is constantly ill because of her persistent hunger, for both food and love, and anxiety about her survival, both physical and emotional. But her text also exhibits another level of distress because of the lack of means of self-reflection—the dis-ease of effacement. In this case, mirroring represents more than social conformity. It is self-definition and expression.

Eileen Chang displays a similar relationship with reflective surfaces. However, her attitude is anything but passive. In "Intimate Words," an autobiographical piece, she describes lodging with her aunt and constantly, clumsily crashing into glass doors, shattering glass tables and gashing herself. Chang's sense of discomfort, living in a borrowed space, is metaphorical of women's general lack of ease living in a society designed with little consideration for women's needs and comfort. More than just distending the social fabric, Chang's movements stretch and rend the space around her. As she tried to make her space conform to her needs, she sometimes broke the things that confine her movement, but often also hurt herself badly in the process. She writes about her defiance of her father in order to go to school as a child, then to attend college as a young woman. She was severely punished by her father once, who beat her unconscious, then confined her unattended till she managed to escape a year later.

There is no doubt that women strove to write in very restrictive and inhibiting social environments. It is not without reason that Xiao Hong's autobiography was written by Secret Murmur. However, if, as De Lauretis and others have shown, the idea of a woman is artificially constructed by men, it is also this fabrication and arbitrariness that affords women the opportunity to manipulate their own construction and effect for their own purposes and according to their desire.

In writing about women in the third person, Eileen Chang joins the chorus of feminist critics on women's passive object position. However, in her own reflexive textual confrontation, this representation becomes highly complex. In a scene in Chang's autobiographical essay "A Child's Words Are without Inhibition" (Tongyan wuji), mirroring is brought into focus as a metaphor of self-representation. In this scene, Chang, who has just been bullied by her stepmother, runs into the bathroom and rehearses lines of revenge in front of a mirror. Her stepmother teases her for empathizing with her brother, who has just been reprimanded. Behind this taunt is an underlying accusation of Chang's attempt to imitate or even identify with a boy instead of dutifully staying within the bounds of a girl's sensibilities. In the bathroom, Chang creates an imaginary dialogue in which she becomes the observer of an image of her self-creation: "I stood in front of the mirror as if it was a movie close-up. I watched my tears flow down my twitching face. I gnashed my teeth and said, 'I will have revenge. I will have revenge one day.'"[30] This clandestine performance is meant for the stepmother, who represents the adult world or the dominant society and whose authority is absolute, whether just and rational or not. Chang's enactment in front of the mirror, which she imagines to be a movie screen, is a form or self-expression—the cinema is a public form. As a result, her sense of self is divided in the process. In the role of the observer, she self-consciously and reflexively watches her effect on this screen in order to assess how she, in the role of the object, might be evaluated by society. Chang edits her reflected self to fit the frame of the screen. Here she illustrates the process that De Lauretis describes, in which female sensibilities and expression are conditioned, manipulated, or cut to fit particular expectations.

In its role of mediation, the mirror is an ideological tool. The representation has little to do with re-presenting an objective, originary truth. In fact representation is a result of artificial manipulation according to a desired effect. Chang self-consciously arranges her image to create a dramatic situation, to make it fit a pre-text. Uttering the stock lines, "I will have revenge; I will have revenge one day," she strikes a common female filmic pose—wronged, anguished, and tear-stained—traditionally, the only feeble expression of protest against injustice for women.

However, on close examination, one discovers that this mirroring is a lot more complicated than a woman's submitting herself to enframement in De Lauretis's schema. There is a double reflection process. On the first level is the public screen on which a female drama is enacted: spectator enframes the object. On the second level is the mirror on which this enactment is reflected: Chang becomes the spectator who watches herself watching the enactment. The description here is of the moment of self-recognition, when a traditional object duplicates the procedure that objectifies her in the first place: the object sees herself as an other. Chang, the object, claims the subject position as the spectator in this *duplicitous* stance, while remaining the object in regard to the dominant scopic relationship. In fact, in this moment, there are three aspects of self, the spectator who represents the dominant ideology, the direct object of this spectator, and the self who watches and designs the enactment on the screen. In this mirroring scene, Chang experiences the objectification of herself through the mirror and is simultaneously split between identifying with the ideological subject position that judges her enframed self and the traditional object position that receives the gaze. The process does not stop here, but continues in further splitting off to become a standoff between the complicit ideological subject who self-regulates, the object, and the unreflected presence beyond the screen that manipulates the two. This unreflected presence, laments De Lauretis, is the "true" self left out of representation and suppressed.

However, it is precisely this lack of fixity that allows Chang to slide fluidly back and forth between the poles within the scopic exchange and even beyond this equation. In so doing, Chang reveals the total artifice of the so-called self that is publicly displayed and also any idea of a "true" subjectivity within. Feminist critics bewail women's construction by ideology. However, rather than succumbing to or refusing this construction, Chang embraces it gleefully, manipulating the idea of her self to her heart's content, precisely because it is artificial. In the following, we will see how, in the end, the reality of a woman is uncaptured and uncompromised, because unreflected.

Unmasking in Mirroring

In a 1934 essay, "Some Conjectures about Theatrical Masks" (Mianpu yice), Lu Xun discusses the use of traditional theatrical masks in traditional drama. In traditional theater, the different human prototypes are identified by the different *mianxiang* (painted faces). According to Lu Xun, these are evolved from masks used in the Six Dynasties (743). Both the masks and the *mianxiang* completely cover the natural faces of the actors. Each of these masks represents a character type. Each of these types, in turn, has a specific dramatic function in the drama and correspondent formulaic code of gestures. The *mianxiang* do not represent particular individuals, but are metaphors of human attributes and emotions such as faithfulness, loyalty, martial prowess, buffoonery, and wickedness. They also signify social roles such as young scholars, middle-aged loyal ministers, and young filial daughters. The audience does not see individual faces, but identifies a world of inferences and associations in each hyperbolic human type. The audience of traditional theater is used to seeing the *mianxiang* as figures that are meaningful.

However, Lu Xun argues that these traditional masks no longer signify in the twentieth century because social semiology has changed and with it the sense of reality:

> In his article in the *Drama Weekly* No. 11 (*Zhonghua Daily* supplement), Mr. Bo Hong discusses the issue of opera masks. He admits that Chinese operas employ symbolist strategies: "For example, white symbolizes cunning, red, loyalty and bravery; black, ferociousness; blue, evil spirits; gold, good spirits, etc. In the West, white is used to symbolize innocence and purity, black stands for sadness, red for passion, golden yellow for glory and loyalty. The use of color as symbols in Chinese operas is actually no different; it is just simpler and cruder." This appears to be an accurate assessment. However, on second thought, doubts begin to set in. These symbolisms such as white for cunning, red for loyalty and bravery, are limited to the mask. Applied elsewhere, white no longer means cunning, nor does red, loyalty and bravery. . . .
>
> Of course, masks have their meanings, but I don't think they are symbols. The stage sets and spectators' expectations are also no longer the same as the ancients. Masks have only become superfluous. There is no need to preserve them.[31]

Audiences used to be able to read profound significance in the masked faces of traditional theater. However, audiences and readers of the new era find these figures ineffectual. Lu Xun argues that since their meanings are not universal, these theatrical masks cannot signify across time. Beyond the particular ancient operatic world, they are valueless and meaningless.

Lu Xun was not the first, nor the only one, to criticize traditional drama. The reform of the theater is part of the general discussion of the May Fourth literary revolution. Qian Xuantong's description of the traditional opera in his 1917 letter to the *New Youth* magazine editor, Chen Duxiu, as "painted, powdered, overmannered, and obscurantist," perhaps best summarizes the alienation the new audience felt toward the figurative faces of the traditional actor.[32]

Used as a metaphor of representation itself, the theater as described by Qian Xuantong, just like the literary language *(wenyan)*, represents a system of expression that had ceased to be meaningful in the twentieth-century reality. In fact, Chen Du Xiu's criticism of the literary language as "arch, obsequious, elaborate, and empty" and like a "painted and powdered dirt idol" echoes Qian's deprecation of the classical theater.[33]

Translated from May Fourth metaphorical language, mannerisms and affectations of traditional theater represent the social rules of an outdated world that circumscribe individual behavior. The repossession of one's body is a well-known aspect of May Fourth iconoclasm, from the breaking away from family control, to women's escape from their inner chambers, to rejection of the practice of arranged marriages. Natural faces and movements in modern drama reflect personality and individual feelings, thoughts, and actions. The plain face, as opposed to the painted, is a symbol of the assertion of an individual will against the dictates of traditional structures of dominance, namely the patriarchy. May Fourth critics regard as unnatural the formulaic facial designs in traditional drama. Because one's face and costume no longer have meaning on the surface level, such matters as individual quality and essential nature are no longer perceivable on one's face. In this way, an individual also easily escapes social detection and control. However, precisely because the "natural" faces of modern drama are "unreadable," they suggest occlusion. Occlusion of interiority is a result of the change in signification conventions.

In the *Autobiography of a Woman Soldier* (*Nubing zizhuan*, 1936) Xie Bingying uses this trope of the painted face versus the natural face to represent the struggle between fulfilling traditional duty and the desire for self-expression. The title of Xie's book refers to both her experience as a volunteer soldier in the late 1920s, a rare enough feat for a woman at the time, and her continuous battle against different social injustices against women. When Xie returned home from her military service (in the Northern Expedition of 1927), she was immediately forced into a prearranged marriage. Xie describes with irony her being made up by her mother and another older woman on her wedding day:

> Although I had been growing my hair out for half a year, it was still too short to cover my forehead. This was one thing that troubled my mother most. The woman who had been asked to make me up and remove my facial hair was Chang's mother. She combed my hair over with fragrant oil till it shone, then she started to paint my brows and apply rouge and face powder. "Aunty Du, I do not need any of this. Just let me be in my natural face *(benlai mianmu)*." I firmly and rudely pushed away her hand. "Every girl has to do this on her wedding day. Moreover, you are going to be such a beautiful bride. A little bit of rouge and powder, you will look just like a fairy. Haha!" I knew that she was mocking me. My skin had become quite dark from exposure to the sun during my army days. There were freckles on my cheeks. Her wish to apply makeup to me was only to make me look like a clown [literally, comic actor] on stage. I refused her good intentions because I felt too humiliated.[34]

Xie was carried away in a bridal palanquin to her in-laws' house: "I sat in the palanquin, lifted my veil, and looked at myself in a little mirror hanging against my chest. I felt I had become the clown in an opera. I almost laughed out loud to myself."[35]

Xie was being prepared for the traditional roles of a wife and a daughter-in-law. To be forced to have makeup applied is to be painted with an appropriate mask *(mianxiang)* for her imminent performance. In trying to paint over Xie's face, Aunty Du and her mother attempted to paint her into a picture-perfect bride who would conform to conventions and propriety, covering up the willful individuality she constantly displayed. However, Xie's insistence on her "natural face" *(benlai mianmu)* revealed her determination in rejecting the role and life story of a traditional woman.

In the excerpt above, a crucial self-reflexive moment occurs when

Xie, costumed and seated in a palanquin, raises a mirror to herself and then laughs to see her own reflection. Xie's smile to herself, hidden from direct sight of the people around her, hints at the presence of subversive private thoughts despite her appearance of capitulation. In the end, we discover that Xie managed to negotiate her way out of consummation of her marriage and eventually ran away from her in-laws' household and regained personal freedom. Convincing him that she would never return, she was also finally able to obtain a divorce from her husband.

When she saw her costumed self in the mirror, Xie laughed. However, Xie's laugh is difficult to interpret. Should she not be angry or worried or sad at her impending fate? Unlike the bridal mask that the older women tried to paint over her, Xie's natural face does not have meaning on the surface. Xie can no longer be read and interpreted in the "bridal" role despite the fact that she was dressed for it. Because of the unreadability of her face, the figurality of her costumed image is also disrupted. She laughed when she became aware of the fact that all her signs were wrong. She was dressed as a young bride, but her behavior was contrary. The symbolism of the traditional stage, or world, has lost its efficacy. Her mirror did not capture her object state, but this particular moment of her self-knowledge.

The painted or masked face is without "deep, private" meaning because signification is completed upon the surface level; the mask itself is meaningful. In contrast, Xie's unmasked, naked face is without surface signification. Her mysterious laugh implies duplicity—surface signs do not correspond to private meaning. We are left to assume interiority.

The naked face is enigmatic because its signification is no longer obvious or fixed. Numerous times, Xie uses puppetry as a metaphor of how an individual is manipulated by society with fixed codes. Her autobiography is about breaking these social codes, especially the three symbols of womanhood: bound feet, pierced ears, and a marriage contract. In an early episode of Xie's autobiography, she writes about her being marked as a woman:

> On the morning of the "Birthday of the Flowers" (the twelfth of the second month), my mother waited till I was fast asleep to pierce a hole in each of my earlobes. When I started from my dream in pain, she had already strung pieces of red string through them.

"Good. Of your important matters, I've already accomplished two," my mother said to me very happily. The three important matters she had to perform for her daughter turned out to be (1) foot binding, (2) ear piercing, (3) marriage.

"That's right, there is still one thing to destroy me you haven't done yet," I replied angrily, which again brought on a great scolding from her.³⁶

Xie is gradually prepared and marked for the role of a traditional woman with all the right signs: the specific costumes, makeup, mannerisms, and finally, life story. Xie's insistence on her naked face *(benlai mianmu)* and her refusal of the bridal mask renders her role and its meaning indistinct. Her looking into the mirror on her way to being a bride, contrary to conventional understanding of women's mirroring, is not about conformity. It represents existence of independent thought that is contrary to social expectations.

Similarly, in the short story "Love in a Fallen City" (Qingcheng zhilian), Chang describes this process of subversion through a moment of the heroine's self-mirroring. This story follows the adventures of a young divorcee, Bai Liusu, in her search for independence and personal fulfillment. Having divorced her abusive and profligate husband, Liusu takes refuge in her brother's household, living in subservience and humiliation. A well-meaning relative tries to convince her that the way out of her demeaning situation is remarriage. This suggestion gives her much pause, as it would violate social conventions. Pondering the stifling atmosphere of the family hall, feeling the oppressive presence of the ancestors (tradition) whose portraits hang from the walls bearing down upon her,

> Liusu gave a cry, shielded her eyes with her hands and ran stumbling upstairs . . . and tumbled into her own room. She switched on the lights, flung herself against the standing mirror and scrutinized herself carefully. Still good, she was not too old yet. . . . From the terrace, she could hear her fourth brother playing the *erhu* again; the pitches of the same melody rose and fell with vigor. Liusu unconsciously tilted her head, threw a theatrical glance to one side, and made a hand gesture. In front of the mirror, she did a little performance. The music did not seem to be just the *erhu* anymore, but a full orchestra of strings and pipes playing a sad palace dance. She

made a few steps to the left, then went a few steps to the right. She seemed to be in step with the rhythm of a long-lost, ancient dance. She suddenly smiled—*a secretive [yinyin de] smile, a smile that seemed not to harbor good intentions [buhuai haoyi]*. The music suddenly stopped. The *erhu* outside was still going on, but the story of loyalty and filial piety that was the story behind the music no longer had anything to do with her.[37]

The family hall in the Bai household is an ancient, timeless world, and Liusu runs to her room to escape its oppressive force. In the rest of the story, after this initial moment of reckoning, Liusu willfully challenges family propriety and openly pursues her happiness in a risky liaison with the playboy Fan Liuyuan, finally marrying him. As for Xie Bingying, traditional theatrics is, for Eileen Chang, a metaphor of the suppression of individuality. The choreographed dance steps, the coded behavior, from the glance to the hand gestures that Liusu rehearses in front of the mirror, symbolize the behavior of an individual circumscribed within traditional expectations. Like Xie Bingying, Liusu performed in an unmasked face. In contrast to a *mianxiang* that designates a typology and life story, Liusu's naked face lacks signification according to traditional codes. When she gazes at herself in the mirror, the charm of the tradition's hold on her breaks. Her smile signals duplicity—lack of correspondence between what she appears to be and what she is. She starts to dance out of step. Her behavior, from that moment, also lacks synchrony and identification with her environment, revealing her alienation from the traditional society. In Liusu's mirroring moment, she identifies a self beyond the subject and the object of the gaze.

In both stories, Xie Bingying and Bai Liusu are forced into traditional roles. They perform in full regalia of their womanly roles. Their self-reflexive smiles on their unmasked faces, however, immediately disrupt the signification of all the surface codes of their dresses and gestures. Smiling into their mirrors, they refuse the pure performativity of outward compliance. Indeed, very soon, both women dance out of step. Their subsequent behavior also falls out of step with traditional social order.

The act of mirroring in these literary instances brings to view the various sides of the modern heroines—the observer, the object, and the object divided between the reflected exterior and the suggested presence of an alternate self—De Lauretis's unrepresented "in-between." In the reflective moment, the split of the self becomes manifested. The women's mysterious smiles that refuse signification suggest the presence of the unreflected, uncaptured "in-between" that perverts the old society's dominant system of meaning.

The Changeable Subject

Chang is constantly aware of the fact that woman as a social category is merely a cipher, created according to social expectations. Thus, much of her writing is a nod to this condition, no matter how ironically. She deliberately exposes the artifice of her creation and mocks the reader's desire that she tries to fulfill at the same time. By this means she not only undermines the reader's gaze by reminding him of the delusion of his "Pygmalion" power, but also tells the reader that he is ultimately beholden to her literary manipulation. It is she who gives him the illusion that he has created her according to his desire. In the opening of "Intimate Words" (Siyu), perhaps Chang's most personal and autobiographical piece, she makes fun of our gullibility as readers of the artificial effects of writing:

> "Intimate words overheard in the deep night; the moon sinks like a golden basin." I suppose even if you did not intend to exchange intimacies, at that hour your words would become intimate words. I do not want to pretend what I have to say here is any great secret. Under pressure from Mr. Editor, this piece of writing has been completed in a great hurry. That is why I might have been a little too unrestrained. What I have written are not things that require any thought. They have always been there, perhaps as part of the setting of my subconscious. So let us pretend that this is a night when "the moon sinks like a golden basin," and someone is whispering, murmuring in your ear.[38]

Here, Chang makes it clear that the feeling of intimacy in her writing is a literary effect, created for different purposes, from appeasing editors to sheer financial consideration. Despite the seemingly personal subject matter, the writing has less to do with revealing the "true" authorial subjectivity than fulfilling "market" demands. Chang explicitly demonstrates that her posture of sincerity as a writer is a strategy, no different from the mirroring scene in the same piece, in which she manipulates her own image in the mirror to create a particular effect on her "viewers." Carolyn Heilbrun might have argued that women's writing is circumscribed by male language and male desire. However, Chang's writing pokes fun at this readerly delusion. She understands the artificiality of herself as a woman designed according to an ideological perception. However, it is this arbitrariness that she relentlessly mines and exposes in her writing, deriving much hilarity from the fact that as she owes her existence to readers, while readers rely on her literary sustenance for their fantasies of power. Readers who willingly receive as true the literary effects cultivated by the writer are as much dependent on her to affirm their ideological world as she is dependent on them to affirm her existence. Understanding this reciprocity in the exchange between readers and writers, Chang is able to restore balance to this traditional relationship that favors the gazer at the expense of the object of the gaze.

In the scene in which she presents a filmic rendition of herself, her reflexive examination of her mirror image is to estimate the effect of her tears on her spectators. The condition that brought about the tears may have been genuine, but she presents herself, from facial expressions to her "monologue," according to the specific impact she wants to evoke for her imagined spectators. In a work reminiscing about her daily life as a child, "A Child's Words are without Inhibition" (Tongyan wuji), Chang gives a memorable description of a childhood conversation with a school friend. She reveals the rhetorical device she used to create the sense of intimacy between her friend and herself, the effect of which went beyond even her own "authorial" expectations:

> One evening, a school friend and I were taking a stroll along a corridor in the dormitory in the moonlight. I was twelve. She was a few years older. She said, "I am very fond of you. I don't know if you realize it." Because of the moon and because I was a born storyteller, I quietly and solemnly said, "As for me . . . aside from my mother, there's only you." She was very touched at the time. Even I was moved by myself.[39]

In this passage she not only upsets the balance of power between the reader and the writer, she also plays on the notion of authorial subjectivity. As she peels back the emotive surfaces, we realize that there is not necessarily a corresponding emotive being. The emotional atmosphere of this whole scene is achieved through the rhetorical strategies of storytelling. If the object of the gaze is an effect of ideological sight and configured according to the needs of the plot, it is neither permanent nor predetermined. Unlike the heroines of her works (and Xiao Hong, who lacks mirroring moments), she is neither affixed nor petrified into an aesthetic object. As the author of her own texts, manipulating the conditions between herself and her gazers, she does not succumb passively to the male gaze. Here, Chang deflates the most important assumption in scopic politics—a stable subject that generates a specular object.

As we have seen in Xie Bingying's attitude toward her bridal dress, traditional costumes have lost their power to prescribe specific feminine roles and behavior. Modern women's clothing became changeable; their identities also became mutable. The mercurial nature of modern women is expressed in Chang's essay "Records of Changing Clothes" (Gengyi ji), which explores the history of Chinese women's fashion. In this essay, Chang dilates on the obvious theme of how women dress themselves according to the ideological standards of propriety and beauty in different eras. However, more significantly, she also expounds on the notion that women's identities, like fashion, are accumulated exterior codes and can be changed according to different situations if women have the will. A caricature of Chang appeared in a Shanghai periodical (together with two other glamorous writers, Su Qing and Pan Liudai) titled "Lipsticks and Fountain Pens" (Kouhong yu gangbi) in which the caption reads: "Eileen Chang, who dazzles with her extraordinary attires and strange costumes" [Qizhuang xuanren de Zhang Ailing].[40] Known for her flamboyant personal style, Chang obviously considered clothing an integral part of her persona. The curious title of her essay, "Changing Clothes," is used ambiguously in both a verbal and an adjectival sense, either changing of one's clothes or the changing of fashion, suggesting that her discussion of women's fashion is not undertaken merely as a passive historical observer, but as an evolving subject who mutates through changing societal conditions. "Changing Clothes" is easily an essay about changing subjectivity. Women are signs put together according to contemporary taste, needs, and meaning. However, more importantly, Chang also shows that it is women who manipulate the signs.

Chang challenges the perception that women are fixed ideas produced by patriarchal authority. If a woman is an object of gaze, cut and framed according to male desire, Chang shows how this artificial woman ultimately has the power to manipulate the desire. In the instant Chang peers into the mirror at herself, she evokes the general reader's sense of familiarity of a suffering female. She then immediately unsettles this familiarity by revealing the literary device she used in creating its effect. Here is Chang's answer to the Pygmalion myth, poking fun at this delusion of power. It only works, because *she* has meant it to work.

The Self as Literary Commodity

Recognition of the artifice of her endeavor as a writer gives Chang a particularly playful attitude toward writing itself. Perhaps for this reason, she was considered an "unserious writer" in her days. Even today, her works stride the line that separates literature from commercial texts.[41] Many writers of her generation, especially male, regard their works with seriousness, driven by a strong sense of moral obligation toward society. Even her female counterparts, such as Cao Ming, the later Lu Yin, and most famously, Ding Ling, regard writing as a social and political mission. Their writings reflect their self-perceived social positions as intellectuals who felt an imperative to be leaders. Whether intended or not, writings of this period have been consistently read in the social realist mode. In contrast, Chang has a deliberately and provocatively casual attitude toward her work, which resists most pragmatic interpretations. She might have been called decadent or even unpatriotic.[42] In reality, she was less sanguine or had a less privileged attitude toward the notion of authorship than many of her politically engaged contemporaries:

> Recently I saw a couple of lines in an English-language book satirizing the kind of writers who are overly interested in themselves. I thought the description was most appropriate: "They spend their whole lives staring at their belly buttons, trying to see

if there is anything that might be of interest for others to look at as well." I wonder if I also might be seen as exhibiting my navel. But I decided to go ahead with my writing anyway.[43]

Chang is obviously aware of the criticism of women writers' "typical" penchant for omphaloskepsis. However, rather than attempt to justify or reject such an accusation, Chang admits that her writing is self-serving, "spitting out her feelings to her heart's content *(Yitu erkuai)*."[44]

With the same candidness about her pursuits as a writer, Chang reminds us constantly about her banausic motivations. In the same essay, she describes a practice by which her family tried to determine the kind of person a newborn would become by placing various symbolic items on a tray before a baby and watching what it might instinctively grab. There were two contradicting accounts about Chang's choice. One reports that she picked up a writing brush, the other, a gold ingot. A reader can't help but compare this sardonic self-assessment with the numerous encomiums of famous men with descriptions of precocious childhood acts that mark them for greatness later on in life.[45] Demystifying the notion of talent, Chang tells the story of how, having earned five dollars for submitting a cartoon to a newspaper, she immediately bought herself a lipstick: "My mother said that I should have saved the five-dollar bill as a souvenir. But I am not sentimental like her. To me, money is money. It can buy me whatever I want."[46]

Women's writing may have suffered criticism and neglect because of their perceived sentimentalism and narrowness in scope. However, Chang loses no opportunity to make fun of the grandiosity of male writers. This self-importance, she implies, is a luxury few women can afford. How can any woman talk about things of national importance when personal survival is at stake? Writing is a vocation for men, but for women, Chang argues, it is a matter of subsistence. Su Qing, a woman writer, a contemporary of Chang's and of equal popularity in Shanghai, wrote an essay titled "My Own Room" ("Ziji de fangjian," 1944), a distant echo of Virginia Woolf's *A Room of One's Own*. Su laments her lack of privacy, personal space, and money when abandoned by her husband. She was forced to board at a relative's home with two young children and had to endure their growing resentment toward her. She finally managed to find employment as a journalist and columnist and set up her own home amid vicious rumors that she had achieved these positions in exchange for sexual favors.⁴⁷ Obviously empathetic to her predicament as a modern, self-supporting career woman, Chang quotes Su Qing:

> This year, I have been a self-reliant petit bourgeois. Concerning professional women, Su Qing has this to say: "I look around me. I bought everything, even the nails in this room, with my own money. However, what joy can I have in this fact?" These are words of great wisdom indeed. The more one thinks about them, the more one realizes the loneliness behind them.⁴⁸

For both Su Qing and Chang, no matter what other noble ambition they might have had, their writing is first and foremost a pecuniary pursuit, for survival. In "Poetry and Nonsense" (Shi yu hushuo), Chang describes her decision to write on a traditionally highbrow subject matter, poetry, in response to an illness that kept her home with nothing to do and nowhere to spend her money. This enforced home-stay and writing are described sardonically as beneficial to both her physical and fiscal health. Chang never misses a chance to point out the poignant relationship between money and a woman's writing:

> In the summer, when I had nothing to do at home, or there was heavy manual work I couldn't do, I would write essays on Cézanne's paintings, books I had read, or the religious practices of Chinese people—it is ultimately a civilized pursuit. I decided that this was the month of refinement *(fengya zhiyue)*, so I decided to become classy all the way and write about poetry.⁴⁹

In spite and because of the great popularity of their work, Chang and Su Qing turned, in an ironic posture, their writings and themselves into a kind of commodity in this new trade between readers and women authors. Calling themselves the "petit bourgeois," they participate enthusiastically in this material economy. In the transaction between the writer and her readers, women, the traditional object of the power trade, now become active brokers of their otherness. No one understands more than Chang how women are objectified, fetishized, and commodified, as we have seen in her various depictions of women in her short stories. If Lu Xun put into literary currency the image of cannibalism in describing the consumption of individuals by the demands of traditional society, it is Chang who raised this notion of the consuming of women to a new consciousness.[50]

If writing is seen as a kind of material exchange, the subject matters and the subjectivities in writing are the commodities traded. In the spirit of such commercialism, Chang fragments her world into a veritable emporium. Her essays collected in *Liuyan* are filled with consumer items: fashion, music, art, groceries, cinema—everyday objects and daily effects of the petit bourgeois—even the woman's body. Satirizing her position as an object of the patriarchal gaze, Chang even breaks herself down into a composite of parts in her self-writings. It is not from one center of self that all the stories and situations in her text emanate. Rather, from within all the different societal expectations she arises as different subjectivities from situation to situation. She constructs a vast textual emporium in which she carries out her transaction with the reading public—delivering to them what it desires. As in the changing of clothes, Chang mercurially transforms from one object of desire to another according to the demands of different situations, an intimate confessor ("Intimate Words"), or a loyal and devoted friend ("A Child's Words"). As a good salesperson, Chang anticipates and delivers what the patriarchal consumer wants, estimating the financial returns and laughing all the way about his delusion of power. But through all these, she remains elusive as a self, neither grasped nor consumed. While Sontag laments that women have been cut and evaluated according to their different body parts, Chang sees how this fragmented self can also be a source of power. Taunting and teasing, the traditional object of desire now controls the gazer, by now withholding, now provoking, and now providing fulfillment of his desires. The male desire that is supposed to entrap women also entraps the gazer himself.

This is where much of the recovery work in women's literature fails. In "The Female Body and Nationalist Discourse," Liu strenuously protests against the fact that the seriousness and reality of women's voices are usurped by nationalist rhetoric and calls for a revisioning of all women's writings.[51] However, it is more important to recognize that certain writers, such as Eileen Chang and Su Qing, consciously reject such a grandiose social scheme or historical mission. Maybe they *are* socially unconcerned, as they stand accused, and they are *not* apologetic. They hold a fundamentally different attitude toward writing—not mimetic, not social realist, and not didactic. And they should be allowed to be as they wish, without having agendas put into their mouths in the name of revisionism. As Theodore Huters pointed out, the problem with the study of modern Chinese literature in general is a predominantly realist reading, and as such, a nationalist agenda, even now.[52] Even those writers who professed to reject this principle and have been thus rendered unimportant in literary history are given elaborate justifications in order to resurrect them from neglect. This ultimately pins them back in a place they resisted.[53]

In 1995, Chang was discovered dead alone in her Los Angeles apartment. There was a general lament of the loss of a "literary talent," and many readers were both shocked and titillated that a journalist attempted to search through Chang's garbage in order to find out the details of her last days. While there was an outcry against such indecent prowling, the content of Chang's garbage was nevertheless eagerly sought after.[54] In the industry of "Chang studies," there are many writings about Chang that display a garish curiosity about her personal habits and private details. Many readers confuse Chang's own life—ungraspable as a subjectivity in her works—with her stories. The air of mystery surrounding Chang, indicated in such books as Yang Yi's *The Extraordinary Woman Eileen Chang* (Qinuzi Zhang Ailing), or Shui Jing's *The Art of Eileen Chang's Fiction* (Zhang Ailing de xiaoshuo yishu), testifies to the almost worshipful gaze lavished upon her.[55] As an object that stays within the frame of the gaze, she nevertheless upsets the alignment of power. In this way, even in the most barbaric consumerism in which the constructed woman is offered up and cannibalized as a commodity, Chang as a person remains elusive above all.

Conclusion

The relationship between women and their mirrors is an age-old symbol of the uneasy heterosexual contract between women and the masculine world. Within this exchange, the subject and object seem to align themselves along predictable gender lines, with men controlling the position of power as the gazer and women occupying the position of the object. Chang's self-commodification attests to the possibility of self-representation as both subject and object at the same time. Chang's writing about herself complicates the traditional relationship between women and their mirrors (as symbols of the aesthetic and behavioral norm) by which they anxiously measure themselves. She is an object, also a subject; the observer, as well as the observed. In Chang's mirror scene, she duplicates her presented identity as an enframed object, yet unexpectedly controls the power dynamic from within this frame. She thus uses the structure of familiar male gaze, but only as a commentary or perversion of it. She proves that the object of the gaze is not fixed in either time or space, but evolves continuously through fabrication.

Chapter Three

Nationalism and the Gestural System of Self-Expression

A study of modern Chinese autobiography would not be complete without a discussion of Yu Dafu, who famously proclaimed that all literary writings contain elements of the autobiographical.¹ Without doubt, Yu is one of the most personal, sentimental, and melodramatic writers, and as such, regarded as a representative voice in the rise of individualism and romanticism in modern Chinese literature. For convenience of argument, I distinguish between individualism and romanticism, identifying the former as an ontological state, while the latter is a literary effect. The tendency toward bathos is a particular literary fashion in the early May Fourth period. Writers particularly associated with the early Creation Society, such as Yu Dafu, Zheng Boqi, the poet Guo Moro, and the dramatist Tian Han, are renowned for their "romantic" proclivity. Reading their personal narratives, one is constantly compelled into the mire of the "psychological" melodrama of the author. However, as I repeatedly show in this volume, the notion of interiority is more rhetorical than psychological. In this chapter, I argue that the appearance of interior depth and intimacy in Yu Dafu's writings is an effect of the "gestural system" of representation. This strategy, particularly identified with Yu's "psychological fiction," is in fact, all about body and surfaces.

The question is, why this emphasis on the autobiographical and one's physical body at a time when China's national survival was an all-consuming issue for most intellectuals? The paradox in Yu's writings is immediately evident—despite the seeming solipsism, his writing is tightly connected to, if not instigated by, nationalistic concerns. As a result, the nation and the individual share the same expressive space.

In this chapter, through a reading of Yu Dafu's autobiographical works, I examine how highly personal and individualistic expressions are conjoined with the most urgent social and political concerns. Continuing my discussion of the effects of the language reform and the related search for true expression, I explore how and why melodramatic strategies, particularly the focus on the body and its gestures, are a literary form of Chinese individualism as well as nationalism.² In short, this chapter is an examination of confessional writing and its place in modern Chinese nationalism.

Reading Yu's Autobiography

Because of Yu's use of intentionally intimate literary forms such as diaries, letters, autobiographical accounts, and rhetorical devices of confession, such as melodramatic exclamations and ellipses, readers often assume that Yu's narration is all about himself and his feelings. The confusion of form with content in Yu's writings has been the source of much scholarly speculation and discussion. Michael Egan long ago pointed out the problems of analyzing Yu's writings based on an unquestioned premise of identification between him and his characters.³ Egan suggests that the weakness of the psychobiographical reading in early scholarship is that it frequently results in judgmental conclusions about the author as a person instead of real discussions of his or her writings.⁴ However, Egan's reading ignores the extrinsic condition of the writing and confines the understanding of Yu's works within the protagonists' myopic textual worlds. Thus, in his discussion of "Sinking," instead of evaluating the sociopolitical relevance of Yu's melodramatic exuberance, Egan complains that the infamous outburst, "China, Oh my China! Why don't you grow rich and strong," is a stylistic failure, an "afterthought and irrelevant to the development of the story."⁵

More recently, Kirk Denton attempts to connect Yu's works to an intellectual lineage. He evaluates their seeming awkwardness and contradictions within the context of a particular May Fourth intellectual dilemma. Yu's "Sinking," Denton claims, demonstrates the paradoxical desires to destroy traditional bonds that suppress individualism, on the one hand, and to seek self-identity and self-affirmation from tradition in the face of Western imperialism, on the other. He thus sees Yu's nationalistic sentimentalism and solipsism as embodying the generation's conflicting relationships with both the tradition and the West.[6] Denton interprets Yu's work as an inadvertent testament to the generational search for identity or subjectivity. However, this reading is just as unsatisfactory as the approaches to which he objects. In his intention to raise Yu's works beyond the personal, Denton's reading slips into cultural generalities.

Such efforts to distinguish the writer's life from his writing are insensitive to the text. Yu himself obviously intended the confusion. He wrote in four different highly personal genres: fiction of "things around oneself" [shenbian xiaoshuo], autobiographical essays, diaries, and an autobiography. Between 1921 and 1937, he produced twenty-four different collections of diaries for publication. His *Nine Diaries* includes entries from December 1934 to February 1936. His autobiography, *Dafu zizhuan*, was written between 1936 and 1937. Many of the events recorded in the diaries were rewritten in the autobiography. Likewise, much that appears in the autobiography and diaries had earlier incarnations in short stories or became fodder for eventual fictional elaboration.

The narrator of the diaries and the autobiography, the author and the protagonists of the fiction are superimposed so as to be completely indistinguishable. Fiction and facts, the author and protagonists, overlap in an intricate *textum*, to use Roland Barthes's term.[7] Through the palimpsest of texts, the adumbration of the author appears as the sum of all the different impressions, real and fictional. Yu's work reflects a complete, deliberate continuity between the intertextual and the extratextual world. It is important to connect the signification of his writing to the historical. However, it is equally necessary to regard it on the level of rhetorical construct and textual effects and give heed to Yu's assertion that his works be read *autobiographically*—that is, with attention to the individual consciousness within the forces of history. Autobiography as a form or the use of "I" as a signifier is a cultural or political act that needs to be deciphered. As we will see in a later section, Yu regards the individual as firmly engaged in and intertwined within the historical process, whether as a victim or an active agent—not merely a product.

The Reading Contract

As a form of literature, Philippe Lejeune argues, autobiography has all the instabilities of this category. As such, the traditional attempt at differentiation of fact and fiction is a futility. This is only too evident in the case of Yu's writings. According to Lejeune, the power of autobiography is derived, not so much from the veracity of the information relayed, but on the strength of the autobiographer's name. He asserts that autobiography is definable as a contract established between the reader and the writer on the premise of an *assumed* realness of the autobiographical subject, regardless of the actuality. The subject has the legality of the name of the author and all the abiding properties. The content itself is secondary. The "autobiographical pact" between the writer and the reader depends on an absolute acceptance, on the part of the reader, of the truth content of the autobiography. Once this agreement is established, the writer has no obligation to continually prove him- or herself.[8] Autobiographical truth is just this: a speech act that is based on contractual understanding rather than epistemological authority. Accordingly, the reading of autobiography should be a consideration of the form rather than the content.

Obviously informed by the nominalist position, Lejeune's understanding depends on the idea of the effect and power of language as a social system of signification because of, despite, and in spite of, the authorial will. In the same vein, James Fujii, noting a similar tendency of the author/narrator confusion in Japanese I-novels, argues for maintaining the critical attention on the level of rhetorical surfaces. (The I-novel was at its height of popularity when Yu was studying in Japan. Yu and the rest of the Creation Society writers were heavily indebted to this kind of writing.)[9]

> [D]iscussions built around [biographical details] tend to promote an essentialist view of the subject, suppressing the very narrated (constructed) nature of subjectivity. Attention to the rhetorical strategy helps restore that which is occluded by the installation of the subject as a given.[10]

This position on the value of language offers a way out of the author/narrator, truth/fiction conundrum that particularly plagues the reading of Yu's works.

According to Lejeune, in autobiography, the narrator of the text steps out of his or her role in the narration to assume the name in the authorial contract with the readers. To read Yu's autobiographical writings is to observe this contract established upon the power and the aura of the name to the fullest extent and to suspend our insistence on factuality. This is neither to suggest nor deny that the literary creation has any intrinsic equivalence to the actual person. What we know of an author is only what we are allowed to know through writings and certain circumstantial information. What we are able to grasp of a writer is only that which is available in the form of rhetorical and figural constructions—tropes, metaphor, allegory, metonym—and the contextual conditions of the writings.

The Melodramatic Voice as Gesture of Inarticulation

In chapter 1, I discuss the commonly held idea among young intellectuals of the May Fourth era that the vernacular is less infected by the ideologies of the past world than is classical literary language and is thus more able to express the feelings, thoughts, and sensibilities of the new generation. This led to the notion that since the voice is a natural and direct conduit of one's interior world, the new writing should foreground the fluency of speech—the vernacular.

When we compare Yu's works with Chen Hengzhe's piece published in 1917 with its focus on speech in writing, it is hard not to notice the dramatic difference between these two writers. (See chapter 1 for a discussion of Chen's story.) While Chen's "phono-text" is unquestionably groundbreaking, it nevertheless leaves the reader puzzled, if not bewildered, by the constantly rotating roster of characters only known to us through their banter, which just barely reports their daily travails. The "meaning" of the writing is no more than what one can decipher from overhearing an unknown group of undergraduates giving vent to mundane sentiments about their daily lives in college. The characters presented through the straight verbality lack depth. Nevertheless, Chen's piece is an important beginning to what became quintessentially May Fourth romanticism—the tireless monologue and the obsessive focus on the minutiae of one's private world. Yu is clearly a representative of this phenomenon. However, there are obvious differences between the two writers. What are the possible connections between Chen's one-dimensional creations and Yu's "psychological fiction"?

It is not without reason that Yu has been recognized as the first writer in modern Chinese literature to produce psychological fiction.[11] This designation, as will be apparent in the following discussion, is questionable. However, Yu's characters do exhibit what appears to be an interior depth that is absent in Chen's work. What creates this effect of depth?

In "Humane Literature" ("Rende wenxue," 1918), published in *New Youth*, written directly after the promulgation of the literary reform, Zhou Zuoren advocates a nonelitist literature to further undermine classical writings. He describes the immediacy of the expression of feelings in vernacular writing:

> If we recognize the self as one with the rest of humanity, mixed within the human world, then the general affairs of humanity are also our own. When we speak of the urgent events that affect us, our hearts race and our mouths sputter. We want only to express our genuine thoughts and actual feelings. Naturally we will not have time to work over our sentences.[12]

Zhou not only describes the intimate connection between the self and the world, he articulates the new expression of this relationship. Speech, assumed to be direct and unmediated, is the ideal medium for instantaneous and spontaneous emotional responses. Though it is at times clumsy and inarticulate because there is no time for either refinement or censoring, this writing is considered superior to overwrought literary flourishes because it is unmediated. Hence, it is authentic, honest, and unaffected. It is natural that this new "true" writing includes all groans and gasps and other inarticulate and extralinguistic ejaculations as the writer sputters out his or her emotions. This sputtering is certainly plentiful in Yu's works, which he scatters with ellipses, sighs, and moans as his characters lapse into extreme emotionalism. The narrative of events are often punctuated by nonverbal eruptions:

> I got a room [at an inn] and washed my face. The attendant handed me a sheet of paper and asked me to fill in my name, hometown, and profession. I stared at him blankly for a while. He thought I had probably never traveled before and didn't know the proce-

dure, so he explained it to me patiently. Ah . . . ah, how could I not know? It was only because I lacked courage to write anything down: my name unknown to anyone, the hometown from where I hail, my profession—Ah . . . ah, tell me how I could write these down.

Not being able to fend him off, I picked up a pen and put down a fake name. I put down *foreigner,* and in the blank for profession, I put down *nothing.* Unawares, my tears spilled onto the piece of paper. The attendant was alarmed. He looked at the form and said to me: "Mister, where do you live? Please fill that in. Also, you must put down your profession." There was no other way but to cross out *foreigner* and fill in *Korean.* Under profession I also crossed out what I had written and filled in *drifter.* After the attendant left, I closed my door, fell on my bed, and cried my heart out.[13]

If Yu has always been regarded as a writer who displays great individualism, this distinguishing characteristic of his writing is a result of these spontaneous emotive asides inserted within the narrative of events. Yu's writing is as much dependent upon common narrative details as the alternative system of nonverbal signification. Peter Brooks notices the same strategy in his study of melodramatic effects in fiction, which he traces to the theater.[14] Although Brooks's study focuses on late-nineteenth- and early-twentieth-century European texts, particular Balzac and Henry James, the melodramatic strategies he describes can be observed in many early May Fourth writings as well. Brooks identifies a "gestural system" of signification in melodrama that supplements verbal representation, that is, the use of bodily gestures to relay the verbal in the event of the "inerrable." Hyperbolized bodily movements and vocal gestures, such as sighs, sobs, and exclamations, fill in the inarticulate moments when normal narration breaks down. The verbal and the gestural are different systems that signify simultaneously but independently of each other. The relationship between these two systems is not hierarchical; language is not primary and gestures are not secondary, but they supplement each other. In reading, both the language and the gestures need to be deciphered rigorously. (I discuss this in a later section.)

In comparison, both Chen Hengzhe and Yu have the same penchant for lingering over seemingly inconsequential moments in their writings. Both have a similar emphasis on the dialogic, and an equal disregard for plot movement or even the content itself. In other words, both are interested in the act of telling. The most apparent difference between them is the absence of the gestural system in Chen's writing. As a primary device in Yu's, strong emotions and all aspects of the self that are inexpressible through locution are related through body language that signifies beyond verbal meaning. This difference between Chen and Yu offers an important clue to deciphering the effect of "psychological depth" in Yu's works. The use of the gestural system in writing suggests an alternative truth that is not immediately evident or transparent through verbal language. This occluded reality, which one would naturally take for psychological depth, is a direct effect of gestures.

True to the vernacular movement's emphasis on the voice, much of Yu's writing is a combination of verbal language and the "sputter" of emotions. He tirelessly and obsessively tells and retells his experiences through the various autobiographical and confessional forms. In fact, many of his pieces are about the same events, told in different ways, from different angles and using different strategies and devices until the "total truth" about him surfaces. The act of telling is more important than the stories being told. It is in this approach that Yu remains firmly a product of the May Fourth generation, whose belief in the voice as the carrier of truth is unwavering. However, Yu pushes this instrument of truth to its extreme capacity, going into territories unarticulated or inarticulable before. It's there that the voice falters and has to be relayed by an alternate system.

The Language of the Body

The body as a system is one of the most important elements in the strategy of melodrama. The inability of speech to fully express thoughts awakens the body's expressiveness. The materiality of human bodies and their inefficient contortions in the attempt to convey meaning is what creates melodrama. In Brooks's discussion of *Orphans of the Storm*, he describes the heroine, Henriette, as "wholly seized by affective meaning, of message converted onto the body so forcefully and totally that the body has ceased to function in its normal postures and gestures, to become nothing but text, nothing but the place of representation."[15] Brooks points out that gestures are tropes, a type of catachresis.[16] To read gestures is not to "decode," but to "decipher."

In Yu's works, not only are physical gestures the primary figural element, the body as a whole becomes text. If actors in a melodrama stomp the floorboards of the stage or clap their hands to draw the audience's attention to particular points of emphasis, as Brooks points out, Yu engages in various rhetorical demonstrations (stomping) in his writing. His hyperbolized locutions and blatant revelations of his bodily desires in his narratives are not merely for emphasis, but also to engage the reader's attention on the level of the body, to make the reader concentrate on the body with all its physicality, pulses, and contortions. Meaning is sustained and completed on the level of surfaces—the body and its gestures.

The passionate gesticulations and tropes of hyperbole are results of impulses to make whatever's hidden to come to light till the narrative is complete and the story is fully unraveled. Occluded meanings in melodramatic texts are not necessarily psychological. They might merely be hidden for a while to be uncovered eventually.[17] Rather than relying on the reader to probe the interior recesses of the characters, the characters themselves often strive to uncover and complete the meaning. Melodrama is a result of the energy produced from the struggle to reveal the suppressed. Thus the body is the site on which the events of both internal and external aspects of the self are enacted. Melodramatic writing is thus like a Möbius strip—a continuity of surfaces, without differentiation between the interior and the exterior worlds, the intimate and the public. It is as such that Brooks rejects the notion of melodrama as a psychological text, but refers to it instead as a "theater of signs."[18]

Yu's romantic writings rely on physical gestures and, despite their constant association with psychological fiction, are antithetical to it. The blatant sexual confessions and fantasies in Yu's works might have, at one point, shocked their readers. Even today, some of his works have not lost their power to titillate or disturb because of his insistent revelation of every aspect of his protagonist's intimate experiences. Perhaps what is most problematic about Yu's confessions to a reader today is not the "immorality" of his thoughts, but the bathos that seems disproportional to the situation from which they arise. Yu has a propensity for investing seemingly trivial things with moral or emotional gravity that seems to verge on the irrational or the absurd. This self-importance or egotism often corrodes the authority of his own narration.

For example, in "Returning Home," Yu writes about his financial destitution and his attempt to burglarize someone's house after having recklessly used up all his travel money. While he pondered the ethical implications of this act, his thoughts suddenly gave way to sexual fantasy evoked by a pair of women's shoes he saw on the floor of the room he was planning to enter. When his material need and ethical dilemma, with which the general reader might have been able to sympathize, turns into a fetishistic self-indulgence, he alienates the readers he courts. The significance (literary or figurative) of Yu's sexual fantasy at that particular instance of the story is unclear. Readers endure Yu's soaring rhetoric as his protagonists wrestle over matters of seeming inconsequence. The banality of the events seldom bears out the intensity or grandiosity of his expressions. His so-called transgressions are usually indecencies bound in private thought, never realized in acts that offend. It is the incongruence between the rhetorical intensity and the nature of the narrated events in his writings that makes Yu's works challenging, and, at times, irritating to read. One is tempted to follow Michael Egan in regarding these moments as stylistic failures. For this reason, some readers dismiss his writings as effects of maudlin perversity and are misled into judgment of his psychological condition as a writer. However, reading Yu on this psychological level is disappointing and unproductive.

The protagonist goes from describing his absurd solution to his financial problem to a sudden erotic interlude, thus suspending the natural progression, both physical and psychological, of the plot. These shifts in focus, which seem to have no implicit or explicit meaning in the writing, often accompany moments of mental crisis. At the point of intense internal struggle, a hiatus appears in the narration, which is then taken over by physical gestures, usually sexual. Rational thoughts and narrative logic are thus usurped by the dictates of bodily needs. Reading this passage "melodramatically," we realize that the body takes over signification at the moment of the character's impasse in reasoning or failure in verbal self-expression.

In the same story, Yu again resorts to the devices of melodrama when overcome by scenes of happiness around him, which exacerbate his own misery in having to return to a loveless home, jobless and penniless:

> The moment I got off the train at the terminal, I felt a kind of shame and despair being in Hangzhou's surroundings. If I could describe this feeling with words at the time, the sleeves of my cotton summer gown would not have been soaked with tear and sweat. This is because sorrow that can be articulated by words is not the most sorrowful in the world.[19]

In this passage, Yu not only explains the inerrability of intense feelings, but also how his body functions to substitute for these moments of inarticulation. Similarly, in "Sinking," sexual acts, fantasized or actual, replace or supplement the articulation of the protagonist's complicated and inexpressible feelings of alienation and paranoia. Physical gestures relay locution, making *visible* his discomfort.

The focus on the body results in a constant competition between two states of awareness—the conscious, verbal, and rational on one side and the occluded, bodily, and inexplicable on the other. The latter's signification continuously disrupts the narrative logic. To readers, this seemingly unpredictable, uncontrollable, or bodily is what appears as "interiority" breaking through. Yu's text is about a continuous self-negotiation, not so much to close the chasm between mind and body, but to give equal concession to both. This negotiation is not about suppressing or resisting bodily needs; but about managing them while acknowledging their existence and the need for their expression. Physical impulses are as much reality as articulated truth.

Body and Society

The body is the major signifier in the gestural system. Vigilance over the body, whether another's or his own, whether sexual, sentimental, or fraternal, is a major preoccupation in Yu's writing. In his diaries, Yu frequently belabors himself for the weaknesses of the flesh—slovenliness, laziness, drunkenness, and licentiousness—and urges himself to reform.

I woke up at eight in the morning, and unclean thoughts arose in me again, breaking my month-long resolution to be diligent and to apply myself. Today, I plan to visit for half a day at Yingxia's hotel, bathe, buy a few books I like, have a drink, and reindulge in the weaknesses of my life; then tomorrow, I'll start anew. "Ah, tomorrow, the hopeless tomorrow!"[20]

The well-managed body, functioning in an orderly way, is crucial to one's moral health and as a result, the general health of the society. Yet the body's expressiveness—its desires, physical impulses, contortions, and disorders—disrupts the logic of human language, which is the basis of harmonious human relationships in society. Aphasia that causes misunderstanding is often a tragic device in melodrama, according to Brooks. Resolutions are brought about when verbal communication is reestablished among characters, and hence, understanding, harmony, and social order. In "An Evening in the Intoxicating Spring Breeze" (Chunfeng chenzui de wanshang), the body's usurpation of verbal expression threatens to disrupt normal human relationship. The initial "misunderstanding" between the protagonist and a young woman in the story arises from his unyielding silence about himself. The woman even suspects that he is a criminal because of his secretive and solitary nighttime rambling. When she discovers that he is an intellectual and that he goes out only at night because his clothes are too shabby to be seen in daylight, she is filled with remorse at her lack of sensitivity toward his misfortune. Her sympathy elicits from him a return of deep gratitude. Still without a verbal venue, the intensity and urgency of his feelings explode forth in the form of sexual desire:

When I saw how innocent she was, an unthinkable feeling arose in my heart. I wanted to take her in my arms; but my reason commanded: "Don't give in to such wickedness! Don't you know what kind of situation you are in right now? Do you want to ruin such an innocent virgin? Monster! Monster! Right now, you don't even deserve to love." When that kind of emotion arose in me, I shut my eyes for a few seconds. After listening to the command of my reason, I opened my eyes. I felt that my surroundings had suddenly become brighter than a few seconds ago.[21]

On the simplest level, this is a story about discovering human warmth and exchange of care for one another in a harsh and indifferent world. Being attentive to one another's physical well-being is the ultimate expression of care. The concern between the protagonist and the young woman is initially expressed through food. Their relationship begins with their sharing of treats with each other since they are both desperately poor and can afford little. The man's offering of edibles to the woman gets fancier as his feelings toward her increase, to the point where they become beyond his means. Finally, as his feelings for her intensify, this concern for bodily nourishment is transmuted to a transgressive level of physical desire. The protagonist's emotions toward the young women are complex and profound. It is not mere sexual love even though it is expressed as such. His feelings for her are originally inspired by a righteous dignity over her victimization by society, being forced by poverty into exploitative situations. This sense of social justice, together with his gratitude toward her reciprocal care for him, fuels the protagonist's sexual feelings. The love of the body, and by extension, sexual love, is here intricately connected to social love. Thus the care and love of the body is, paradoxically, an inherently social response. It is a mistake to read the bathos and sexual expressiveness in Yu's writings as solipsistic or even psychological.

The Historical Subject

Though Yu's writings are constantly labeled as "individualistic" or "egotistical," the sense of social engagement in them is indismissible. They demonstrate his belief that every detail of the self is of universal and historical relevance and significance. Private emotions thus share the same expressive space as social issues in his writings. Zheng Boqi, in a reminiscence of the early Creation writers, explains this seeming paradox in the works of his confreres of the literary society (1923):

> We are like bubbles in the torrent of the times. The works we create will naturally and inevitably be colored by the times. However,

we should not stop at this subconscious inference. We should hold on to the times and make a conscious effort to articulate our present. We should use forceful methods to express the times, the way of life and thought, so that people will be able to reflect on and evaluate their own lives. Therefore, we have a heavy responsibility toward the present.[22]

The sentimentalism of the Creation Society writers is an expression of their commitment toward the world rather than a retreat into an interior space, as their "subjectivism" has always been regarded. Yu sees his protagonists as representatives of history, set within the coordinates of the historical and social conditions and metonymically joined to the greater society. The historical is implicated through them and is manifested through them. A fellow Creation Society poet, Guo Moro, writes in his autobiography, *My Childhood* (Wode tongnian), "The motivation for my writing is constant: to use myself to illustrate the entire era."[23] Similarly, Yu believes that he is a "great 'I' who can represent all the nations of the world," using the language of *dawo* (the great "I") and *xiaowo* (the small "I") in currency during that era.[24] (I discuss this in the following chapter, on Hu Shi.)

Because of the notion of the sagittal connection between the self and the world, the individual and the "I" of humanity, the investigation of the self and the knowledge of the self logically become the source of knowledge of the world. In this reversal, even the most private of all activities becomes wrought with universal significance. The writing of autobiographies, diaries, or autobiographical fiction is thus about the writing of universals through the trajectory of the self. As a result, despite the seeming egotism of autobiographical writings, Yu justifies their relevance as the nation's text: "Diary writing benefits investigative researches. It relieves historians from the dry historical facts and lets them see an individual's record of his society at the time. This is a fact that cannot be denied."[25] On another occasion, he similarly asserts the historical relevance of his diaries: "Diaries are useful in historical researches. They are records of the sentiments of real people in real society. They are to supplement dry historical data, and are actual facts that should not be buried."[26]

In accordance with the contemporary view of the relationship between self and society, Yu believes that individuals are social beings, immersed in the social and political currents of the times. Their expressions cannot, but be political or historical. Even the most private experience has social meaning. By the same token, even the most personal writings are "social texts."

This universalism, however, does not usurp the importance of individual specificities. Further discussing the nature of diaries, Yu anticipates his readers: "As for us readers, our primary motivation is to pry into other people's private matters. This *curiosity* [original in English] is the greatest motivation in our reading of fiction."[27] Through the highly confessional nature of his writing, Yu induces his readers to attend not only to the historical events, but to himself as a social and historical being. Readers are thus to invest in Yu the writer as well as his stories.[28] Through his complete divulgence of both inner and external aspects, Yu creates a "total subject" or "total citizen" who not only asserts his participation in the world in his physical presence, but through his emotive being as well. He is a complete public being, whose life, inside and out, belongs wholly to the historical process.

Yu's success in creating social beings can be seen through his readers' enthusiastic reception of his works. His collection in which the short story "Blood and Tears" (Xue yu lei) is included sold over twenty thousand copies at its first printing.[29] The Hong Kong–made Western suit that Da, the protagonist, wears also reputedly became an instant fashion. Referring to Yu's representative influence in society, his contemporary, Shen Congwen comments, "Dafu only knows how to write about himself. But he *is* youth—*us*."[30] Yu and his works speak to his generation in a way that pure romantic solipsism never can. Thus the use of sexuality in Yu's works, contrary to his critics' claims, transcends Yu's personal psychology or egotism.

Yu's style of individualism is an oxymoron since it is firmly imbricated within the society at large. The individual is tied to the society. The devotion toward his body expressed in his diaries is by extension a dedication to the welfare of his society. The individual body represents the nation. The care of the body is ultimately a gesture of national stewardship, and the care of the self is national preservation. In the urgent rhetoric of national salvation in China in the 1930s, this is translated into an intense obsession with the body.

The Health of the Body

Because of this perceived contiguity between the self and nation, the health of one's corporal being is an important measure of the corporate health of the nation. The body's perverse desires or illnesses point to the reverse truth, that of society's corruption and decadence. The body and all its related issues, such as health and sexuality, are the commanding metaphors of Yu's tale of himself and the nation. He begins his *Autobiography* (Dafu zichuan) with the following description of China's state of disease and its equivalence to his own physical conditions:

> I only wish to write about one thing; that is, in the middle of the night on the third day of the eleventh month of the twenty-second year of Guangxu was the birth of a yet unfinished tragedy with a rather weak plot.
>
> The twenty-second year of Guangxu (1896) was the third anniversary of China's defeat in the Sino-Japanese war. The court was daily issuing guilty verdicts, running official academies, repairing railroads, talking about politics and negotiating treaties with different countries. The slumbering lion of the East, having been hit on the head this time, seemed to be waking up. However, while it was still in its sweet dreams, its internal organs had rotted from indigestion. No matter how good the doctor might be, prescribing suitable treatment to the problems would not be easy. The rot had already spread through different organs in places above and below. The people of this defeated country—especially the little people who were just born are, of course, deformed, paranoid, and hysterical. . . .
>
> . . . I was not even twelve months old when I developed stomach problems because of malnutrition. I was ill for over a year, developing from weakness to fever, from fever to convulsion. Everybody from high to low in the family was exhausted by this young life. Between the spring and summer of the third year after I was born, my father died of fatigue.[31]

Significantly, in Yu's autobiography, incidents of his own life relay, even mirror, the events of the nation. Two primary symbols of male power and dominance in Yu's universe are eradicated at his birth. The patriarch's demise is immediately followed by the degradation of the dynasty.³² The birth of a deformed child is directly connected to the decline of the family and the floundering of the kingdom. The personal world forms a seamless continuity with the greater, historical world. The individual becomes a synecdoche of the nation. The nation also becomes a metaphor of the self.

Yu describes the situation of his household after the death of the patriarch: "This is the point where the prologue of the tragedy ends, and from now on, only a cast of orphans and widows will appear in the play proper."³³ The new society in which the young protagonist grew up is the weakened domain of the family women—all the male members have left or died. Thus the melodrama of the deformed fledgling, riddled with diseases and mischance, begins the narrative of the new, emasculated society. The "feminine plague" in Yu's family, to his despair, envelops the entire generation. His schoolmates in Hangzhou exemplify this new age of decadence and feminization:

> Hangzhou is, after all, the provincial capital. Most of my fellow students were sons of the country gentry who wore satin and indulged in meat. How many students there were in my class whose clothes and accessories were lovely, whose skin was soft and fair, whose gestures, delicate, and whose speech, quiet and gentle. What surprised me was the phenomenon of the constant companionship between older students and younger boys. In the elementary school in Jiaxing, this kind of practice existed too. However, it was definitely not as widespread as in Hangzhou. There were a few students who didn't think it humiliating being regarded as a woman. They put on fragrance, makeup, and face powder and affected behaviors that showed off their wealth.³⁴

It is also in a demasculinized position that Yu regards the village woodcutter, Ah Qian. In the general atmosphere of feminine decadence, Ah Qian becomes a model of strength of a "normal," masculine world. His physical quality is strikingly different from Yu's peers. Even his world of the rowdy taverns or the mountainous wilds is antithetical to Yu's cloistered, feminine world of the schoolhouse and home. Of course, Ah Qian's male power is most evidently displayed in sexual terms: his dark skin, sinuous, muscular body, and rich, masculine voice. When Ah Qian took Yu to the hills one day, the ravishing effect of their climb together on the feminized protagonist was unmistakably sexual:

> We climbed higher and higher. The colors of green and red on the mountain made me dizzy. The sun shone directly on the mountain slope, and from the grass and trees and the earth, arose a particular smell, making my breathing difficult. Even Ah Qian began to get hot. He took off his worn padded jacket and threw it to the ground. He made me sit down to rest on a large piece of rock, then went off alone to chop wood and gather wild fruits, wearing an undershirt, singing a song from the operas. I turned around and stood on the rock, and gazed toward the big river, and felt a deep sense of magic.[35]

The individual body, as we have seen, is for Yu a site on which one experiences one's social and political reality. Thus, Ah Qian's body is a political symbol. His male strength and particular sexuality is the very hope of the weakened and feminized nation. However, as with all other symbols of strength of his era, Ah Qian eventually succumbs, drowned in an accident after a drinking bout. At this incident, Yu exclaims: "The death of Ah Qian took away my dreams and my youth."[36] Ah Qian represents a hope that a rigorous new China will succeed the old defunct dynastic patriarchy. With his death, the depletion of China's strength and hope is complete.

Yu's diminishing sense of self is in direct correspondence to the rise of his estimation of Japan, China's major military antagonist in the 1930s. While China revealed all the signs of feminine weakness, Japan was in a state of overwhelming masculine health. Yu bewailed the slow feminization of Chinese men and the unhealthy, "thin as the day lily" beauty conventions of Chinese women. In contrast, he marveled that Japanese women were strong, healthy, and just like men in their physical abilities.

Yu's autobiography was written between 1936 and 1937, on the eve of Japan's all-out invasion of China. His work symbolically opens with a commemoration of China's humiliating defeat in the first Sino-Japanese war of 1894—the beginning of a series of military as well as diplomatic defeats of China by Japan. With Yu's description of the emasculated condition of himself and his generation, he genderizes and sexualizes the contest of power between China and Japan. In its weakened military state, China became the helpless woman, subjected to Japan's virility. Lydia Liu charges that such uses of women's bodies to articulate the experience of the nation silence women's self-expression: "The raped woman served as a powerful trope in anti-Japanese propaganda. Her victimization is used to represent, or more precisely, to eroticize China's own plight."[37] Liu's point is that in such a substitution, women's expression is usurped by the rhetoric of nationalism, and as such, women's real suffering is silenced. However, I argue that it is precisely to reinvest this overarching and totalistic discourse of national survival in intimate and individual (male or female) meaning that Yu and his protagonists themselves take on this feminized self. It is with an understanding that the most serious violation is felt on the level of the individual body.

I mention Yu's vigilant care of the physicality of his compatriot women. One discovers that he applies the same attitude in the surveillance of his "enemies." In his autobiography, he writes about his impulsive spying on Japanese women, hiding behind bushes, secretly walking in on his landlord's daughter during her bath, and other similar, sexually compulsive behavior. These activities, however, are always followed by angry outbursts at himself, self-loathing, remorse, and shame. If individual conditions equate with the national situation, one surmises that these self-flagellations are more for his lack of courage to openly confront the "powerful" Japanese women, than for the "immorality" of his impulses and behavior, as they are generally interpreted.

One day, in a rush of drunken courage, Yu decided to attack the very emblem of the Japanese threat to his manhood (and nationhood). He charged into a brothel, intending to prove his masculinity through confronting the ultimate symbol of female sexual power—a prostitute. However, the incident ended in defeat for him. His reaction to the incident the morning after suggests he was the ravished, not the aggressor:

> I woke up around noon the second day. I extended my arm in the quiet room and touched a soft, warm body, and remembered in confusion my wildness and madness the night before. I felt as if I was being doused on my head with ice water on a hot summer day.

> ... I looked at the clear sky through the glass window and then at the pink confetti scattered beside the pillow. Helplessly, I let flow two strings of tears.[38]

In interpreting a similar scene in "Sinking" (Chenlun), the fictionalized version of the same incident, Denton suggests that for Yu, Japan is the quintessential symbol of successful Westernization. The protagonist's rush to the Japanese brothel symbolizes his generation's heady embrace of progress and change. Thus, "[t]o yield to his desire for this Japanese prostitute would be to concede his national inferiority and relinquish his national identity to the West."[39] However, Denton argues that the protagonist is ultimately able to preserve his national identity because he passes out without engaging in sexual intercourse with the prostitute, thus preserving his "purity of desire of his motherland."[40] In "Sinking," the narrative ends with the protagonist contemplating suicide by the seaside. Denton refers to this as an "existential moment" in which the protagonist realizes that his "individual identity is profoundly threatened by the collapse of the cultural whole."[41] Nationalism implied in Denton's reading is limited to the idea of preservation of tradition, an alternative to progress and individual identity that is equated with national culture. Following this argument, the protagonist's self-preservation from defilement is a last-minute nationalist awakening—China's prodigal son's return to tradition. However, in the story, his "embrace of tradition" is only a result of the failure of his sexual mission. The "purity" of tradition is barely saved through the good fortune of our hero's impotence, passivity, and powerlessness. The protagonist's sense of defeat and suicidal contemplation at the end of the story does not support Denton's explanation. The protagonist's action is more than a matter of identity or cultural crisis.

There is no doubt that Yu's personal pain is in alignment with the trauma of the times. However, Yu's response is beyond the personal. It is about himself as an individual, but this sense of individuality is in terms of Yu's understanding of the corporate unity between the self and the nation. The compromise of one's body equates the prostration of the entire nation. To read Yu's writing as a personal event diminishes the idea of nationalism to a notion of culture. This kind of discussion of intellectual mentality further slips into abstraction, which ends up taking away from the historical specificity of the condition of the writing.

In the autobiography, the brothel scene is the pivotal event that concludes the work. Yu's autobiography has a very strong teleological pattern. The time scheme of the work is set between the two Sino-Japanese wars. It opens with the defeat of China in the first Sino-Japanese war and the decline of the old order. It ends at the brink of the second. Autobiographical closures usually happen either at a completion of the metamorphosis of the subject in the mode of bildungsroman, or at the autobiographer's arrival at an epochal juncture of his or her life. The end point of Yu's work is significant for both himself and the nation, both on the verge of a transforming experience. After leaving the brothel, he boards a streetcar and the narrative ends in a freeze-frame in front of the Japanese Imperial Palace:

It is not worth it! It is not worth it! My dreams, my future goals, and my passion for my country—what is left of them now? What is left of them? I felt a wave of remorse in my heart, a well of warm moisture in my eyes. I draped on an old gown from the brothel, slumped against the wall, and sat like that in a daze, sobbing continuously to myself for I really didn't know how long, until that woman woke up. After she accompanied me to my bath, I had a few cups of warm wine. It was then that I recomposed myself. Three hours later, I leaned against the window of an automobile, brows tightly drawn. When it drove toward the snowy high plains of the Imperial Palace grounds, I felt a wave of emotions I had never experienced before surging through my mind. I felt as if in one short night, last night, someone had taken apart the flesh and bones in my body.[42]

Yu's tremendous grief about his night of misadventure at the brothel is clearly explained in this passage as sadness over a failed political mission. The equation between sexual power and military dominance and conquests is obvious. The experiences of the individual and the nation are contiguous and inseparable. After the protagonist's "defeat" in the brothel, he feels that his whole structure of being is violated and altered. The Japanese Imperial Palace, the most potent symbol of Japanese imperialist strength and military might, looms in the moment of Yu's sense of dissolution. Against such a symbol of power, the portent of China's doom is clear.

What Yu's writings reveal is the complex position of the "I" in its metonymic relationship with the nation. The speaking subject must speak for both the new generation and the nation. However, despite these alliances, the voice in Yu's confessionals must also speak about the experience specific to an individual within a particular space and time, confronting particular historical circumstances. Yu's rhetoric of the body efficiently incorporates the representational value of his existence as a historical subject without losing sight of the specificity of the individual subjectivity.

Conclusion

This constant equation between self and nation is beyond mere assertion of individual representation or even identity. History, in Yu's view, is more than "objective" facts and data. Yu's writing is an effort to view the historical through the individual and to understand how it is lived and experienced on an individual level.

The physical body is the site on which the grand narrative of nationalism is invested with individual meaning. In Yu's writings, it is individual suffering and fear that one hears amid the din of history. Yet the bodily performance in Yu's writings and his focus on his bodily desires are also, paradoxically, methods of transcending the realm of the individual to express the condition of the nation. When Yu Dafu writes about himself relentlessly, he is not just interested in his own being. He is a synecdoche of the nation. His experience is the experience of the nation. When he speaks of his pain and hurt, it is China's pain and hurt that he evokes. His impotence is also China's impotence. The watchfulness over his physical self and the obsessive documentation of the self are inherently social and nationalistic acts.

The gestural system is a particular form of expression of nationalism. Through this, the imbrication of self and nation is revealed. Nationalism for Yu is not a vague sense of belonging, or nostalgia for tradition. It originates from a very intimate, yet social, realm of caring for the self and others. Individualism is nationalism.

Chapter Four

Names and Destiny

*Hu Shi's and Lu Xun's Self-Nomination
through Autobiography*

Names are fundamental markers of one's social identity. In autobiography, a name can be a metaphor for an individual, and the manipulation of one's name reveals the relationship between an individual and his or her society. The process of "coming to" a name is both a metaphor of personal growth and an acquisition of social presence. The different methods of self-naming and, in turn, the different textual organization in an autobiography to record this process, reflect different ideas of nomination and individual authority in society. Concerning these issues, how an author arranges the narrative of his or her name is often more important than what constitutes his or her life story. In this chapter I will examine the autobiographical works of Hu Shi and Lu Xun, exploring the relationships between their ideological compulsions represented by their names and their self-narratives.

Names, Faces, and Identity

As we have seen previously, Philippe Lejeune offers a useful model for autobiographical definition, focusing on the relationship between the author and the reader. Here, I continue to explore Lejeune's ideas on the connection between autobiographers and their names. According to Lejeune, autobiographies, like histories and biographies, are "referential texts." "They claim to convey information about a 'reality' that is external to the text and hence is subject to the test of *verification*." Lejeune thus introduces the notion of "referential contract" in autobiographies.[1] His method calls for discipline on the reader's part to suspend disbelief in order to fully participate in the reality premise of the work. Readers must be willing to enter into an "autobiographical contract with the author of an autobiography, to affirm the identity of the author in the text. In this way, the contractual name of the author is a signifier and signature of his/her ontological reality."[2]

In my discussion of Eileen Chang, I distinguish three parties in the autobiographical moment—the reader, the author, and the object—all represented by the same name.[3] The autobiography is in essence about the object and not the author despite the fact that the object is the namesake of the author, existing in the name of the author and signifying the author. It prospers on the credit of the author's name while the author's actual self is suspended from the text. The author and the object are allogamous, bound by shared proper names. However, they are not one and the same.

In Lejeune's schema, autobiography is as much a matter of form as a contractual relationship between the writer and the reader, ultimately to be completed through the accreditation of the reader. Under the contract of reading, the identification between the author and his subject is affirmed. Lejeune asserts that "[w]hat defines an autobiography, for the person who reads it, is above all a contract guaranteeing 'identity' sealed by the name of its signer."[4] Accordingly, the identity of the autobiographical subject is not created through a representational or cognitive reality, but is based on a legal, contractual speech act—a legal name.

Onomatology, naming, is an important topos in modern Chinese autobiography, more significant than representational likeness. Names are denotations of identity. Eileen Chang illustrates this awareness of the signification of names by devoting a chapter in her *Liuyan* (Flowing words) to discussing the semiotics of names, borrowing the Confucian dictum, "The names [of things] must be rectified" [bi ye zhengming hu], as the title to her essay. Chang believes that an individual's name is more than a cipher by which one is referred; it is a code by which an individual is *called into being*. Therefore, Chang claims that poor people often name their children Ah Fu (wealth), Da You (great abundance), and so forth.[5] A name is a heraldic code of a person's destiny:

> The naming of a person is a kind of minor or small-scale creation. A grandfather of the old days would put his feet up on a foot-warmer in winter and while smoking his water pipe, come up with a name for his newborn grandson, who would become whatever he was called. If he was named Guangmei ["illuminating the lintel"], he would try his best to make the household shine in pride. If he was called Zuyin ["in the shelter of his ancestors"], or Chengzu ["continuing from his ancestors"], he would always remember his ancestors. . . . However, aside from fictional characters, there are very few people whose names really reflect their real substance. (Very often, it is exactly the opposite. A name represents a need, a lack. Nine out of ten poor people have names like Gold, Wealth, or Abundance.) However, in the end, the name will merge with the person's looks and behavior, and become an air about him. Therefore, naming a person is a kind of creation.[6]

Eileen Chang also explains at length how she received her official name from her mother instead of her father. Her mother, who lived separately from her father throughout most of their abbreviated marriage, gave Chang her name when she registered her in school against the father's will. The fact that she received her official name from her mother had great symbolic value to Chang. It commemorates the birth of an individual consciousness through inheriting female determination and defiance. As a result, despite the fact she found her name rather common and vulgar, she claimed she would never change it.[7] An author's attitude toward his or her name, especially family name, often reflects the status of his or her membership in mainstream society. Chang's identity is built upon a lineage of female triumph over traditional patriarchal control. In May Forth writing, it is often through erasing the patrilineal information in their autobiographical works that writers express their rejection of the traditional society. One's name is often a direct symbol of one's relationship, positive or negative, to familial and social affiliation and is an important code in autobiography.

Names, whether inherited from one's family or self-selected, are indicators of one's ontological reality. After Xiao Hong escaped from her father's violently abusive home and embarked upon a literary career, she adopted different pen names, each an implicit description of her mental state and her relationship with the dominant society in different moments of her life. Her most celebrated works, *Tales of Hulan River* (Hulanhe zhuan) and *Field of Life and Death* (Shengsichang) were written in the mid-1930s while under Lu Xun's mentorship. These works reveal her at her most mature and socially committed as a writer. She adopted the nom de plume Xiao Hong, "Red" (as in the Red Army), for her works.⁸ However, her autobiographical *Market Street*, which records her unhappy life with her domineering lover, San Lang (Xiao Jun), is published under the name Qiaoyin ("secret murmur").⁹ This work, as I discuss in chapter 2, records her life of dependence and submission. Her self-estimation at the time is well reflected in her choice of name.

By the same token, writers' attitudes toward their filial connections often reflect the claims of dominant social forces on them. Yu Dafu's romantic alienation, Xie Bingying's rebelliousness, Xiao Hong's temerity, and Hu Shi's conservatism are all mirrored in how they deal with their pedigree in the opening of their autobiographies. As mentioned, Eileen Chang claims matriarchal connection. Yu Dafu's sense of alienation from society is reflected in the events of "regicide" and "parricide" as the prologue to his personal tragedy. Xie Bingying's *Autobiography of a Woman Soldier* (Nubing zizhuan) begins with her "life-and-death struggle" with her mother at birth. Hu Shi, in *Self-Narration at Forty* (Sishi zishu), however, devotes a chapter-long encomium to his parents, celebrating his father's heroism, uprightness, and accomplishment as a loyal minister of the Qing court and his mother's traditional virtue as a self-sacrificing and evasive wife.

Hu Shi's Great-Men Texts

In his preface to *Self-Narration at Forty* (1937), Hu Shi laments autobiography's lack of significance in Chinese literary history.¹⁰ As an intellectual leader who played a prominent role in motivating progress in society, Hu Shi considered it his mission to spearhead the development of autobiographical writing by personal example. Furthermore, he compiled a list of China's great men, who, he hoped, would respond to his call and contribute their writings as well. Hu's list includes such eminent men as the editor of *New Youth* magazine and founder of the Chinese Communist Party, Chen Duxiu; the National Peking University chancellor Cai Yuanpei; and the financier and philanthropist Hong Xiling. Hu hoped that the works of these important men would, first, establish a legacy of greatness, and then serve as both inspiration to, and historical documents of, China's modernization.

Hu's emphasis on personal testimonials reflects his indebtedness to the Qing political thinker Liang Qichao, who believed that individual greatness is a primary motivating force of history. In Liang's view, history writing is a dynamic performance. Not merely is it a passive record of the past, it is authored and determined by prominent individuals of the present:[11]

> History is different from other subjects in that it specifically records the activities of human beings. A heroic act of a single person or a group of people can lead to great changes in history. If one were to eliminate the activities of the most powerful, I am afraid it would be questionable whether history would still be the same.[12]

While the individual is assimilated within and conditioned by history, according to Liang, he is simultaneously an active force that propels historical development.[13] Since individuals constitute the entirety of society, Liang describes the relationship between an individual and society as dialectical, between a part *(jubu)* and the organic whole *(quanbu)*. Accordingly, an individual exists, not in isolation, but as a crucial strand in the entire social weave. Liang thus believes that it is only through the experience of an individual that one can understand the history of a society or humanity. For this reason, he is a strong advocate for the writing of biographies:

> From whole *(quanbu)* to part *(jubu)*—what does it mean to go from whole to part? History is a whole and is a unity. A perfect history is an incorporation of the events of the whole body of humanity. Only this can be considered history. Since it is a whole and is a unity, recordings from different places are only small pieces of the machinery in the entire organization. Without understanding the

whole, there can be no understanding of the parts; without understanding the world, there can be no understanding of China. The biography, which I am going to discuss, is a part drawn from the whole. Whether one is investigating a person or an event, ultimately, it is but a part of the whole. Although the scope is very narrow, one should not forget that this is part of a whole.[14]

Using the updated terminology of *xiaowo* (small "I") and *dawo* (the great "I"),[15] Hu Shi renews Liang's premise, believing that an understanding of China is necessarily through the lives of its people, especially eminent people. Autobiographies of the famous are crucial documents because it is these people who create history, and thus records of their lives are records of the entire machinery of the society. In this view, autobiographies mark the intellectual lineage of a people and are important sources for historical research:

We baldly narrate, without adornment, the miscellaneous affairs of our childhood, hoping that those who have great achievements in society will also, like us, baldly record their lives without adornment in order to provide material for historians and to blaze new trails for students.[16]

Since these prominent people are the determining forces of history whose acts and words directly affect the direction of societal development, the articulation of these individuals' lives moves history's narrative forward. The records of the eminent can inspire and anticipate an ideal future because those who read them will also be spurred to great achievements and contribute to development. As such, autobiography has both constructive and didactic purposes. Given China's political weakness and social fragmentation in the first half of the twentieth century, autobiography seems to be a suitable remedy.

Hu's notion of history is a metalepsis; it is forever in the future, to be created and yet forever addressed as the past. By extension, an autobiography also articulates both the future and the past; it is both backward- and forward-looking at the same time. It is both performative and constative as a rhetorical system. The writings of great men have important implications in the greatness of a nation. Accordingly, autobiography is an important literary mode in China's striving toward modernity.

Self-Nomination

The beginning of Hu Shi's autobiography is a lengthy tribute to his father and his achievements as a loyal minister of the Qing court. The second chapter is ostensibly about his mother, celebrating her role as a virtuous wife. However, her existence actually functions as supporting proof of her husband's greatness, with numerous descriptions of her respectful gazes upon him. In turn, these encomia of Hu's parents serve to illustrate Hu's own distinguished lineage and thus affirm greatness as his birthright. The authority of the father is transferred to the son. The introductory sections on his virtuous parents prepare his readers for his own eventual eminence.

Aside from his biological lineage, Hu's autobiography also charts the intellectual inheritance and development of his childhood and formative years. He first became aware of his own destiny for greatness when he was in Shanghai pursuing his studies in the China National Institute. It was there that he had a "spiritual awakening" through, especially, Yan Fu's translation of T. X. Huxley's *Evolution and Ethics* and Liang Qichao's voluminous collection of political essays in the *New People's Miscellany* (Xinmin congbao). Perhaps most significantly related to Hu's interest in biographies are Liang's numerous sketches of European thinkers such as Hobbes, Descartes, Bentham, Rousseau, Kant, and Darwin. Through Yan Fu's translations, Huxley's social Darwinism captured the imagination of young intellectuals at the time. They responded to Darwin's ideas with such enthusiasm that many changed their names as pledges of their new way of thinking.[17] Joining his young coterie with their newly acquired appellations such as *Yang Tianze* (Natural Selection Yang) and *Sun Jingcun* (Struggle-for-existence Sun), Hu also adopted a name to reflect his new allegiance—*Shizhi*—derived from the phrase *shizhe shengcun* (survival of the fittest), which is both descriptive of his intellectual world and proscriptive of his society at the time.

Hu's newly developed sense of commitment to society was further nurtured by the student unrest at the China National Institute, a secondary school he was attending. Students of the school banded together to protest certain "undemocratic" acts of the trustees. Many students even withdrew from the school to establish a rival New China National Institute. Hu served as the secretary of the student association. The students received a great amount of attention and support from the general society and eventually eradicated what they deemed unjust in their school. With this event and the publicity around it, Hu began to appreciate his sudden propulsion from his childhood's domestic arena into adult society. He became, at that moment, a "new citizen" of China, occupying a notable social and historical position.

The young intellectuals at Hu's school formed an elite and exclusive idiomorphic society with their Darwinian rhetoric. The membership is identified by their new names, made up from the vocabulary of the new thinking. Personal appellations that incorporate ideas of struggle, selection, and survival, illustrate the students' strong desire for social progress and renewal. Through these new names, the young men presented themselves to the society. Their names reflected their sense of social mission and conviction that they would be the ones to propel China toward evolutionary success. For Hu Shi and his coterie, self-naming equals societal nomination.

Hu ends his autobiography at the culmination of his early career. He was awarded a Boxer Indemnity scholarship through Qinghua University to study in the United States. Hu Shi marks this occasion by jettisoning his old name, Hu Hongxin, which to him represents his state of immaturity and youthful dissipation. He uses *Hu Shi* to formally promulgate a new beginning for himself, a new identity, and a new career: "When I was in school, I used the name Hu Hongxin. This time, as I was planning to take the [scholarship] exam in Beijing, I was afraid I would fail and would be laughed at by friends and other students, so at the last minute, I changed my name to Hu Shi. From then on, my name became Hu Shi."[18] Hu Shi is of course the name by which all his achievements are known to us today and recorded in history. His acquisition of the new name indicates his official initiation into society and marks a new phase of his social participation. It also signifies his arrival at the status of a historical being. It marks his evolution from the boy, Hu Hongxin, who had little sense of himself and his relevance to the society in the beginning of the autobiography, to Hu Shi, a self-assured young intellectual who was just embarking upon the most significant phase of his career at the end of his writing. Charting the process of his progression from Hu Hongxin to Hu Shi, his autobiographical narrative is motivated single-mindedly toward this apex of self-reinvention.

Hu Shi's autobiography illustrates how the author and his namesake infer each other. The autobiography of Hu Shi is really the story of Hu Hongxin because the narration terminates at the point where he adopts the name Hu Shi. The autobiography is really about Hu Hongxin's coming to this name. The significance of this work, however, is derived from the weight of the name Hu Shi as the author's namesake and not Hu Hongxin, the subject. The appellation *Hu Shi* is a dynamic marker in modern Chinese literature and history, representing a respected intellectual leader of the 1920s. The name encapsulates significance well beyond the life of Hu Hongxin, while *Hu Hongxin* remains a mere cipher outside of the text. The autobiography is about how the author, Hu Shi, suspends his own identity to become "Hu Hongxin" in the work and how the author and subject coincide at the end when the autobiographical subject (Hu Hongxin) becomes the author (Hu Shi).

The resemblance between the subject and the author in Hu Shi's autobiography is a result of the process of onomatology—naming and invocation. The name *Hu Shi* is metonymic of his life and thoughts. Through this name, the autobiographer reveals or constructs his position of influence in society. Hu's different nomenclatures are not mere significations of personal identity, but represent his sense of nomination to significant positions of power.[19]

As the substantive in autobiographical discourse, the subject's name is the metonym of the author's existence and identity. The process of nomination is thus a driving theme in many modern autobiographies. The coming to a name is equivalent to coming into being. It is with this understanding of onomastic power that Hu Shi had hoped to recreate a new China through the invocation of great names in his work: Cai Yuanpei, Chen Duxiu, Hong Xiling, and so on. He had hoped that through the self-writing of these great men, China would be moved toward modernity. Thus the writing of autobiography for Hu is a fulfillment of Lejeune's theory of the relationship between ontological identity and public contractual promise. Hu believes that autobiography has the performative function of promoting social change.

Hu Shi probably couldn't agree more with Lejeune, who asserts that autobiography is exclusive to those who occupy public spaces, politically or culturally. Only those who own prominent spaces in society are in positions to convince the public of the authority, and thus reality, of their textual self. But more importantly, only those with name recognition can effect social development through their self-articulation.[20]

According to such an understanding, the "autobiographical space" is related to onomastic power, privileged to those whose names are recognized by the public, the *youming de* ("the famous," or literally, "those who have recognized names"), those whose names exist in the public consciousness, imagination, or discourse, or those who are cultural symbols. By extension of having names *(youming)* they have faces *(youmianzi)*.[21] The face as an imagistic register is meaningless unless it is recognized or claimed by the reading public. In Paul de Man's terminology, autobiography is about the "giving and taking of face."[22] In this sense, it is the public, the readers, that designates its autobiographers. In the same way, it is the public that names its social heroes. The process of naming, as illustrated by Hu Shi's autobiographical project, fulfills all the connotations of nomination.

Linearity and Modernity

Published in 1937, Hu's autobiography is written in a surprisingly old-fashioned, annalistic form, a typical pre–May Fourth biographical form. Hu wrote his life events in a bare-bones prose, an annotated chronological list of events more than storytelling. Therefore, Hu's work sometimes reads like a curriculum vita—a fitting submission, considering his self-nomination to social eminence. Hu believes that national and personal progress is best expressed through the traditional historical forms of annals and chronologies *(nianpu)*.[23] At face value, the lists of data in these works are the best way of conveying facts with minimal interpretive distortion through the experiences of writing and reading. According to Richard Howard, prior to his autobiography Hu Shi experimented with the form by writing the *Chronological Biography of Zhang Xuecheng* (1922). This Qing historiographer, whose importance is exhumed by Liang Qichao, was significant to Hu's idea of the "great-man text" of autobiography.

In the *Biography of Zhang Xuecheng,* Hu expands on the pre–May Fourth form, substantiating the rigid chronological skeleton of conventional annals by concise annotating, which he believes to be necessary in creating a sense of developmental causality. Hu writes in the preface: "A *nianpu* that only records events one by one but does not describe the origin and development of ideas is of little value. Thus I have decided to write a detailed *nianpu* of Zhang Xuecheng in which I will not only record the events of his entire life, but also record the process of his intellectual development."[24]

In his autobiography, Hu follows his own maxim of chronological accuracy by listing painstakingly each book he read and each writer who influenced him in his formative years. These factual details are then strung together by an overarching structure that creates a sense of directed progression in the writing. Within such a framework, Hu organizes the otherwise heterogeneous and simultaneously occurring events of his life in a formula of cause and effect, along a strong temporal imperative. He thus eliminates the appearances of randomness and presents a determined, forward-looking linearity toward a personal and textual goal. He also uses a large number of hard figures, such as tabulations and lists of things in his writing. Calendrical classifications, for example, divide the narrative into distinct periods. The narration of each event is prefaced by conjunctive temporal designations: "I was born on the seventeenth day of the eleventh month of the seventeenth year of Guangxu's reign (17th of December, 1891)."[25] "During the Jiawu year (1894), at the beginning of the Sino-Japanese War . . . my father entrusted his family to [my uncle] in their transport back to his hometown of Huizhou."[26] "Two months before my father's death, he wrote a will."[27] "In these nine years (1895–1904), all I got was the two words, 'reading' and 'writing."[28] These dates and the prepositional leads in the writing, such as *during, before,* and *later on,* connect the incidents of disparate or similar nature in a long concatenation of causes and effects. This particular grammatical structure in Hu's writing contributes to the sense of causal, spatial, and temporal relationships among divergent things, situating them in specific and meaningful contexts. This kind of organization forces logical connections among outwardly unrelated events and gives meaning, intention, and teleology to the random.

The teleology of Hu's work is the fulfillment of all the anticipatory temporal clauses that introduce the different sections of his life. In such a way, Hu's life is meaningful, logical, and historically relevant, and thus important. This organization, as I will show, is more than a stylistic preference or an objective decision, but reflects Hu Shi's particular social values and ideological position.

Hu's autobiography is obviously written with didactic purposes in mind. Because he is a "great man," his life story is exemplary. The sum of his experiences points to one climactic end when it will be revealed. The structural organization of Hu's writing reflects the development of his thought and character. This individual progress, from an ignorant, dissolute boy to an enlightened intellectual, parallels the ideal social development of China, from tradition to modernity. Hu's vision of human history, as that of individual life, is evolutionary, from infancy to maturity. Just as he achieved intellectual sophistication at the end of his autobiography, China also supposedly arrived at the modern enlightenment of the twentieth century.

The Ideology of the Autobiographic Order

Despite his position as an avant-gardist in the intellectual revolution of May Fourth, Hu Shi's autobiography reads in a curiously archaic and conservative style. If his work seems old-fashioned compared to that of Lu Xun, Yu Dafu, and Xie Bingying, who also produced autobiographies around the same years, it is surely not because of the actual experiences of his life or the substance of his thoughts, which are committed to social progress. It is in the structure of his work that, despite himself, he reveals his rigid alignment with the old patriarchal ideal. In classifying different kinds of autobiography, Wendy Larson identifies two major modes. Each reflects the author's social beliefs. First, the "circumstantial autobiography" is a "textual construction that relies on references to ancestry, position, and local status, creating an intellectual figure that is firmly entrenched within the signifying institutions of society."[29] Larson suggests that the majority of orthodox official biographies are "circumstantial" texts. The alternative to this form of autobiography is the so-called impressionistic autobiography exemplified by Tao Qian's parody, "Master Five Willows." This ironic work, an anti-autobiography, which asserts his eremitism and anonymity, is a demonstration of his refusal of conventional social relationships. Regarding Tao Qian's work as a paradigmatic text, Larson explains that the writing of an impressionistic autobiography reflects an authorial stance that is withdrawing from the affairs of the world.[30] She believes that in the intense political climate of the 1920s and 1930s, such an antisocial stance was impossible. She thus qualifies all the autobiographical works of this period as circumstantial.

By Larson's definition, most May Fourth writers' works are circumstantial because of their firm commitment to social issues, Hu Shi's being a primary example. Hu's autobiography indeed conforms to Larson's notion of circumstantial autobiography. It is premised on cooperation with and affinity to his society. Following the autobiographical conventions of the imperial era, he begins his work by establishing his affiliative and filiative connection to the patriarchy. He expresses his sense of participation in the patrilineal logic and organization that he inherits from his forebears. While affirming the authority of the past and progressive evolution to the future, Hu's founds his view of history and his writing on the solid status quo of the present. There is neither ambiguity nor discomfort in Hu's participation in his society. His life story is an affirmation of his vocation as an intellectual leader, a title and position conferred upon him by society, just as his father had been appointed by the court and acknowledged by the populace under his jurisdiction. Hu's autobiography is a declaration of his societal and historical position. Despite the fact that all Hu's intellectual innovations are meant to challenge certain old customs of thinking, writing, and speaking, he is unwilling to take apart the basic epistemic structure by which the traditional notion of society and history is framed and in which he is a privileged member.[31]

However, very few May Fourth writers actually sympathized with Hu Shi's program. Many young iconoclasts perceived themselves as aberrant to mainstream society and were antagonistic toward it. In their political stance, the May Fourth generation rejected traditional social structures; in writing, they also refused established narratives and textual conventions. Understandably, they also rejected the old autobiographical form, the structure of which repeats patriarchal societal organization. May Fourth autobiography therefore displays an unmistakable sense of disinheritance from the past.[32]

Lu Xun's Autobiography

Lu Xun's autobiographical work is an important deviation from the circumstantial text. It displays a total rearrangement of the traditional order of perception—social, temporal, epistemological, even ontological. However, although it lacks the formal characteristics of a circumstantial autobiography, as with all of Lu Xun's works, it is unquestionably a piece of social commentary.

Lu Xun's peripatetic *Morning Blossoms Picked at Dusk* (*Zhaohua xishi*, 1927) is regarded as a miscellany *(zawen)*.[33] Many pieces in it are autobiographical. The individual essays are usually read separately without assuming causal or thematic connections among them.[34] Unlike Hu Shi, whose temporal clauses link events in a concatenation that leads to one moment of fulfillment, the only element that seems to unify Lu Xun's work as a whole is, literally, the binding of the book. The title, which metaphorically refers to the content as memory blossoms from the dawn of his life, his childhood, describes only a part of what the book contains. It includes a number of scholarly expositions on traditional legends and literatures, though most of these pieces begin with a personal anecdote explaining his interest in them. For example, he includes elaborate discussions of "Wuchang," the mythical death messenger, and "Pictures from the Book of Twenty-four Filial Pieties" (a classic collection of stories about exemplary sons) in the middle of his work, and then further elaborations in the afterword, combining anecdotes with sophisticated research and discussion. Aside from these studies, there is also a biographical sketch of an acquaintance, Fan Ainong, whom Lu Xun first met in a rather unpleasant encounter in Japan where they were students. Fan's death at the end of the narrative closes Lu Xun's "autobiography." If "memory blossoms" reflect the "theme" of the collection, as the title suggests (morning being the past, dusk the present), some of the essays mentioned above would seem completely out of place.

False Metaphors

How does one make sense of the textual incongruities in Lu Xun's collection? One might consider the stories of filial piety and the lore of the death messenger as having metaphorical associations with youth and death, as two possible thematic strands in Lu Xun's work. By definition, a metaphor is a concrete emblem that stands in for an abstract essence. The choice of the emblem for a metaphor is usually based on its resemblance to the original quality it represents.³⁵ The meanings of the words or attributes used as emblems change according to their usages in different situations. Therefore, metaphors derive their meanings through associations within the contexts of the works in which they appear. A metaphor is only meaningful within a very particular context. Lu Xun's use of Wuchang or the *Book of Twenty-four Filial Pieties* is beyond the function of metaphors. They do not merely substitute for the original meaning. In fact, their individual monadic worlds usurp the original meanings they were "supposed to represent." In Lu Xun's work, entire chapters are devoted to the expositions of mythical figures, discussing their history, evolution, and significance in society. However, he makes no obvious attempt to connect them to the narrative itself. These essays constitute their own complete discursive worlds. Lu Xun then injects them wholesale into the various worlds of his past—texts within texts— yet none of them has any figural relationship with another. All together, these writings produce an impossibly gnarled *textum* in Lu Xun's work. One is hard put to say whether Lu Xun's autobiography is about childhood or death, or, for that matter, any identifiable theme.

Lu Xun uses superficial links among the chapters to create an aura of metaphorical relationships among his various textual matters, such as childhood with the *Book of Twenty-four Filial Pieties*, death with Wuchang. However, Wuchang and the *Twenty-four Filial Pieties* have mere emblematic value in relationship to the "themes." They are devoid of representational or symbolic function in the work despite their forced contiguity in the notion of a unified text. Similarly, though the title of Lu Xun's work, *Morning Blossoms Picked at Dusk*, suggests a metaphorical potential for an autobiography, we discover that only a little more than half of the essays can loosely be identified as records of the author's past. The actual substance of the writing does not fulfill the intention expressed in the title.

Lu Xun's work challenges the common notion of plot cohesion in realistic or historical time, expressed through the delineation of events along successive and causative order. Edward Said's examination of linear forms in nineteenth-century European biographies or historical novels problematizes the notion of temporal chronicity and its ideology. Arguing that the temporal scheme of a novel is conditioned by social ideology, Said describes the chronological compliance in these writings as a "wedding [of] a mimetic, verbal intention to time." The assumed common experience in terms of notions of communal time and space is institutionalized in the novel form. Subversions of such coercions are also manifested in the temporal arrangements in the novel. Writers create a "private arrangement between an original character . . . and that character's version of time." As a result, Said observes, there is often tension within realist novels between the need to observe the linear form and the desire to individualize such a temporal scheme: "The difficulties presented by Realism derive from its ambiguous attitude toward these arrangements made between time and character, arrangements which seek to replace the bonds of community with the creative subjective freedom of unfettered emotions."[36] One can also assume that similar manipulating and individualizing time as a way of subversion is also a strategy in autobiography, a genre that relies on the idea of verisimilitude.

Previously, I argued that the linear temporal order in a narrative, as exemplified by Hu Shi's work, reflects the perspectival organization of the existing patriarchal norm. Hu Shi regards himself as a motivating factor in historical and societal development, as a *xiaowo* (small "I") complementing the *dawo* (great "I"). His work thus observes unproblematically the operating structure of society, to affirm "the bonds of community." In return, he is nominated to a position of eminence in society.

Hu Shi decries the dearth of modern autobiography in Chinese literature. His concern is perhaps justified in terms of circumstantial autobiographies that observe a strict monochronicity in the name of objectivity and historical accuracy. However, since embedded in this kind of writing is the organization of the existing patriarchal ideology, it is natural that writers who refuse such designations will also eschew such a textual organization. Once this structural qualification of autobiography is removed, one can hardly be sympathetic to Hu Shi's lament.[37]

Lu Xun's autobiography lacks progression in a chronological or causal sense. The juxtaposition of different temporal layers and thematic material creates a heterogeneous textuality overall. One simple and undeniable reason for this mix of subjects and styles is that most of these essays were published separately and were then collected by Lu Xun much later. However, if we take them as a whole—as the reader is encouraged to do by the author's anthologizing—the violence of joining these divergent titles under an arbitrary object of autobiography creates definite effects on the reading experience and the production of meaning.

The complex arrangement of Lu Xun's work is not totally haphazard or random. There is a loose sequence among the different events or things that represents the different stages of his youth: his relationship as a small child with his nanny, Ah Chang; the death of his father when he was an adolescent; then study in Japan as a young adult. From a discursive or narrative point of view, Lu Xun's essays do follow a vague outline of a temporal movement that is chronological, but not necessarily progressive or teleological.

The notion of plot, however, is largely eradicated in Lu Xun's work. If the prominent figure of the author's self in Hu Shi's writing is derived from the cohesiveness in the plot, then the shattered teleology in Lu Xun's must articulate an alternate notion of self. One recalls Eileen Chang's mirror experience described in chapter 2, in which she confronts the multiple aspects of her self through an act of reflection: her imagined spectator, herself as the subject, herself as the object, and the subject as the object. In the multivalence of Chang's perception, the notion of a unified, articulable self is impossible. Likewise, Lu Xun's work is a mosaic where there can be no assumption of causal relationships among the different pieces in the narration, no logical association among the different objects of the autobiographical gaze, and no logical genitive continuities. For example, Lu Xun's hatred for cats as a small child does not lead to his eventual study of medicine in Japan. His account of Wuchang the death messenger has no direct contribution to the narration of his father's death. His relationship with his nanny, Ah Chang, does not cause his interest in the *Classic of Mountains and Oceans*. Nevertheless, all these events are coterminously arranged in the work. The expositions on the *Book of Twenty-four Filial Pieties,* Wuchang, and other seemingly unrelated pieces in the writing are apostrophes, having neither tropical nor topical function in the general scheme of the work. They intersect the narrative pieces and, thus, obstruct textual cohesion and destroy the possibility of any dominant teleological focus in the work. These interruptions prevent one from succumbing to an interpretation based on an expectation of causality and consequentiality in textual motivation. Hence denouement is also disallowed.

We recall that Hu Shi's temporal clauses and conjunctions form connective tissues among earlier events and later happenings as the causes and consequences of each other. They prescribe a sense of progression toward a final culmination and fulfillment. In Lu Xun's ultimate "later on" at the end of his work, his own narrative is replaced by another's—Fan Ainong's life of disappointment and final suicide. This conclusion violates the rules of autobiographical endings. At the point of denouement, Lu Xun's text turns in focus, aiming away from the literal self to another figure, who becomes an emblematic figure of the disenchanted Chinese intellectual youth. What the reader discovers at the end is not completion and fulfillment, but confrontation with a sudden analophon.

The Ending: The Departicularization of the "I"

The ending of Lu Xun's work is extremely problematic. How do we understand a nominally autobiographical work that interrupts our reading in the autobiographical mode by shifting its subject?

In many of Lu Xun's short stories, images of young, defeated idealists like Lu Xun's "substitute," Fan Ainong, appear over and over. In "In the Wine Shop," Lu Weifu's "muddling through" helped him avoid thinking about his life, realizing that striving for a hopeless future or trying to live up to past aspirations were both futile: "The future? I don't know. Just think: Has any single thing turned out as we hoped? Of all that we planned in the past? I'm not sure of anything now; not even of what I will do tomorrow; not even of the next minute."[38] This sentiment duplicates Fan's in *Morning Blossoms* and is echoed in Lu Xun's words in the preface of the volume:

> It certainly gets hot early in Kwangchow [Guangzhou]; the rays of the setting sun shining through the west window force one to wear nothing but a shirt at most. The water-bough in a basin on my desk is something quite new to me, a lopped-off bough, which, immersed in water, will put out lovely green leaves. Looking at these green leaves and editing some old manuscripts means that I am doing something, I suppose. Doing such trifling things, although really tantamount to death in life, is an excellent way of banishing heat.[39]

Lu Xun's disillusionment in the individual's ability to effect changes in society is invested in the numerous characters of young idealist intellectuals in his stories. Fan, in his autobiography, is one among many of such defeated young men who reenact the role of the well-known mythological giant in his *Call to Arms* (Nahan) preface, who lifted the gates of the benighted and backward traditional society to let children pass through to enlightenment and happiness.[40] However, given Lu Xun's tremendous pessimism about his world, Fan's suicide at the end of the work—he is crushed by the weight of society—is as inevitable as the death of the giant, crushed by the weight of the gate.

Fan's death at the end of Lu Xun's self-narrative immediately draws our attention to Lu Xun's association with his protagonist. The parallels between the situations of Fan and Lu Xun in the writing are apparent. Like Lu Xun, Fan was a returned student from Japan and once harbored the same, if not a stronger, enthusiasm to lift China out from its dark ages. Both men aspired to become the mythological giant who lifts the gate of hell. However, Fan, before there was any significant trial of strength, died of fatigue and frustration. The similarity between Fan and Lu Xun is obvious. That Lu Xun uses Fan as a surrogate to tell his own story is also obvious. Through Fan, Lu Xun not only bewails the futility of individual effort but also predicts his own demise from the same conditions. By using the ending of Fan's story to substitute for his own, Lu Xun also violates some rules of autobiography. He manages to write beyond the conventional limit and prescribes an ending for himself beyond his present. Contrary to the conventional movement of autobiography, which, as Georges May describes, is "a long backward glance," Lu Xun's work is nostalgic and proleptic, retrospective and prospective, simultaneously.[41]

Lu Xun's use of a surrogate death in *Morning Blossoms* demonstrates a familiar strategy in his writings, a process that Leo Bersani might describe as "departicularization." Often, Lu Xun's narrators occupy a seemingly objective stance as observers in his short stories and even in the autobiography. While the authority of the narrator is affirmed, personal feelings become the general social ethos, and individual experiences embody universal truth.[42] Lu Xun's personal disillusionment invested in characters like Fan reflects those of the young intellectuals of the period in general. However, while individual experience is used to reflect a common condition, Lu Xun's ubiquitous first-person narrator is an automatic signifier of subjectivity. Embedded within Lu Xun's works, therefore, are the double impulses of the private and the public, self-expression and didacticism.[43]

There is a further layer in the relationship between the "I" of the narrator and the narrated objects in Lu Xun's writing. Lu Xun has created many protagonists who seem to have great emotional depth and sensibility: the narrator who regrets the class barrier that has developed between him and his childhood friend, Run-tu, in "My Old Home"; the "I" who listens sympathetically to the hopelessness of Lu Weifu in "In the Wine Shop"; and the narrator who is unable to alleviate the mental suffering of Xianglin's wife in "The New Year's Sacrifice." However, these narrators are often mere observers or listeners. It is only through describing the conditions of others that their subjectivity is foisted upon them from outside. (This is contrary to the sentimental writings of Yu Dafu or Lu Yin, for instance, whose romanticism is a result of attention to the individual within.)[44] Witnessing the conditions of Xianglin's wife in "The New Year's Sacrifice" evokes an intense self-awareness in the narrator. The state of her being claims a direct correlation to the state of his conscience. The narrator is startled and then haunted by Xianglin's wife's question of whether or not there is hell after death. This becomes a moral crisis for him because he cannot commit to a position:

> [B]ut by simply concluding with this phrase "I am not sure," one can free oneself of all responsibility. At this time I felt even more strongly the necessity for such a phrase, since even in speaking with a beggar woman there was no dispensing with it. However, I continued to feel uncomfortable, and even after a night's rest my mind kept running on this, as if I had a premonition of some untoward development. In that oppressive snowy weather, in the gloomy study, this discomfort increased.[45]

The physical condition of Xianglin's wife thus becomes the symbol of the narrator's moral vacillation.

The narrator in Lu Xun's works is often an empty vessel whose three-dimensionality as a character is a result of the external affects that accrue around him.[46] Conversely, it is only through the impotent gaze of the narrating subject that the tragedies of the voiceless masses are given reflection and representation. The objects rely upon the vessel of the narrators to give expression to their experiences. The relationship between the narrative subject and object is symbiotic in Lu Xun's works. Neither exists convincingly without the affirmation of the other.

Similarly, the "I" of Lu Xun's *Morning Blossoms* contributes little to its own pathos. The "I" is a conduit for the expression of characters such as his father and Ah Chang. Conversely, Fan becomes a subjectivity for Lu Xun himself. These external beings fill out the inner dimension of the "I." The self is a composite of people and events and is given substance through their narratives.⁴⁷

The story of Fan Ainong, a narrative object, serves as a substitute resolution for Lu Xun's autobiographical subject. Contrary to the conventional metaphor of the mirror in which the object is the reflected image, the double of the autobiographer in *Morning Blossoms*, Fan, is the specular other of Lu Xun's autobiographical act—the alterity to Lu Xun's ipsity. The relationship between the reflected image and the mirroring subject is no longer symmetrical. The differentiations between the subject and the object are no longer absolute. Lu Xun's autobiography is hence a text that turns inward and outward at the same time, traveling between pathos and ethos.

The Allegory of the Name and the Duplicity of Adult Language

Similar to Hu Shi's work, in Lu Xun's *Morning Blossoms* the issue of naming is a prominent trope, but of a totally different nature and with a totally different consequence. Hu Shi's name is a metaphor of himself. Lu Xun's name is a catachresis, a paradox. This seems to be the moral behind the story of the snake beauty in his chapter "From the Hundred Herbs Garden to the Three-Flavored Schoolhouse," in which Lu Xun narrates the end of his childhood freedom and the beginning of his schooling experience. Lu Xun begins this narrative with a legend connected to his childhood playground, the "Hundred Herbs Garden." In the tale, a young scholar hears someone calling his name in the garden. When he responds to the call, he discovers to his delight that it is a beautiful woman. A monk who happens to pass by immediately notices an evil aura about him and realizes that he is under the influence of an unclean spirit. He tells the scholar that since he has responded to the call, the woman, who is actually a snake demon, will come and devour him that night. The monk gives the scholar a box as a talisman. That night, the scholar hears a stirring in the garden. Suddenly, a ray of light shoots out of the box. Then all returns to silence again. The scholar discovers later that a centipede spirit in the box killed the snake demon. As a lesson to his tale, Lu Xun laments: "The moral at the end is: Therefore, if you ever hear a stranger calling your name, you must never respond. This story made me feel the perils of being human poignantly."[48]

Previously, I discussed how, according to Hu Shi, an individual's name represents one's self-volition and fulfillment of social nomination. It articulates the agentive role of the self in society. For Lu Xun, however, an individual's name identifies the violent antagonism between the self and society. Hu Shi's work is about social nomination, while Lu Xun's is about the elision of one's self.

The struggle between the self and society is expressed in Lu Xun's comparison between the child's world and the adult's world. While the former represents individual freedom, the latter describes social strictures. In Lu Xun's childhood reminiscences in *Morning Blossoms,* the Hundred Herbs Garden symbolizes the untrammeled childhood world of individual freedom: "There was a very big garden behind our house. It was believed to be called the 'Hundred Herbs Garden' . . . it was my childhood paradise."[49] The vigor of life suggested in the name is fulfilled by the profusion of sensate delights that it provides:

> I need not speak of the green vegetable plots, the smooth, slippery coping around the well, the tall honey-locust tree, or the purple mulberries. Nor need I speak of the long shrilling of the cicadas among the leaves, the fat wasps couched in the flowering rape, or the nimble skylarks that suddenly soared straight up from the grass to the sky. Just the foot of the low mud wall around the garden was a source of unfailing interest. Here field crickets droned away while house crickets chirped merrily. Turning over a broken brick, you might find a centipede. There were stink-beetles as well, and if you pressed a finger on their backs they emitted puffs of vapor from their rear orifices. Milkwort interwove with climbing fig which had fruit shaped like the calyx of a lotus, while the milkwort had swollen tubers.[50]

Lu Xun's beloved childhood garden was filled with colors, sounds, and spectacles. The name of this garden captures its lushness, exuberance, and abundance. This Edenic realm of sensual joy contrasted sharply with the village school that he was forced to attend, a world of dullness and deprivation ruled and civilized by fussy adults. Through the respective descriptions of these two realms, Lu Xun illustrates the paradoxical human states of innocence and knowledge. The acquisition of knowledge, especially book learning, necessitates his expulsion from his childhood paradise. It could not have escaped Lu Xun that his narrative of the loss of innocence parallels the Old Testament myth of Adam and Eve and their exile from Eden after their ingestion of the fruit of knowledge.

In the biblical myth, Adam's fall from grace is attributed to the temptations of the woman, Eve, who in turn is an agent of the snake. Similarly, in Lu Xun's legend, a beautiful woman, who is also a snake, threatens the demise of a young man. Lu Xun's exile from paradise is concomitant with his acquisition of knowledge, as is the case of Adam's expulsion from Eden. Earthly learning is the source of the downfall for both.

Treating this myth from a psychoanalytical perspective as the basis of the human subconscious, Maire Kurrik's reading, which gives metaphorical significance to the story of Adam and Eve and humanity's moral struggle, also has implications for Lu Xun's story. Kurrik defines knowledge as the ability to judge between the desired and the undesirable as the good and the bad. This ability to differentiate is manifested by the ability to say both "yes" and "no" to different things. In other words, knowledge is the power to both affirm and negate. Before his acquisition of knowledge, Adam's role in the Garden of Eden is solely to affirm the goodness of God's work. Using the language of ego activity, Kurrik interprets this power of differentiation as the beginning of the split between the superego and the ego and the distinction between internal desire and outward behavior:

> It is also interesting that this area of the negative and the negated which God creates as an excluded or an outside can only be expropriated, brought inside, by an act of eating. This is reminiscent of Freud's idea of the bodily origin of negation. We affirm what we take in and negate that which we do not wish to take into the body. The body is the barrier between the inside and the outside.[51]

In this interpretation, human culture develops from the splitting of the self and is characterized by inhibitions and negations, a point that forms the basis of Freud's differentiation between instinctual, bodily desires and the cultural repression of their expression. The act of ingestion further creates cognition of the differentiation between one's interior and exterior, between one's ego and superego activities. This in turn, marks the beginning of duplicity and secrecy. The ingestion of an apple is the cause of Adam's fall from grace. This act of ingestion marks the separation between outside and inside, exterior phenomena and internal emotions, the natural world and the human world, visage (outer appearance) and trait (self, feeling) and finally, between language and intention.

Notwithstanding the Freudian language, Lu Xun's world is also fraught with paradoxes: between innocence and knowledge, childhood and adulthood, sensuality and repression. Lu Xun's Hundred Herbs Garden is a prelapsarian realm of self-unity and linguistic purity. The sensate language in his description of the garden is one of affirmation, reflecting the unity between phenomena and substance. However, he is prohibited from responding to the snake's summons. The destruction of the self as a result of responding to one's name is the first sign of the separation between language and meaning. The name is a metalepsis of the self. It is an empty metaphor because it is a sign of oneself without substantiation. It embodies neither one's outward nor inward attributes. Thus one's name, which is one's sole representation in society, can be seen as a displacement of one's reality by a cipher and a suppression of the real self. The name is a symbol of disjunction between the self and its representation. When one answers to and acknowledges a connection to this empty sign, one accepts the meaninglessness of oneself. The name is thus a negation of the substantial self.

The snake-beauty's threat to devour the scholar's body if he answers her call is a threat of the compromise of oneself if one submits to the total representational power of one's name. The reality of our selves will be reduced to a pure linguistic cipher. Our responding to our names lets the society of disjunctions and duplicity overtake our selves. Thus we lose forever connections to any real meaning. To respond to one's name when called by the snake-beauty is to let one's reality and autonomy be usurped. To answer to one's name is to exist in unfulfillment of the true meaning of the self. It is the death of the self. Thus Lu Xun bewails the peril of answering to one's name.

The chapter "The Hundred Herbs Garden and the Three-Flavored Schoolhouse" is strategically placed in an otherwise desultory work. It functions as a symbolic divide between Lu Xun's wholesome childhood world and the degradation of adulthood. It also marks the division of the many polarities at work in Lu Xun's text—child/adult, nature/culture, freedom/restriction, variety/insipidity, intention/language, and so on.

The schoolhouse, which represents the adult world of knowledge and learning, is described in direct contrast to the garden, a realm of naturalistic, sensate delight. Not only is the physical structure of the schoolhouse an obvious distinction from the untrammeled nature in the garden, this schoolhouse is significantly named "Three-Flavored Studio." The paucity of sensuality of the place and the dull insipidity of the activities there are embodied in the name itself—a direct contrast to the exuberance of the garden.

It is in his schooling that Lu Xun first experienced adult duplicity, lies, farce, and hypocrisy. The old tutor is a pathetic and pretentious fool cloaked by the appearance of civility and decorum. Mrs. Xian in the chapter "Miscellany" turns out to be a vicious tease and a malicious gossip behind her demeanor of kindness. His own father's appearance as an upright gentleman belies his willfulness and arbitrariness. Lu Xun recounts in "The Fair of the Five Fierce Gods" that just as the whole household was joyfully getting ready to go to the village spirit festival, his father suddenly issued an order that nobody was allowed to go to the fair until Lu Xun memorized a passage from the classical text *Jian luè* (Outline of history). Lu Xun remarks that although he finally managed to learn the passage, his enthusiasm for the trip was completely dampened. In Lu Xun's description, the adult world is hypocritical, superficial, and unreliable. There is neither logic nor consistency in the signs that adults use to represent their meaning and intention: signs have no link to their referents; things are not what they seem.

Similarly, the "civilized" language of the adult culture has no true signification, a point that Lu Xun makes through the chaotic reading aloud of old texts by the children in the schoolhouse:

> Then all of us would read at the top of our voices, with a roar like a seething cauldron. We all read from different texts: "Is humanity far? When I seek it, it is here." "To mock a toothless man, say: the dog's kennel gapes wide." "On the upper ninth the dragon hides itself and bides its time." "Poor soil, with good produce of the

inferior sort interspersed with superior produce; its tribute, matting, oranges, pomelos."[52]

The children are chanting jumbled, disconnected lines from classical texts, such as the *Analects*, the *Book of Changes*, and the *Book of History*. The incomprehensibility of the children's chant reflects the condition of the ultimate divorce between language and meaning. Detached from their original contexts, the texts that the children recite are meaningless gibberish. The chanting is merely a formality without meaning. The children adopt adult speech without meaning what they say, just as adults say what they don't mean. Again, it is an instance of form separated from, even usurping, content.

The absurdity of the children's reading not only illustrates the duplicity and meaninglessness of adult speech, but also ridicules classical culture. Classical writing, which is supposed to be the essence of Chinese civilization, becomes risibly irrelevant and pathetically outmoded in the children's riotous reciting. Through the children's voices, Lu Xun demonstrates that, separated from the monadic context of the classical literary world, classical language exists only as empty signs. These old writings have lost their power of signification in contemporary society.

To oppose an old language that has lost its potency is, of course, the whole idea behind the May Fourth language reform. *Wenyan* is regarded as a defunct language of a bygone age; it is riddled with dead metaphors, stale allegories, and other apophasis and linguistic tropes that will not say what one means. It is inferior to the vernacular, a natural language that comes from "real" and immediate emotions in response to one's surroundings.[53] To Lu Xun, the world defined by the *wenyan* culture is formal, artificial, and hypocritical. It destroys the world of linguistic unity and purity one finds in the Hundred Herbs Garden. Lu Xun's vehemence against classical language is revealed in the opening of the chapter on the *Book of Twenty-four Filial Pieties:* "I must search in all the four directions for the severest, direst curse for those people who oppose the vernacular or create obstacles for the adoption of the vernacular."[54] In a satirical ending to his tale of his childhood paradise, Lu Xun laments how it has been turned into an overgrown wasteland after it was sold to the Zhu family.[55] Zhu is, of course, the last name of the neo-Confucian arch-patriarch Zhu Xi (1130–1200), whose annotation of the Confucian classics, the *Four Books,* had defined Confucian culture since the thirteenth century.

The irony of Confucianism's emphasis on the teaching of "rectifying names of things," of calling each thing by its proper name and each person by his or her correct title, could not have escaped Lu Xun. It is only when relationships conform to their names, Confucianists maintain, that people will be placed correctly in their various social stations and harmony will prevail. As Lu Xun points out in his snake legend, however, it is precisely this social labeling that oppresses the individual. It represents a death of self. Lu Xun's indictment of Confucianism's emphasis on bookish learning and destructive influence over one's natural inclinations and individualism is expressed in his suggestive descriptions of the Hundred Herbs Garden after it had been purchased by the Zhu family: "It has been seven or eight years since I last saw [the garden]. To be sure, there were only a few tufts of wild grass left in it. But it once was my paradise."⁵⁶

Conclusion

Hu Shi, as we have seen, regards his name as a social insignia. It is a metaphor that articulates his condition as an individual—a survivor, and the nominated. The acquisition of his new name is a beginning to a successful career. It is a self-conscious determination of the meaning of his life. Hu Shi believes in the correlation between self-volition and social progress. His autobiography, a "great-man text," is a record of the fulfillment of the protagonist's predetermined ordination to greatness. The beginning narration of his eminent lineage and precocious acts of early childhood are thus important proofs of his claim of greatness in the work. The narrative structure also reflects this specific teleology of the gradual assumption of his societal nomination. As in all traditional "circumstantial" autobiographies that employ the linear scheme, development from childhood to adulthood is regarded as a personal and an intellectual progress. It is through such "great-man texts" that Hu Shi articulates the great process of China's modernization.

Unlike Hu Shi's work and against the traditional circumstantial autobiographical convention that it exemplifies, Lu Xun nowhere mentions his name, his date of birth, or his lineage. To be called by one's name is to be conditioned by the forces of adult society that work to negate one's self and break down its unity. For Lu Xun, our social appellations do not embody the meaning or substance of their referents, but usurp the actuality of the referents. By nomination, one is reduced to a mere cipher.

Lu Xun rejects the social system that attempts to label and thus place him. He therefore rejects the model of temporal linearity in his textual organization that articulates the particular structure of the patriarchal ideology. Although Lu Xun begins his collection with narratives of childhood events, they are not arranged to reflect any developmental sequence. The child in Lu Xun's writing is static. It is unconnected to, or rather it is in polemisis to, the adult state. The transition to adulthood is sudden and violent, and this movement (if there is a coherent one) is devolutionary. The rest of his experiences after this childhood state are repeated proofs of the end of vigor and the end of self.

Hu Shi sees himself as a promoter of a new language and culture. Aside from his advocacy of the vernacular, he discusses the new short story and drama as well as new autobiographical and biographical writings in his numerous "instructional" essays.[57] His leadership in modern Chinese letters is apodictic. Hu Shi's writing is sure-footed and unproblematic because he stakes his views upon solid, traditional notions of truth, logic, and reality based on an incontrovertible language of facts and numbers. In this sense, he remains the true "realist." However, for this same reason, his work also seems strangely dated. Lu Xun's fragmented text, which is riven with tension caused by rotating polarities, violates the traditional premise of historical time or reality. In Lu Xun's linguistic world, the traditional divisions between objects and subjects, inside and outside, no longer hold. It is in the works of Lu Xun that we find the effects of the new literary mentality.

In my reading of Hu Shi's and Lu Xun's works, I have shown that the relationship between an individual and a society is reflected in his or her textual stance. Hu Shi's narrative affirms the time and place of his social origins by "wedding a mimetic, verbal intention to time."[58] Lu Xun's fundamental questioning of the old institutions of perception, expression, and knowledge, and their referential efficacy in this new era, results in new rhetorical tools and a new narrative structure.

Chapter Five

A Moral Landscape

*Reading Shen Congwen's Autobiography
and Travelogues*

The material reality of location in travel literature is more than just a trope in its function. In travelogues, the narrating subject defines a presence in the literary locations he or she visits, which is ideological. It is with this view of narrative that I propose to analyze Shen Congwen's (1902–1988) sojourns to western Hunan and his childhood home of Fenghuang in his two works *The Autobiography of Shen Congwen* (*Congwen zizhuan*, 1930), and *Random Sketches on Travels to Western Hunan* (*Xiangxing sanji*, 1936).[1] Autobiographies and travelogues have often been interpreted as a kind of metaphoric journeys in search of self through revisits to a personal past. Similarly, Shen's writings are often read as a form of romantic nostalgia in his search for an alternative to modern, urban decadence in the simplicity of the rural world of his childhood.[2] In these interpretations, the land Shen depicts becomes a part of his imaginary or subjective universe. In this chapter, however, I argue that the land has both physical and symbolic functions as a political and cultural entity. In my reading, I not only relate the autobiographical self with the writer's temporal milieu, which I have sought to do in the previous chapters, but his geographical location as well. In this way, I locate the writer in a political and ideological relationship to the land in which he travels. In so doing, I examine the moral implications of the acts of writing and reading.

Shen's use of autobiographical strategies in writing about the Hunan countryside is significant. Like Yu Dafu, Shen's interior landscape is directly connected to the society at large. More importantly, however, these writings are particularly revealing of his idea of his position in the sociopolitical terrain and his problematic relationship to the objects of his narrative gaze. In the reflexivity of the autobiographical act, Shen turns his potentially damaging objectification of the countryside into a self-critical perspective on the morality of representation. Using autobiographical writing as an analogy to the act of reading, Shen also makes us apply the same self-criticism to our own gaze on landscape as a literary object.

The Political Implication of Reading and Writing

Disciplines of knowledge or ways of observation, such as geography, cartography, and topography, are shaped by the ideologies that employ them. This has been well argued in recent years by scholars from Edward Said to Mary Louise Pratt.[3] From the angle of literary production and consumption, Franco Moretti extends ideological geography to include the immediate sociopolitical coordinates of the writer's world. The activities of writing and reading are clearly circumscribed by external geography, from the location of plot action—countryside or city, which country or which city, even which parts of the city—to social or economic factors, such as distribution of books or libraries.[4] Equally emphasized in Moretti's theory of reading are the social conditions of writing—the writers' and the readers' notions of their world based on class and politics, material conditions that dictate publishing, marketing, and reading. This means physical locations in writings are by definition referential regardless of the content or plot. Moretti's reading thus removes creative production from the sole agency of the writer to a more diverse set of material parameters.

In view of the emphasis on location in recent literary discussions, one should reassess the importance of geographical locations in Shen Congwen's writing to the meaning of his work. Shen is especially renowned in modern Chinese literature for his evocations of the bucolic countryside and lives of minority groups and country people from his travels in western China. Past scholarship often treated such travels metaphysically, as processes of self-discovery. Leo Ou-fan Lee places Shen in a tradition of Chinese travel writings, connecting him directly to a lineage that begins with Xu Xiake (1566–1641), often considered China's first modern geographer and professional traveler. Lee argues that through this history of travel writings, one can delineate the development of literary subjectivity in Chinese literature. The importance of Shen's journeys to the interior of China for Lee is more psychological than actual. They represent a particular stage in the development of a literary subjectivity and illustrate the developing relationship between the self and society in modern Chinese literature.[5]

More often, scholars associate Shen's works with native-soil literature, a genre that is thematically defined by a search for a rural utopia as an alternative to the urban experience. Rosemary Haddon identifies three characteristics in native-soil writing: It is an urbanized narrator's depiction of his or her rural, childhood home; it contains an allegorical meaning evoked by the countryside; it describes socially marginal characters.[6] Zhu Xiaojin points out that the trajectory of native-soil writings is usually from a perceived dichotomy between the city and the countryside.[7] These two locations allegorize, respectively, the urban world of wickedness despite appearances of morality and decency, and the naturalistic world of innocence, free from the pretenses of class and social rules. Returning to nature is thus a remedy to urban dwellers for their moral weaknesses and the spiritual degradation brought on by rapid social changes in cities. Zhu suggests that Lu Xun's urgent call for people to return to their original, natural state of freedom from artificial morality precipitated the native-soil movement in the 1930s and 1940s.[8]

Both Zhu and Haddon describe native-soil writers as "sojourners in cities," implying that their identification is with rural sensibilities and that their perception of the city is based on these sensibilities. The countryside is their spiritual home, while the city is a place of alienation. In this convention, Shen's literary travels are a pilgrimage in search of spiritual redemption.

This reading of native-soil writing is demonstrated by Peng Xiaoyan. She argues that Shen attempts to show the way for social reform by leading us through an idealized landscape populated by romanticized visions of peoples who are closer to nature, therefore, purer and simpler, and as such, wiser. She thus also claims that Shen's writings transcend the strictures of realism ("chaoyue xianshi" [going beyond realism]). His travels are allegorical pilgrimages to the land of enlightenment. The countryside is the salvation of China as a utopic reconstruction.⁹

Likewise examining Shen in terms of native-soil writings, David Der-Wei Wang finds a much more complex concern with humanity. Wang argues that Shen's writings are a journey through the human "heart of darkness." He believes that through a strategy Wang terms "critical lyricism," Shen transcends the limits of realism, of mere portrayal of phenomena, to an investigation of the roots of human pathos and passions. Shen's writing is thus about the interior landscape. The land that he depicts is not a concrete, material reality, but an "imaginary nostalgia" on which Shen's hopes and fears for humanity are imprinted.¹⁰

Shen's journeys into China's interior have thus far been interpreted as a literary trope and an allegory in function. In these various readings, the places of Shen's travels reveal more of Shen's subjectivity than the actual locales and the peoples he writes about. As a result, the places described are important insofar as they are part of the author's internalized universe, an imaginary landscape, or mythical sites of an urban intellectual's dream of utopia.

The Relationship between Writing and Social Power

In order to place Shen's writing and native-soil literature in their general context, it is worth making a brief excursion into the concurrent folk-literature movement in the 1930s.¹¹ This movement arose from an anthropological or ethnographic interest among urban intellectuals in the various customs and cultures of peoples in the different regions of China, particularly minorities and tribal groups. This so-called Going to the People *(daominjian qu)* movement was instigated and led by a number of scholars at Beijing University, including Deng Zhongxia (1897–1933) and Zhou Zuoren (1885–1967), and later, the prominent historian, Gu Jiegang (1893–1980).¹² This academic interest in the countryside often contributed to, or arose from, romantic visions of tribal peoples as a version of the "noble savage."¹³ This would support Peng's and Zhu's observations that the thematic principle of native-soil literature is mainly a search for lost innocence in the countryside and among "primitive" peoples.

Regardless of whether investigations into tribal cultures directly contributed to the interest in native-soil literature, they reveal the power relationships at the time between urban elites and country people, especially ethnic minorities. Critics of ethnographic practices have maintained that writing is a kind of technology of power that exercises dominant relations through representation.[14] The intellectual attitude toward the countryside and tribal groups can be characterized as an "imperialistic nostalgia," in Renato Rosaldo's terms. This kind of self-righteous affection for powerless or marginal peoples effaces the obvious inequalities between the two groups.[15] It is not important whether Shen is connected, directly or indirectly, to this contemporary fascination with the countryside. What is significant is that the countryside, perhaps never an innocent trope in Chinese literature in general, is a particularly politicized metaphor in Shen's cultural context. The attitude of "imperialistic nostalgia" is particularly poignant in the case of western Hunan, the site of Shen's writings, given the history of hostilities between the Miao minorities and the Chinese central government. (This will be discussed further below.) By reading Shen's depiction of the countryside as merely a part of his subjectivity and his personal story and by ignoring both the conditions of the production and consumption of his writings, we bury the actual politics of the region. By reading Shen's writings of western Hunan without regard for the question of location, we become unreflective participants in a historical erasure. Shen's landscape would be reduced to a space produced through the literary imagination of an urban intellectual as a sanctuary from urban oppression. As such, the countryside is appropriated by the privileged gaze of the city and of intellectual culture. Reading becomes a kind of tourism, which, as I will demonstrate below, is a form of violence.

Surveying the Historical Site

Shen's writings are born out of the violent discourse of conquering and subjugation. In beginning an autobiography by evoking the authority of official documents, Shen places his personal experience squarely in the larger history of the land. He thus makes abundantly clear the connection between political conditions and his life. It is appropriate, then, that we bring into consideration Shen's self-identity vis-à-vis his experience and his personal relationship with the land about which he writes so profusely and obsessively.

The landscape Shen reproduces through numerous textual details, some shockingly explicit, is more than a figment of literary fantasy or imaginary yearnings for the past. The mention of western Hunan evokes historical images of its Miao (Hmong) inhabitants, Fenghuang being one of the three districts along the western borders in which the Miao tribes settled in great numbers.[16] The history of the Miao people in China is a long and bloody one. Their relationship with the central governments during the Ming and Qing periods was marked by displacement and various extermination and pacification campaigns. These were compounded by numerous uprisings against the local authorities and by internecine warfare. The largest and most disruptive insurrections were the so-called Miao Rebellion from 1854 to 1873. The twenty-year war resulted in unimaginable devastation in this region.[17]

Shen came from a military family. His grandfather, Shen Hongfu, was a general in the Hunan army during the Miao insurgency. In 1864, he was appointed provincial military commander in the Hunan company and later, the "Grand Defender" (*zhenshou shi*) of Yunnan, the heartland of minority presence and a center of the maelstrom.[18] Shen's father and brother were also military officers who made their careers in the various wars in Hunan. Fenghuang, where Shen was born and grew up, is in the southwestern border region. In his own description, the very existence of this little town represents the aggressive policy of the Qing government toward the Miao people. According to Shen, Fenghuang's first mention in a historical work is in the military document *Miaofang beilan* (A manual for the defense against the Miao).[19] The function and aim of such a composition are obvious from the title.

Fenghuang was established as a garrison town. During the Republican period, armies of different allegiances, government and private militias, raged through the countryside, carrying out various military campaigns. More than once, Shen describes the Qing policy toward the Miao peoples as repressive, noting that many places in Fenghuang still bear the traces of the bloodbaths that occurred there. Shen frequently describes in his writings the aftermath of the massacres and carnage of war that he saw as a child, first in the Miao suppressions, later in the various warlord militias, and finally, during the campaigns against the warlords themselves. Shen's writing about Fenghuang and western Hunan is set against this bloody history.

Shen's telling and retelling of the tales about this region cannot be read as neutral, since in many different ways he is deeply imbricated in a lineage of violence. That is, he hails from a military family and served in the military in his early career variously as a foot soldier, an army secretary, and a recorder. In the first section of his autobiography, Shen situates himself very clearly in the historical conditions of his writing. It is willful ignorance on the part of the reader to disregard this broad context, laid out for us at the onset of his work.

Through his writings, Shen re-creates this invasive experience for his readers. He opens his *Autobiography* with a description of Fenghuang. However, this description is not the usual autobiographical mise-en-scène. In leading us into the region through his writing, Shen duplicates the experience of military surveillance and invasion. He prepares the readers for an exploration of the region, ready to open before us historical documents (especially of military history) and military manuals. However, conceding that official records are boring, he finally inserts, wholesale, an earlier essay of his that provides a general topographical description of the region.

Shen literally spreads out before us an ichnographical description of Fenghuang, pinpointing individual locations, so we can better penetrate the area and view it with greater accuracy:

> If a curious person examines the old maps of a hundred years ago, he should be able to find, on a very isolated corner around north Guizhou, eastern Sichuan, and western Hunan, a small dot named *Zhengan* (Like other dots, in reality, it should represent a town, and in this town there lived about three to five thousand people. . .).[20]

This description in Shen's writing gives us an aerial perspective in which we first encounter the land as a dot on the map. Then in a gradual descent, the dot enlarges and specific details come into view. This movement of the perspective mimics telescopic adjustments through which our privileged panoramic perspective is maintained. We are able to gather information about this locality without actual contact with the people and the place, nor entanglement in its banalities.

Shen inscribes this region in the bureaucratized language of government policies and military management. Thus we "enter" the town of Fenghuang through perspectives that could only be possible through organized knowledge, such as history, geography, cartography, and technologies of sight, such as telescopic, panoramic, and aerial ranges. The introduction to the town is, in this sense, a discursive invasion.[21] Shen then takes us through the actual landscape and architectural sites, the turrets and other military structures. During our tour, he reveals the bloody history behind these sites: "Because of the repressive policies of the Qing over the last two centuries and the resultant rebellions, blood had stained every public road and every blockhouse red" (4). However, Shen tells us that all of that history is now over. The army camps have been turned into civilian residences; the forts are destroyed and the people are all "assimilated" *(tonghua le*—transformed to become *like us)*. Shen's narrative encircles the area, just as the natives have been circumscribed within the history of Chinese conquest, and then assimilated.

In the next section of the introduction, Shen provides general ethnographical information, including the economic activities of the people. As Shen's prose continues, we are led to an even closer inspection of the individuals at their daily chores. We are now near enough to tell even the details and the colors of their clothes. Shen's description of Fenghuang is full of delightful, bucolic details. As the tour continues, we as readers imbibe the pleasures of the land:

> The water of the river is clear year round with many mandarin fish, carp, and crucian carp. The larger ones are bigger than a human foot. In the houses along the shore, one can often see tall, fair women, who are adept at smiling when they see people.[22]

The description of the landscape flows seamlessly into an appraisal of the physical attributes of the local women. These smiling women by the river, as readers of Shen's *Travels* will come to know, are prostitutes. Here, Shen exposes the intrusiveness of our readerly position vis-à-vis the natives. Our pleasure in the scenery exerts an erotic power as our gaze turns on the fair-skinned women. The bond between power and pleasure here is explicit. At this point our gaze turns exploitative, as we understand that the objects of our gaze can be possessed. This visual imposition at such a minute level of everyday life is, in Edward Said's words, a "micro-physics of imperialism."[23]

Indulging in sensual pleasure and aesthetic experience, Shen continues his description of Fenghuang:

> I ran about too wildly during the day, wandering all over, watching, hearing, and smelling different things: the smell of dead snakes, of decaying grass, the odor of the butcher's body, the smell from the kilns where bowls were fired after the rain. Although I could not describe them all with words, I could distinguish them easily. The noises made by the bats, the sigh of an ox when the butcher pushed a knife into its neck, the cry of the big yellow snakes hiding in pits and caves, the faint splashing of fish in the dark—all these sounds were distinct in my ears and I remember them very clearly.[24]

Shen's sensual celebration of the countryside in his introduction is disconnected from aspects of daily life. It reads like the "highlights" of the pleasures of local exotica that one might find catalogued in a tourist pamphlet. The journeys that Shen undertakes in these works are not, as Peng Xiaoyan or Leo Lee have argued, pilgrimages for self-enlightenment or self-discovery, but a travel guide of the region, fully equipped with maps, historical information, and topographical records. Inscribed in a language that coincides with the political mapping of the land, the text leads the outsider, the metropolitan reader, into the territory. Seeing through the eyes of a truant child or a tourist or a voyeur, the perspective on Fenghuang is distant and detached, lacking both commitment and empathy. We observe other people's tragedies and wars, but we are disconnected from our own complicity as readers in the violence of Shen's description.

The Civilized Landscape

In 1930, when Shen was in Beijing, firmly established as a writer of the Beijing school *(Jingpai)*, he wrote for an urban readership or, at the very least, a lettered and, as such, elite readership. The city-country dichotomy that Zhu delineates in native-soil literature is not a simple spatial or even cultural differentiation, as he suggests. As the "Going to the People" movement illustrates, this dichotomy is a result of complex social, political and cultural contests between members of the dominant urban elite and marginalized peoples in the countryside.[25]

Writing for his particular readership, Shen's narrative and aesthetic perspectives do not belong to the native peoples of western Hunan, but reflect the elitist gaze of the cities. The language and references that Shen employs in many of the descriptions of the countryside affect an urban or elitist taste. In the chapter "A Friend Who Wears a Beaver-Fur Hat" in the *Travels*, landscape painting is used as a special code of sublime exchange between Shen and his friend, a colorful local character who lives by the Xiang River. Shen insists on relating to his friend on Shen's rhetorical terms—in the language of art connoisseurship. This particular dialect of friendship is not one that reflects a delight in the guileless simplicity of peasants but one that appreciates the rare sophistication of a country eccentric who has acquired the taste and learning of a cultivated gentleman. The friendship is conditioned upon their mutual fluency in the elitist culture:

> "This doggone scenery is really like a painting!"
> "Naturally! But whose painting?" I said. "Brother, whose painting do you think this looks like?" I deliberately wanted to test my friend to see how much he knew about Chinese paintings.
> He laughed. "That son-of-a-bitch Shen Shitian; he paints with bold strokes, just like a bandit."
> I naturally disagreed with this kind of wild exhortation. . . . Honestly speaking, there was an air of heroic desolation in the naturalness and elegance of the scenery that came to us through our windows.
> He seemed to have understood my silent thought. He then said, "Look, old man, this crop of the mountain, this clump of trees, that spread of the treetops, that wash of light mist—really! Only that wild dog, Wang Lutai, could have painted it!"
> This time, he "guessed" right. I said, "This time you've read my mind. I was just thinking how similar this scenery is to Wang

Lutai's scrolls. You have a fan painted by him. I knew you would recognize it."[26]

The landscape and scenery are compared to scroll paintings. They are transformed into figurations and, finally, figures of speech in which the immediacy of the actual physicality is completely "civilized." The landscape is thus inscribed within the gaze of the urban intellectual by the language of culture and becomes the site of intellectual aesthetic sublime.

In the same way, Shen transforms the scenes of battles and slaughtering that he witnessed as a child into the picturesque. The violence and the urgency of the original sight is turned into a tableau vivant—as an artistic endeavor:

> I had already heard many stories about battles. It was always "mountains of human heads, rivers of blood." In the operas, it was also always, ". . . thousands of soldiers, tens of thousands of horses; it is hard to tell who is winning, who is losing." However, aside from the story "Qin Qiong Mourning a Head," in which one could see the wooden head being maneuvered about on a crimson platter, I had never seen a real battle or things like severed heads before. [Now,] over there was a big pile of these bloody things chopped off from human necks.[27]

As before, Shen's description of his childhood world relies heavily on the aesthetic language of classical culture, in this case, lines from the operas. In another instant, he describes the sights of death and destruction as "brilliantly colored pictures" [yanse xianming de tuhua].[28]

Shen thus builds his description of the countryside upon various existing cultural forms: literary writings, maps, legends, paintings, and dramatic images. He transcribes all experiences into the language of *textual* culture. He refers to his childhood education as reading a little book, and his peripatetic exploration of the sensual world of sight, smell, and sound as reading a big book. The titles of chapters in his *Autobiography* reflect such comparisons: "My Reading of a Small Book and, at the Same Time, My Reading of a Big Book" (chapter 3); "I Have learned Many Lessons, Yet I Still Cannot Give Up the Big Book" (chapter 5).

The experience of the countryside is thus appropriated into a discipline of knowledge, attainable by the metropolitan intellectuals among his readers.

Perhaps one of the most famous literary evocations and the most obvious example of the acculturation of the countryside is Shen's description of the town Taoyuan (Peach Spring) in his *Travels,* an allusion to the famous Peach blossom spring *(Taohuayuan).* Peach blossom spring is a topos in Chinese literature of utopia created in the essay "Taohua yuan ji" (Peach Blossom Spring) by the Jin dynasty poet Tao Qian (365–427). Shen's writing about the Peach Spring in western Hunan, which became a popular site among literati visitors because of the nominal association, captures how an actual locale could be reimagined by the urban elite. Determined to experience the textual Peach Blossom Spring as a reality, intoxicated by the imaginary aura of the great ancient poet and his terrestrial paradise, these romantic travelers ignored the actual condition of the real place in order to indulge in their fantasies. Shen writes about their carving their names and mediocre poetry in different places to mark their presence in this little town, and thus asserting their possession of a literary property that is entirely fictional.

The actual Peach Spring has nothing to do with the literary myth. Shen's vernacular and "secular" version[29] is not inhabited by peaceful peasants and fishermen, but is teeming with characters from the demimonde—adventurers, gamblers, petty politicians, and military men. Shen describes the bravado of these colorful characters; in the same light-hearted tone, he portrays the desperate plight of the prostitutes when old age and illness overtake them. However, for the literary-minded visitors to Peach Spring, the sordid details of the lives of these women and the rest of the local inhabitants are invisible, displaced by the beautiful illusion evoked by the textual Peach Blossom Spring. The natives' urgent struggles for survival recede into the background as part of the "local color." In this way, Shen tames the wildest and most barbaric conditions into a language of culture and aesthetics. While readers ramble through the realm of civilized pleasure, the crises of the original landscape are suppressed and erased.

Shen's works represent an urban discourse on a nonurban, peasant world and an intellectual discourse on a nonlettered world. Through an elitist dialect, Shen converts an inarticulate experience into language, mapping and sanitizing so that urban readers could also now own the experience of the land designed according to their pleasure. Shen, the urban writer, is the constitutive subjectivity of the whole countryside. With his consciousness at the forefront of the writings, the Fenghuang inhabitants retreat to a static and anachronistic world, untouched by history, politics, and culture. The annexation of western Hunan into the consciousness of urban and intellectual travelers and readers is thus accomplished.

In this vein, one could read Shen's writing in the tradition of conquest narrative and consider the history of western Hunan in terms of the exploitation of the Miao and the other rural inhabitants. One could then regard Shen's position as an urban transcriber and an interpreter of the countryside, or, a "native informant." If language and culture are directly aligned with power, is Shen's work inadvertently circumscribed within the rhetoric of power? In other words, can one write outside of one's subject position in society? Through many hints of cynicism in his writing, as in the description of the Peach Spring intellectuals, one realizes that Shen is fully aware of his own literary violence toward the countryside. Both the history of this area and Shen's relationship to it are too complicated to be summarized by a simple plot of a dichotomized contention between the dominant and the marginalized. Shen's works are multilayered. He courts his urbane readers with the beauty of his writing. While we become entranced by his texts, however, he forces us into confrontations with our own violence.

Ambivalent Alliances and Double Perspective

Conventional scholarship on Shen's travelogues and autobiography has been based on the idea of the author as a given unity, so much so that the investigation of the rise of authorial subjectivity has become the focus of investigation.[30] However, Shen's self-representation in his writings constantly calls attention to the paradoxes of his position. His particular historical and sociopolitical situation is a demonstration that the authorial subjectivity is both as concrete and as fluid as all historically situated subjects. In order to decipher the multivalence of meanings in Shen's writing, and to evaluate his own vision of himself and his life, it is necessary to examine Shen's intricate and duplicitous connection to the history he writes about as well as the sociocultural vectors in which his experiences are inscribed.

I mentioned earlier the participation of Shen's family in the history of Miao repression. If he had seemed unperturbed by that association, later he openly dedicates his writings to the Miao peoples:

> The healthy blood of your nation flows in my veins. However, in my twenty-seven years of life, half of it has been swallowed by life in the city. I have been poisoned by a disease inculcated by a hypocritical morality and have become weak and insincere. All the elements of my personality that deserve to be called noble, such as passion, bravery, and honesty, have completely dissipated. I am no longer worthy to claim descent from the same nation as you.[31]

In the 1980s Shen finally revealed his matrilineal filiation with the Miao peoples. Both his grandmother and mother were tribal members.[32] The moral conditions for Shen as a writer of the western Hunan countryside is thus a highly charged issue, so much so that most readers choose to only read the benign side of Shen's works and disregard the bloody aspects. However, it is precisely upon the intersection of his allegiances that Shen formulates his vantage point—between Miao and Han, country and city, the illiterate and the lettered, the dominated and the dominator—stressing his affiliations in opposing worlds.[33]

Shen's identification of himself as a *xiangxia ren* (country fellow) to his readers and urban colleagues is perhaps ironic and a self-parody, but it also illustrates the dialectical condition of his existence. He perceived himself as being on the margin of the system. Doubtless, he viewed his connection with the country peoples and his experience as a child in western Hunan with great nostalgia and sentimentality. However, his ability to assert his country identity is due to the fact that he was a city dweller who has deliberately abandoned the country. In the actual countryside, his *xiangxia ren* identity loses all potency. On the other hand, his country friends see him as belonging to the urban milieu, identifying him as a *Jingpai* (Beijing school) writer. Shen's claim to be a *xiangxia ren* in the city and an urbanite in the countryside gives him the privilege of a double vision that is rooted in his simultaneous identifications with the dominator and the dominated.

Deirdre David argues that it is possible to recover the ideological position of an author through examining the ending of a novel.³⁴ In the same way, one can surmise how Shen rated his two worlds through the resolutions of his two works. In his autobiography, the last chapter is tellingly titled "Yige zhuanji" (A chance for change). Shen ends the narrative of the first part of his life with his abandoning of the countryside for Beijing. This decision to leave is a result of an epiphanous experience during his illness following a friend's accidental death. This death made him ponder the ephemerality of life and the possibility that he might also suddenly die without any real, heroic cause, trapped in the limited world of the countryside. Immediately, thereafter, he left for the city, escaping what he perceived as the narrowness and insularity of country life.

In the concluding chapter of *Travels*, "Yige aixi bizi de pengyou" (The friend who loved his nose), Shen tells of the career of a friend from a military school. For a while, this young man, who had always dreamed of heroic deeds, seemed to have made good in his various adventures around the country as a military man. He wrote letters to Shen in Beijing, mocking Shen's worthless endeavors with his pen and his association with the "storytellers" of the "Beijing school." However, years later, when they met again unexpectedly during Shen's travels, he told Shen about the senselessness of many things he saw while roaming the countryside as a soldier. He wanted to follow Shen to Shanghai to "try his luck with Mao Dun and Lao She" and write stories.³⁵ In both the *Autobiography* and the *Travels*, Shen not only condemns the violence and ruthlessness of the countryside, but also reaffirms writing and the literary culture of the cities.³⁶ This problematizes the inclusion of Shen into the native-soil genre as Peng, Zhu, and Heddon have defined it.

As much as to Shen's seeming nostalgia toward the countryside, his writings also owe a debt to his alienation from it. However, it is also true that Shen's unique vision of the countryside and country people illuminates the decadence of modern city life. By identifying himself as a "country fellow," he affirms a life of natural vigor and honesty that city dwellers lack. Both poles of his cultural displacement, as an urbanite in the countryside and a country fellow in the city, are important in forging a critical stance in his writing.

While reviling the ruthlessness and ignorance of country people, Shen understands well the implication of his affiliation with prominent institutions of power, such as language and culture, that enables him to write about the peasants and natives—the dominated. Shen's unique position of in-betweenness allows him to be both critical and sympathetic to his different associations simultaneously. He understands the relationship between these paradoxes, their embodied values and their violent relationships with each other. He writes about the countryside both as a *xiangxia ren* and an urbanite. He writes both to damn the countryside and to condemn the urbanite's attitude toward the countryside. In this circularity, as I will discuss below, his writings are ultimately self-critical; readers of his works, seeing through his eyes, are also forced into a kind of self-criticism.

Morality and Writing

It is easy to gloss over the violence in Shen's works because it seems so incongruous and irreconcilable to his otherwise gentle world of romantic love, folk songs, and primitive wisdom. It is unsettling when he uses the same level of rhetorical intensity to relate events of drastically differing moral dimensions. Shen writes about the butchery of war—the heaps of decomposing human heads and strings of human ears hung on city gates—with the same lyrical and placid prose and with the same equanimity as he writes about clear running rivers and handsome Miao women. His writings contain much that would appear to be moral inversions. He narrates macabre scenes of poking at the severed heads of the executed with sticks, throwing stones at wild dogs hovering around half-eaten corpses, and boys toting home the heads of their freshly executed fathers and uncles, as if he were creating tableaus or "colorful pictures." His landscapes, expansive and peaceful from a distance, are filled with death and decomposition upon close encounter.[37] He treats the outcasts of society and small-town prostitutes with seemingly indiscriminate appreciation and indulgence. All this provided much fodder for the moral police who have charged Shen's writing with cultural chauvinism and decadent insensitivity.[38] How is one to evaluate and understand the seeming moral ambiguities in Shen's writing without being reductive and judgmental?

Shen understands literature's affiliation with a long tradition of sociocultural tyranny, and its connection with the ruling and elite classes. The question is how he can elucidate the oppressiveness of this act of gazing and writing of an other, while using a literary tool that is so steeped in the politics of oppression. To see the countryside from an urban perspective, whether idealistic or didactic, is destructive, because the act of seeing dislocates the objects of sight from the original context into the purviews of one's own. This perspective also reduces the country to a silent object.

What role do we, as readers, play as we follow his travels as tourists and sojourners in our detached voyeurism of the land, reading the effects of his gaze, turning, as he does, the reality of other people's lives into our own cultural possessions or fantasies? A careful analysis reveals that this kind of poetics of pleasure is intricately linked to an epistemic violence, not merely his, but ours as readers as well. Shen both deploys and satirizes the pastoral vision of the countryside and utopian rhetoric. Shen's writing not only displays his in-betweenness in relation to these two worlds, but also his double perspective as an autobiographer. In his reflexive gaze, Shen the writer duplicates as the reader. At the same time, he is the object of his own gaze as an autobiographer—the "country boy." Shen's writing is thus an exploration of how his role as a reader of the world reproduces the aggression against the less powerful under an illusion of nostalgia and utopia, and how this oppression is repeated when his writings are read by us. He simultaneously examines the power of readers and reveals the political consequences of the readerly gaze from the perspective of the receiver of this gaze. By acknowledging his belligerence as a reader of himself, he brings into scrutiny the morality of the act of reading itself.

Shen's interstitial identity thus creates a double entendre in his writing. His double vision of the country clearly differentiates him from the native-soil writers and helps him overcome their damning perspective. The complex trajectory in his writing cannot be fully analyzed through the simple formulae of native-soil writing delineated for us by Haddon, nor can it be satisfactorily explained in the unproblematized theorization of land in terms of the antagonistic binaries of country-city and peasant-intellectual presented in Zhu's discussions. We need to examine the thematic value of violence in Shen's writing. Shen plays on inversions, reversals, circularities, and repetition inherent in the autobiographical form as a method to transcend the ideological limitations of writing.

The Moral Function of Autobiography

As a child, Shen saw the world around him as littered with disconnected images and disjointed body parts through his still truncated sensibilities. Like the decapitated victim he describes in his autobiography whose head is hung high but cannot see, whose ears are strung up but cannot hear, and whose head is severed from the sentience of the body, Shen also experienced his childhood reality without much self-consciousness or intellectual coherence: "Why are they being executed, and who are these people who decapitated them? There are so many questions in my heart."[39] Later, in his early career as an army secretary, these random fragments are organized into written records. While stationed at Huaihua, Shen wrote, "I was there for a year and four months, and had seen about seven hundred executions. I was able to understand thoroughly under what circumstances these people had been beaten, and why they had their heads cut off."[40] By the logic that follows, the acquisition of writing and reading skills as an adult represents his achievement of sentience and reasoning and thus the ability to organize the scattered images of life into narrative coherence and thus to achieve understanding. The act of writing becomes one of joining all these shards of childhood images and numerals into discursive continuity, giving both reason and logic to the fragments of events.

Hans Kellner contends that the purpose of putting events into a narrative whole is a universal human impulse to create meaning from the debris of the decomposed past. This impulse to historicize, moreover, is to control a chaotic past that is "potentially terrifying in its indifference to the needs of humanity, or perhaps, sublime in its destructive course."[41] As such, history writing rationalizes the violent and destructive elements in human experiences. However, David Der-wei Wang argues that it is insufficient to explain Shen's work in terms of this rationalist or realist project. It is through Shen's "lyrical" tendencies—the exploration of pathos and passions—that Shen is able to map the human "heart of darkness," for him, a terra incognita. Writing is an act of "re-membering." The strength of Shen's writing, Wang argues, is thus the oxymoronic function of his "critical lyricism."[42]

Both Kellner's theory and Wang's reading affirm Shen's remarkable achievement as a historian or interpreter of the times. However, as autobiographical works, there is an added element to Shen's writings that is not accounted for by either Kellner's or Wang's explanation—the strategy of reflexivity and repetition that I alluded to earlier. It is significant that Shen chose to retell, in the particular way that he did, many of his experiences that already had been written into his short stories. Autobiography is a literary form that is concerned with a long, reversed temporal period as well as with historical time. Travelogue, on the other hand, deals with geographical and spatial experiences. These two types of writing constitute a recomposition of the self in terms of temporal and spatial existence. To read Shen's works in temporal terms only, as an organization of the past events, or as a form of psychological reenactment, is to miss a major aspect of his writing. His autobiography and travelogues are reinvestments of his self within a specific location and history, and as such, they connect the singularity of personal experiences to their proper space and time. In other words, not only is Shen interpreting or organizing an objective past; he is also asking a crucial question about the implications of his own experience in terms of both time and space.

Shen's adult experiences are a kind of replay of his childhood activities. If his childhood rambling is random and seemingly meaningless, his adult reexperiencing of the land is a reassertion of his consciousness, as both a social and a historical being, back into this landscape. As a young truant, he wandered around the countryside, collecting visual and aural images of wars and executions. When he became a soldier, his childhood peregrinations turned professional. As a foot soldier, Shen traversed the countryside, leaving destruction and suffering in his wake. Because he had writing skills, he was assigned the duty of organizing and taking down official records of army activities—military operations and executions of prisoners. He turned these images into bureaucratic language and statistics. His curious witnessing of human violence as a child became his official responsibility as an adult. The major difference between Shen as a young boy and as an adult is that the adult had a hand in creating the violent images that the child saw. Moreover, he was made to account for these events as an army recorder—the trials, tortures, and executions of the condemned and the helpless, rebels as well as innocent peasants. His work was to witness and validate the sights and sounds that were already familiar to him from his childhood experiences. In short, his childhood habit of collecting images became a career in his adulthood.

As an autobiographer, Shen reenacts all these past roles once again. The motif of wandering, seeing, and recording his childhood is repeated throughout his life and his works. In this final round, all these fragments of his past are joined into a coherent consciousness fully connected to his historical time and place. If childhood is a disconnected self, represented as a series of truncated experiences—severed heads, strings of ears—his progress toward adulthood is a process of reconnecting the fragments of experience into a historical consciousness, one whose every act and gesture is a significant and deliberate part of history. In other words, in adulthood he is able to place himself within historical relevance together with all the moral issues of such a connection.

Shen's relationship to his past in his autobiography is not merely one long backward glance of nostalgia or idyllic imagination.[43] His past and present are entangled in a complicated involvement with each other. The past is not merely gone and rationalized away, as Kellner would have it, but continually exacts an accounting for, and legitimating from, the present self. How is he himself implicated within this past history he records?

Shen's childhood activities appear innocent and innocuous, because they are separated from a specific historical context and responsibility. However, when the same activities are transposed onto an adult, a historical consciousness, the political meaning of these events is immediately apparent. When Shen said, "I understand thoroughly," perhaps, as an army recorder, it is a comprehension of the violent meanings of the colorful vista of the land of his childhood that he had enjoyed so much. Perhaps it is finally an understanding of the political significance of his sights and his travels. He arrives at this understanding because he is finally able to make the connection between the political, the historical, and his own existence.

The writing of an autobiography, a genre that places great importance on one's temporal being, is an act of placing oneself within history. Self-experience, political geography, and history coalesce when Shen gains coherent adult consciousness in his autobiography, and he is able to join the fragmented understanding of a child into a narrative. In this sense, the notion of "re-membering" in his autobiographical writings contains political significance. This effort to narrativize himself connects his being to its proper meaning and context. In the same way, Shen forces us as readers to connect our visceral awareness with our historical and geographical positions as we direct our gaze upon the textual terrain. Reading Shen's works is a lesson in reflecting on our subject positions and their political and ideological implications, and the degree of our participation in the textual violence toward our "other."

How are readers coaxed into a reconnected consciousness? And how does this consciousness change our understanding of Shen's landscape?

I mentioned earlier Shen's persistence in the picturesque in his writing. He uses the allusion of the utopian Peach Blossom Spring to describe the decadence of the demi-monde. He uses operatic stanzas or references to colorful paintings to describe the bloody mess of war. Irrelevance is a strategy Shen deploys to reveal to us the violence that underlies our customary perception of things. This mixing up of values and priorities is sometimes comical in effect because it creates situations that are absurd. For example, a peasant, his execution imminent, indulges in affectionate thoughts of his ducklings and piglets back home.[44] The cartoonlike figures of peasants, though sadistically tortured, seem to feel little pain or have little sense of tragedy. A simple game of rolling dice casts their lot, either of life or death:

> About one or two hundred were captured everyday, mostly peasants from the Fourth village. They could neither all be released nor all be decapitated. In order to settle this, the decision was entrusted to the heavenly king in whom all the local people believed. A prisoner was led to the yard in front of the main temple of the heavenly king to cast bamboo shells before the god. If one shell faced up and the other down—a *xun* lot—the prisoner was released. If both faced up—a *yang* lot—he was released. If both faced down—a *yin* lot—he was decapitated. Life or death was determined by a cast. Those who were to die went by themselves to the left. Those who were to live went by themselves to the right. Each person had three out of four chances in the gamble. Therefore, among those who were to die, none uttered a word. Lowering their heads, they walked to the left.[45]

Executions are even described as a comedy from which the military officers derived merriment. Consider the scene in which Shen describes the prisoners in Huaihua, where he and his troops were stationed. He records that every time there was an execution, a few officers would gather on a footbridge to watch the excitement. After the drama, they would amuse themselves by recounting the bravado or cowardice and other remarkable behavior of the condemned prisoners being led to execution.[46] In the midst of each macabre comedy, Shen would play his part at entertaining these men, serving his special braised dog-meat. Executions, in Shen's description, are an epicurean burlesque—a distant echo of Lu Xun's world of cannibals in which humans textually consume each other.[47]

In writings about these events, the readers become spectators of the actual spectators of the comedy (again, an effect of Shen's strategy of reflexivity and repetition). It then becomes a moral decision for us to laugh or not as we watch how tragedy turns into a laughing matter in a world of truncated human sensibilities. In this way, the reading of Shen's writings involves a constant moral confrontation with ourselves. We are made to assess the morality of our readerly stance toward the historical events and also how these events are aestheticized and sanitized through textual conventions.

Shen juxtaposes the most bucolic scenes with the most inhuman cruelty, the most mundane and the most familiar with the bloodiest moments. He uses aestheticizing or seemingly innocuous references precisely to problematize them, emphasizing their insufficiency, irrelevance, and inappropriateness to the actuality that they are supposed to represent. Sometimes the resultant irrelevance in his writings is so explicit that its effect is beyond irony. Instead of resorting to humor, readers cringe twice—once at the horrors the writings evoke, once at the casualness with which they are evoked. Shen's tone of seeming indifference exposes the real violence in the world that he depicts—not only the actual suffering and destruction, but how these have been betrayed and de-composed by our conventions of reading and writing. In his strategy of infusing innocence with violence, Shen also brings to our attention our seemingly innocent stance, but violent effects, as readers of texts.

Shen's writing is not about a mythical place and time; it is about a legacy of violence, not just military and physical, but also textual and cultural. These aspects of the past can only be addressed by historical and spatial specificity. The amnesiac and denaturing language of culture, art, and literature constantly evokes an aestheticized image of the countryside, erasing the gory trail of history. It is as if we see the peasants only as strings of ears, disconnected limbs, severed heads, and decapitated trunks. In reducing the natives to mere body parts, readers participate in the campaigns of deculturation of the countryside. The urban readers' acts of primitivizing or idealizing of the countryside obliterate the actual suffering there. The effect is a form of epistemic violence. As we read and enjoy the expansiveness of Shen's land, despite the carnage, we are in effect duplicating the act of the army officers' celebration of a prisoner's death with a feast. Shen, in his role as a writer, enticing us with his euphoric descriptions, is repeating his role in the army, cooking the cannibalistic feast for us.

Shen's depiction of shocking scenes is always through a language of unexpected *a*morality. But if the author refuses to guide us to a moral position, as a realist such as Lu Xun would, then the responsibility for judgment rests solely upon the reader.⁴⁸ Confronted with this kind of writing, we can no longer hide behind the writer's didactic rhetoric, avoiding our own apathy or ambiguity. Abstention from obvious moral statements is Shen's way of interrogating the morality of his readers and society, or at least forcing us into a position of reflexive confrontation.

Reading Morally

In an account from the autobiography, Shen narrates the story of a man condemned for stealing the cadaver of the woman he loved and sleeping with it for a few days before he was discovered. The importance of this story to Shen can be seen in the fact that he wrote about it four times in four different versions. This tale captures a crucial means of understanding how Shen unsettles and questions the aesthetic language and values of the dominant elite (urban/intellectual) culture. The accused necrophiliac is led to his execution, where he is engaged in an exchange with his executioners. The necrophiliac's vision challenges accepted social values of the dominant society:

After a while, he again muttered to himself: "It was so beautiful, so beautiful." Another soldier said, "Lunatic, we are going to kill you. Aren't you afraid?" He replied, "What's there to be afraid of? Are you afraid of death?" The soldier was embarrassed by his retort and tried to scare him by saying, "Aren't you afraid to die, mad dog? In a while, I am going to chop your crazy head off!" That man again smiled gently and spoke no more. That smile seemed to say: "I wonder who the mad dog is." I still remember that smile. All through this decade or so, this image remains, still, peculiarly sharp in my mind.[49]

The condemned man's smile reverses conventional values and expectations: Death is beautiful, folly is wisdom, the executioner is the victim, and silence is articulate. If the military officers had been, as usual, enjoying the execution as comedy, the subject of this comedy is also, by the same logic, reversed. There is something inherently cowardly, laughable, and lamentable about the spectators, the executioners, and the guardians of dominant political, social, and cultural hierarchies—the urban readers.

Upon closer examination, we discover that Shen's landscape is filled with such reversals—subtle but persistent. Dogs devour their human masters, children tote around the heads of family elders. Legality and justice are displaced by luck and superstition. Love is consummated in death. However, these reversals are not lamentable to Shen. In fact, he derives great hilarity out of these seeming tragedies. Shen's comic sense makes us question conventional hierarchies. The bloodstained terrain revealed to us is a landscape inverted, with its bowels turned out. Dogs triumph over their human masters; children replace the heads of society. Shen's writings thus call out for a revisioning of our institutionalized perception. If one reads "contrapuntually," that is, reads with consideration of the intersecting social and political conditions that surround Shen's writings, one realizes the highly political nature of Shen's landscape.[50] And if one reads reflexively, one realizes that it is a place steeped in blood, but aestheticized and neutralized by the rhetoric of our own urban culture. Shen leads us through this process as we reexperience this deculturation, teaching us a lesson in our own moral implication as readers. If we are willing to give up our conventional technology of sight, we encounter a land boiling over in bloody violence that erupts through the patina of calm and civilized literary portrayals.

Conclusion

Shen's writing is often seen as belonging to the native-soil movement, but it contradicts many of the conventions of this genre. It is true that his writings are colored by a hue of utopianism. However, it is also clear that the sense of literary euphoria is very much part of the effect created by Shen through his use of the references and rhetoric of urban culture. This language is carefully selected to sanitize the bloodiness and horrific conditions of the countryside, so that urban readers can traverse the beautified land on a guided tour, marking our presence, making the land part of our cultural property, just as the actual Peach Spring is turned into the Peach Blossom Spring of traditional literary culture.

Shen's effort is far more cynical than sincere. It is only through the juxtaposition of the cultured and beautiful with the utter brutality of truth that we are made to reflect on the effects of our language, of how in the marking of our cultural presence, we erase the traces of others who are powerless. Shen's travels, then, are not merely an exploration of the human terrain, whether it is the rational or the uncanny, but a challenge to the very way history is written and the way human subjects are circumscribed within this writing. Shen's works thus do not so much reflect the reality of suffering in society, like a realist writer's works, nor investigate human nature, like a lyricist's, nor hope for a utopia, like a visionary's. Instead, Shen insists on reconnecting the personal with a greater political context, and through this, he interrogates how we as individual readers contribute to social suffering through our epistemic violence toward marginal groups. Shen's writings are about the violence of representation.

Conclusion

Almost every May Fourth writer, great or small, known or unknown, wrote an autobiography of some sort, either directly confessional, through personal letters or diary entries, or in more formal or conventional narratives. There was a growing sense of individual uniqueness and a feeling that personal experiences provided important testimonies of the generation's struggles against oppressive, traditional society. This surge in self-expressiveness, together with the highly subjective flavor of May Fourth literature, is often said to result from the "discovery" of, or at least a new interest in, interiority.

However inadequate such terms as *romanticism* and *expressionism* are to describe the literature of this period, they do elucidate the tension between the urgent need for individual expression and the driving sense of historical and social mission. Subjective writing, of which autobiography is a representative, is easily associated with all the tropes and topics of modernity, selfhood and individuality, romanticism and sentimentalism, even woman's self-expression and nationalism. Logically, it is in modern autobiographies that the workings of the literary experience of the May Fourth period are most visible. Logically, autobiography is the quintessential May Fourth text. This volume is a study of autobiography's function and place in this era of social change and nationalism.

To this day, the shape of modern Chinese autobiography and, arguably, most literary writing is largely defined by the aesthetic and ideological domination of realism—not merely in how it is written, but also in how it is read. Under the pragmatic and didactic realist imperative, the authorial nature and the surrounding historical conditions are regarded as totally transparent through the text. Literature is regarded as a mirror of history. As a result, scholarship on modern Chinese autobiography, especially, has been subordinate to sociohistorical interpretations of China. Reading and interpretation of this literature have become exercises in recovering and locating correspondences between the linguistic worlds created by writing and the phenomenal world of facts.

The problem with applying a "realist reading," especially in autobiographical studies, is that it reduces the worth of a literary piece to its capacity for verifiable historical facts. How valuable an autobiography is depends on how "true" it is. Autobiography in turn becomes a pragmatic resource for the construction of a psychobiography of an author or a psychohistory of the times. The immediate superficiality of this kind of reading is apparent. It assumes that there is a truth or subjectivity exterior to writing that is recoverable through interpretation.

Autobiography is a kind of writing that hyperbolizes the reader's need to believe in an authorial center and a historical truth external to the work. Autobiographies are composed of records of actual events. They evince the infallible truth of historical reality. However, at the same time, they are "unreliable" because of their obvious subjective trajectory. Hence, autobiography has been considered both realist and romantic, treading upon the very genre boundaries on which literary histories rely for their narratives. In this way, autobiography challenges conventional modes of reading.

Because of this pragmatic criterion of literature's political and social function since the May Fourth movement, autobiographical and other so-called subjective or romantic writings have been dismissed for being "too self-centered" and unworthy to be considered "good" or "serious" literature. Thus autobiographies, as well as an entire body of early May Fourth work, particularly women's writings that are mostly autobiographical, have been elided from serious scholarship. At best, autobiographical writings are treated as an embarrassing, though unavoidable, early step toward greater literary maturity. Although there has been a tremendous effort at recovery by scholars in the last several decades, the usual strategy has been to reinsert possible political and social readings in these works. This indirectly reaffirms all the assumptions and prejudices about this literature.

This kind of recovery work does not account for the blossoming of autobiographical writings during the May Fourth period. Given the great number of autobiographies, if the genre is taken seriously *as literature*, our understanding of modern Chinese literature will be reshaped.

The most important event in modern Chinese literature is without doubt the vernacular reform of 1917. It can even be said that this movement enabled the development of modern autobiography. The language reform is in essence a rejection of the traditional signifying institution. Classical Chinese stands for a worldview and a set of moral principles that the new generation abhorred. The issue here is not the essential dissimilarities between classical Chinese and modern Chinese. I do not make any presumptions about the nature of classical Chinese, nor do I examine its transformation in the process of literary modernization. My interest is in how the new twentieth-century view of language and its literary effects constructed by May Fourth writers comes into existence in dialectic with the old world.

Modern Chinese literature is not unique in displaying a difficult relationship between language and representation. However, the distinct historical rupture in the language system of the vernacular language reform provides a rare opportunity to locate the appearance, at a discrete point in time and space, of a general problem in language and meaning. The language reform, which is concomitant with the rise of modern literature, is more than a change in writing style. It is a fundamental change in how language works. Beyond the epiphenomenon of the movement itself, the new language affects the actual configuration of reality and the production of meaning. This new view of representation contributes to a revised relationship between writing and reality, words and meaning. The result of the language reform makes the typical pursuit of historical truth in the reading of autobiography irrelevant. Instead, the question becomes under what circumstances writing generates the *effect* of truthfulness. In other words, the focus in reading is no longer *what* truth is presented, but *how* the notion of truth is produced and *why*.

Applying this view to the reading of autobiography releases it from the burden of facticity. By extension the effects of subjectivity and interiority that we often associate with this genre are also explained at the level of linguistic construction. In other words, interiority is a new rhetorical effect, a literary trope caused by new methods of representation. It is the *baihua* (vernacular) movement of this period that makes the articulation of interiority possible, which, in turn, produces the *effect* of subjectivity and "psychological depth" in literature and contributes to the autobiographical phenomenon. This change is neither perspectival nor psychological, but political and ideological. It is a result of the transformation of one's relationship to this reality and the way that reality is represented in writing. In short, the new technique or tool of self-articulation—the new vernacular—results in changes in the relationship between the self and the phenomenal world.

Because of the revised notion of truth, verisimilitude can no longer be a sufficient criterion for judging and defining autobiography. Instead of representational likeness, names become an important denotation of identity. Modern autobiography is characterized by the simultaneous presence of three different subjectivities: the reader, the author, and the narrating subject (the homonym of the author). The author and narrating subject infer each other. This onomatology, or logic of the proper name, is an important topos in modern Chinese autobiography.

The identity of the autobiographical subject is not dependent on a representational or cognitive reality, but is based on nomination, a speech act. As such, the relationship between autobiographer and readers is contractual. In brief, autobiography is a nonrepresentational, nonmimetic form of writing in the sense that representational likeness, while an inevitable part of autobiography, is not an end in itself and cannot by itself give definition to autobiography.

Concomitant with the effect of interiority in modern autobiography is the development of a highly sentimental or confessional style of writing. Many authors, especially early writers of the May Fourth period, from Lu Yin to Bai Wei to Ba Jin, to poets such as Guo Moro and Wen Yiduo, share a propensity toward this style. Without doubt, Yu Dafu represents one of the most melodramatic and sentimental voices in modern Chinese literature. This sentimentality is related to a new version of truth in May Fourth, a version of truth that de-emphasizes the primacy of phenomenal likeness as its criterion. As a result, readers are treated to endless streams of intimate monologues.

This romantic strategy and many others employed by May Fourth writers bring out the problem of the relationship between the individual body and national polity, and by extension, the individual and the nation. In the overarching rhetoric of nationhood and the overwhelming concerns of national survival, the individual is in danger of being subsumed. In such a situation, Yu's expression of selfhood is understandably urgent, yet the ideological requirements of the time were to meld individual expression with the rhetoric of nationhood. Selfhood thereby becomes intricately intertwined with nationhood. Yu's body becomes the material site for the discourse of nationalism. His obsessive attention to his own body, which appears to him weak, flawed, and impotent, is more than an "adolescent" insecurity, as psychobiographical interpretations often conclude. The paradoxes between the individual will and social expectations, subjective impulses and civic responsibilities, personal weaknesses and societal imperatives, all materialize on the level of pathology. In Yu's ever more desperate struggle against his own body's desires and in his lamentation over its impotence, one sees the toll of modern Chinese nationalism upon the individual. Sentimentalism and romanticism are the rhetorical strategies of the new subject-citizen of modern China.

In this contest of individual expression and nationalism, women's voices were even more vulnerable. It is not surprising that before the twentieth century, only those who were recognizably the great men of society were granted an "autobiographical space." Women were usually denied this privilege. However, even in the early twentieth century, women were still subjected to all kinds of social coercion. Their writings often reveal their lack of freedom, dutifully reflecting social expectations. However, one can also find evidence of their ingenious resistance to capitulation. Within their works, writers from the outwardly rebellious Xie Bingying to the apparently acquiescent Xiao Hong manage to embed a version of their selves that defies conventional limitations of women's expression. These writers employed a double speech that, on the one hand, pacified their audience and, on the other, gave themselves fulfillment of expression. This duplicity is often represented in women's works by the gesture of mirroring, a moment when the two versions of a woman's reality become visible simultaneously—the mirroring subject presented for public approval in every moment of her life, and the obverse of this subject, one who designs her presentation to the world while laughing at her own artifice. Thinking about autobiographies in terms of mirrors elucidates the properties of this reflexive as well as defiant act of writing.

If Yu Dafu shows that interiority is an effect created by a specific literary strategy, Eileen Chang, with her various mirrors, exposes to us the constructedness and elusiveness of the subject in writing. For Chang, the subject position is a literary effect, just as for others it is a social one. Extending this sense of a fictive self, Shen Congwen demonstrates the multiplicity of our social identities. This multiplicity makes us simultaneously victims and oppressors within an unjust society. However involuntarily or unconsciously, we evolve from situation to situation, from relationship to relationship. Shen shows that it is only when we become aware of all our different selves that we are able to empathize with the oppressed and challenge the unjust, because we are both. Autobiographical writing and reading are thus activities of moral reflection.

Autobiography occupies an awkward place between history and fiction. It is too subjective, idiosyncratic, or unreliable to be a historical or social document, yet it is undeniably an important indicator of the times. Because of this ambiguity, autobiography is often an overlooked genre, ignored by historians and literary critics alike. However, as I have argued, the historical value of autobiography goes beyond its factual contents. Its literary value goes beyond form and style, meaning and plot. Autobiographical writing is ultimately political because it reflects an awareness of the self as a historical, political, and social being. It reveals one's strategy of negotiation with one's society, asserting individuality and challenging the tyrannies that exist in all societies. Different autobiographies are different social and political stances. Although the scope of this study is necessarily limited, the examples selected permit what I believe to be valid conclusions about autobiographies of the May Fourth period. Autobiography is not about who speaks or what is spoken, but how an individual speaks up in society and against what strictures he or she speaks. In this sense, the writing of autobiography is a political act.

Notes

Introduction

1. Stephen Shapiro, "The Dark Continent of Literature: Autobiography," *Comparative Literary Studies* 5 (1968): 421–54.
2. Georg Lukács, *Il dramma moderno*, translation quoted from Franco Moretti, *Signs Taken for Wonders* (New York: Verso, 1997), 10.
3. Ibid., 11.
4. Ibid., 12.
5. Frederic Jameson, *Nationalism, Colonialism, and Literature: Modernism and Imperialism*, Field Day Pamphlet, no. 14 (Derry: Field Day Theatre Co., 1988), 6. It is with a similar understanding of the specificity of the historical that James Chandler locates a particular year of significance in his study of English romanticism in *England in 1819* (Chicago: University of Chicago Press, 1998).
6. David Nivison, "Aspects of Traditional Chinese Biography," *Journal of Asian Studies (JAS)* 21, no. 4 (1962): 457–64.
7. Mao Dun, "Zhuanji wenxue" (Literature of biographies), in *Mao Dun chuanji* (Complete works of Mao Dun), vol. 19 (Beijing: Renmin wenxue, 1991), 538–39.
8. Hu Shi, preface to *Sishi zixu* (Self-narration at forty) (Shanghai: Dongya Tushu, 1939), 1.
9. According to Nivison, there are three main kinds of biographies: historical biography, which is part of the Standard Histories; social biographies, usually epitaphs; and annals. Nivison points out that the earlier historical biographies have a highly dramatic flavor, to the point where they read like fiction. Later historical biographies give essential information in a highly formal way, delineating the subject's family background, his official career in outline, quotations from his writings and anecdotes, which are "often stereotyped and quite false, intended to indicate his character. This portrait of character conceives of the man as falling into a type" ("Traditional Chinese Biography," 458).
10. Pei-yi Wu points out that Sima Qian is the first to use the term *zhuan* to denote the biographies in his *Shiji* (Records of the historian). As *Shiji* is the

first of the twenty-five Histories, Sima Qian's work becomes the paradigm. Pei-yi Wu, *The Confucian's Progress: Autobiographical Writings in Traditional China* (Princeton: Princeton University Press, 1990).

11. Stephen Durrant, "Self as the Intersection of Traditions: The Autobiographical Writings of Ssu-ma Ch'ien," *Journal of the American Oriental Society* 106, no. 1 (1986): 33.

12. Ibid., 34.

13. Nivison defines this type of writing as the biographies found in the twenty-five Standard Histories as well as that commonly practiced in local histories ("Traditional Chinese Biography," 457).

14. James Olney dissects autobiography into three parts: aute (self), bio (life events), and graphia (writing). He explains that different writers emphasize different aspects of these moments. James Olney, *Autobiography: Essay Theoretical and Critical* (Princeton: Princeton University Press, 1988), 3–28. Michel de Certeau refers to traditional biography/historiography based around a moral lesson as "praxeology" and stresses its performative and pedagogical function. Michel de Certeau, *The Writing of History* (New York: Columbia University Press, 1988), 7.

15. Nivison, "Traditional Chinese Biography," 458.

16. Durrant, "Self as Intersection," 36.

17. Hu Shi, preface to *Zhang shizhai xiansheng nianpuxu* (The chronological biography of Master Zhang Shizhai), in *Hu Shi Wencun* (Collected works of Hu Shi), vol. 93 (Shanghai: Minguo Congshu, 1953), 3.

18. Hu Shi, *Self-Narration at Forty*, 5.

19. See Wu, *The Confucian's Progress,* and Stephen Owen, "Singularity and Possession," in *The End of the Chinese "Middle Ages": Essays in Mid-Tang Literary Culture* (Stanford: Stanford University Press, 1996), 16–17.

20. Wu, *The Confucian's Progress,* 15.

21. Quoted from Wu, *The Confucian's Progress,* 15. Original text in Tao Qian, "Wuliu xiansheng zhuan," in *Weijin nanbeichao zhujia sanwenxuan* (Selected prose of various writers of the six dynasties), ed. Wei Fengjuan (Hong Kong: Sanlian, 1988), 226.

22. See Wendy Larson, *Literary Authority and the Modern Chinese Writer* (Durham: Duke University Press, 1993). Tao Qian, for example, is a paradigm of Larson's "circumstantial autobiography."

23. Ibid.

24. Chen Pingyuan, *Zhongguo xiaoshuo xushi moshi de zhuanbian* (Changes in the modes of Chinese fiction) (Taipei: Taida wenhua, 1990), 204–5.

25. See Shih Shu-mei's recent book, *The Lure of the Modern: Writing Modernism in Semicolonial China, 1917–1937* (Berkeley and Los Angeles: University of California Press, 2001).

26. Yu Dafu, *Riji jiuzhong* (The nine diaries), in *Yu Dafu rijiji* (Collected diaries of Yu Dafu) (Xianxi: Renmin Chubanshe, 1984), 261.

27. Stephen Owen ("Singularity and Procession") observes a development in mid-Tang poetics of an emphasis on "singularity" in poetic expression. Owen describes this assertion of individuality in terms of individual style or voice that is reproducible and imitable. He also relates this awareness of the "singularity" of the self to the rise of the notion of possession, both actual (such as real property) and literary. This is different from the emphasis on interior uniqueness that Yu claims in modern literature.

28. This kind of interpretation of Creation Society literature is particularly prevalent among scholarship from the PRC, with a Marxist bent. This is particularly the case toward woman writers whose subject matters are often more personal. I will elaborate on this in chapter 1.

29. See Jeffrey Kinkley, *The Odyssey of Shen Congwen* (Stanford: Stanford University Press, 1987) in the former category; and Leo Ou-fan Lee, "The Solitary Traveler: Images of Self in Modern Chinese Literature," in *Expressions of Self in Chinese Literature*, ed. Robert E. Hegel and Richard C. Hessney (New York: Columbia University Press, 1985), 282–307, and Larson, *Literary Authority*, in the latter.

30. Philippe Lejeune, "The Autobiographical Contract," in *French Literary Theory Today*, ed. Tzvetan Todorov (Cambridge: Cambridge University Press, 1982), 193–222.

31. See Paul de Man's discussion of this genre in "Autobiography as De-Facement," *Modern Language Notes* 94 (1979): 919–30.

32. Lejeune, "The Autobiographical Contract," 203.

33. In Rey Chow's study of Chinese cinema, she makes a similar observation that the beginning of self-awareness occurs at the ultimate specular moment when Lu Xun confronts the image of the public execution of a Chinese spy in Japan. Chow, *Primitive Passion* (New York: Columbia University Press, 1995), especially 4–23.

34. De Man, "Autobiography as De-Facement," 922.

35. Judith Butler, *The Psychic Life of Power: Theories in Subjection* (Stanford: Stanford University Press, 1997), 13.

36. Ibid., 11.

37. See, for example, Leo Ou-fan Lee, *The Romantic Generation in the May Fourth Period* (Cambridge: Harvard University Press, 1973); Zhao Xiaqiu and Zheng Qingrui, *Zhongguo xiandai xiaoshuo shi* (History of modern Chinese fiction) (Beijing: Zhongguo renmin, 1984).

38. James Fujii makes a similar observation about influence studies in modern Japanese literature in *Complicit Fictions: The Subject in the Modern Japanese Prose Narrative* (Berkeley and Los Angeles: University of California Press, 1993), 5.

39. See Mary Layoun, *Travels of a Genre: The Modern Novel and Ideology* (Princeton: Princeton University Press, 1990); Alan Wolfe, *Suicidal Narrative*

in Modern Japan: The Case of Dasai Osamu (Princeton: Princeton University Press, 1990).

40. Zheng Boqi, general introduction to *Zhongguo xin wenxue daxi* (Great compendium of new Chinese literature), ed. Zhao Jiabi, vol. 5. (Hong Kong: Xianggang wenxue yanjiushe, 1962), 18.

41. See, for example, the discussions in Firdous Azim's *The Colonial Rise of the Novel* (New York: Routledge, 1993).

42. I direct the readers' attention to works by Layoun, *Travels of a Genre*, and Fujii, *Complicit Fictions*. See also Lydia Liu, *Translingual Practice: Literature, National Culture, and Translated Modernity: China, 1900–1937* (Stanford: Stanford University Press, 1995). In their various methodologies, Layoun, Fujii, and Liu bring to focus the ideological and chrono-political specificity that dictate the "travels of a genre" or a literary form.

43. Zheng Boqi, 18.

44. Liu, *Translingual Practice*.

45. See "The Discourse of Individualism" in Liu, *Translingual Practice*, 77–102. See also Lydia Liu, "Translingual Practice: The Discourse of Individualism between China and the West," in *Narrative of Agency: Self-Making in China, India, and Japan*, ed. Wimal Dissanayake (Minneapolis: University of Minnesota Press, 1996), 1–34.

46. This is a point emphasized in Edward Said's *Culture and Imperialism* (New York: Vintage, 1994).

47. See, for example, Theodore Huters, ed., *Reading the Modern Chinese Short Story* (New York: Eastgate Book, 1990), 5–6.

48. For example, Lydia Liu's "The Female Body and Nationalist Discourse: The *Field of Life and Death* Revisited," in *Scattered Hegemonies: Postmodernity and Transnational Feminist Practices*, ed. Inderpal Grewal and Caren Kaplan (Minnesota: University of Minnesota Press, 1997), 37–62. Also see Wendy Larson's "The End of *Funu wenxue:* Women's Literature from 1925–1935," in *Gender Politics in Modern China: Writing and Feminism*, ed. Tani Barlow (Durham: Duke University Press, 1993), 58–73. This particular issue will be discussed in chapter 2.

Chapter One

1. Qiao Yigang argues against identifying Chen's works as "feminine writings," a generally vitiated category, because they are often considered limited to domestic and personal topics. However, in doing so, she actually confirms the existing prejudice. See Qiao Yigang, "Chen Hengzhe zhi qi Chuangzuo—lun Zhongguo xiandai wentan shang de yi wei nu Zuojia" (Chen Hengzhe and her writings—on the first women writer in the modern Chinese literary coterie), *Zhongguo xiandai, dangdai wenxue yanjiu* 3 (1993): 197.

2. As with *realism* in the introduction, I am using this term in reference to the specific sense in the late Qing literary discussions. I will elaborate on this in a later section.

3. Mao Dun (1896–1981), for example, criticizes Lu Yin's writings as being arrested on the level of the personal. See "Lu Yin lun" (On Lu Yin) (1934), in *Zhongguo xiandai Zuojia xuan: Lu Yin* (Hong Kong: Sanlian shudian, 1983), 235–42. Even today, many critics still have reservations about the achievements of woman writers. Qiao Yigang's discussion mentioned above is an example. Rey Chow has argued valiantly against such discrimination. She points out that "virtuous transaction" is a form of negotiation between women and their society and this negotiation often colors their work. However, in her argument, women are still seen as passively receiving the influence of dominant society or, at the most, using their ingenuity to clandestinely deflect some of the weight of the oppression. Chow, "Virtuous Transactions: A Reading of Three Short Stories by Ling Shuhua," in Barlow, *Gender Politics*, 90–105. My discussion here asserts that the identifying characteristic of women's writing is a willful strategy that is fully feminine.

4. There has been a plethora of "influence study" in regards to modern Chinese literature, beginning with Bonnie McDougall, *The Introduction of Western Literary Theories into Modern China, 1919–1925* (Tokyo: The Centre for East Asian Culture Studies, 1971). Recently, there is Jingyuan Zhang's *Psychoanalysis in China: Literary Transformations, 1919–1949*, Cornell East Asia Series (Ithaca: Cornell University Press, 1992). Leo Ou-fan Lee also stresses the influence of European thinkers such as Bergson and Darwin on the development of modern Chinese thoughts. In contrast to Zhang, he argues against the actual influence of Freud. See Leo Ou-fan Lee, "In Search of Modernity: Some Reflections on a New Mode of Consciousness in Twentieth-Century Chinese History and Literature," in *Ideas across Cultures: Essays on Chinese Thought in Honor of Benjamin I. Schwartz*, ed. Paul A. Cohen and Merle Goldman (Cambridge: Harvard University Press, 1990), 109–35.

On the front of mainland Chinese scholarship, the array of "influence study" is even more impressive. Just to name a couple: Yan Min, "Shishu wusi wentan jieshuo Nicai xueshuo de yuanyi" (An attempt to analyze the acceptance of Nietzsche's thoughts by the May Fourth literary coterie), *Zhongguo xiandai, dangdai wenxue yanjiu* 7 (1991): 7–10; Tang Zhengxu, *Ershi shiji zhongguo wenxue yu xifang xiandai zhuyi sichao* (The intellectual trend in twentieth-century Chinese literature and Western modernism) (Hunan: Sichuan renmin chubanshe, 1992).

5. For example, Marston Anderson explores the importance of traditional literary consciousness, acknowledged or not, in modern writers in *The Limits of Realism: Chinese Fiction in the Revolutionary Period* (Berkeley and Los Angeles: University of California Press, 1990), 76–92.

6. Although there are numerous different discussions about fiction during

the late Qing, realism dominates, and Liang Qichao's (1873–1929) theorization was most relevant to fiction writing of the period. See Zhu Defa, *Ershi shiji Zhongguo wenxue liupai lungang* (A general outline of literary schools in twentieth-century Chinese literature) (Shandong: Shandong jiaoyu, 1992). For a categorization and discussion of the kinds of late Qing fiction, see Chen Pingyuan, "Lun xin xiaoshuo leixing lilun" (On the theory of the new fiction genres), *Zhongguo xiandai wenxue piping congkan* 2 (1991): 114–25.

7. Translated in Amy D. Dooling and Kristina M. Torgeson, *Writing Women in Modern China: An Anthology of Women's Literature from the Early Twentieth Century* (New York: Columbia University Press, 1998), 87–95.

8. Zhao and Zheng, *Modern Chinese Fiction*, 174–75; Kang Yongqiu, "Xinwenxue de diyiwei nuzuojia, Chen Hengzhe" (The first female writer of the new literature: Chen Hengzhe), *Zhongguo xiandai, dangdai wenxue yanjiu* 6 (1990): 77–82; Chen Hengzhe, *Xiao yudian* (A little raindrop) (Xinyue shudian, 1928).

9. Liang Qichao, "Xiaoshuo yu qunzhi zhi guanxi" (The relationship between fiction and the governing of the masses), in *Zhongguo wenxue pipingshi* (History of Chinese literary criticism), ed. Wang Yunxi and Gu Yisheng, vol. 3 (Shanghai: Shanghai Guji, 1991), 608–9.

10. I use the term *realism* here not to indicate the particular nineteenth-century European literary school, but to describe a general principle of "re-presenting the real" in literary writing.

11. Admittedly, late Qing realism differs significantly from May Fourth realism. The former relies on the strategy of eyewitness reportage. The latter often reconstructs a scene in which the readers can be the eyewitnesses themselves. However, the dependence on perspective is equally important for both kinds of writing.

12. See Firdous Azim, "The Subject/s of the Novel," in *The Colonial Rise of the Novel* (New York: Routledge, 1993), 10–33. Also see Mary Louise Pratt, *Imperial Eyes: Travel Writing and Transculturation* (New York: Routledge, 1992).

13. See, for example, Nancy Miller, *Subject to Change: Reading Feminist Writing* (New York: Columbia University Press, 1988); and Teresa De Lauretis, *Technologies of Gender: Essays on Theory, Film, and Fiction* (Bloomington: Indiana University Press, 1987).

14. A point that Azim, *Colonial Rise*, makes in her discussion of the realist novel is its imperialistic quality, not simply in its thematic matters but in its being and its rise. She explains that the construction of realism's subject and object positions contribute to the differentiation between self and "other." Further, she argues that the subject position is constructed through the *obliteration* of the "other."

15. Ideology is used loosely in this essay to indicate notions of standard and normalcy in behavior as upheld by dominant groups in society. As the domi-

nant group who establishes such maxims is often associated with the traditionally more powerful male gender, ideology here is used in close identification with the patriarchy.

As a form of "normalizing" and controlling, the power of ideology is insidious. It is not often articulable as a cohesive/reified antagonist, but as deleterious and all invasive. Everyday exchanges become forms of ideological regulation. This leads Roland Barthes to conclude, in *S/Z*, trans. Richard Miller (New York: Noonday Press, 1990), that there is no language site beyond (bourgeois) ideology. Hence Carolyn Heilbrun asserts on different occasions the impossibility of a real woman's text as long as women have to articulate themselves with the tool of the patriarchy. They will only find themselves mouthing the patriarchal rhetoric—inadvertently, albeit unwillingly. See *Writing a Woman's Life* (New York: Ballantine, 1989).

16. Jonathan Crary, *Techniques of the Observer: On Vision and Modernity in the Nineteenth Century* (Cambridge: MIT Press, 1996), 12.

17. Anderson, *The Limits of Realism*, 76–92.

18. In Guo Shaoyu, ed., *Zhongguo lidai wenlunxuan* (Selections of essays on Chinese literature through the ages), vol. 4 (Shanghai: Shanghai guji, 1980), 258.

19. Anderson, *The Limits of Realism*, 76–92.

20. *Wenxue yundongshiliao xuan* (Selections from the documents of the literary movement), vol. 1 (Shanghai: Shanghai jiaoyu, 1982), 69.

21. Ibid., 123.

22. One is perhaps immediately reminded of the "Great Preface" (Shi daxu) of the *Book of Songs* (Shijing). As far as the origin of emotions is concerned, very little challenge is posed to traditional poetics. However, just as the "Great Preface" points to the difficulty of recording ephemeral individual emotions, Fu also targets the issue of putting emotions down in writing. As Marston Anderson has observed concerning writers such as Ye Shaojun (1894–1988) and Zheng Zhenduo (1898–1958) who borrowed the Neo-Confucian notion of "the investigation of things" *(gewu)* as a basis for their literary theory without direct attribution, many theorists of the May Fourth generation drew on an older literary heritage. Rather than saying that their ideas were derivative, it is more pertinent to regard them as inadvertent and unwilling students.

23. *Wenxue yundongshiliao xuan* (Selections from the documents of the literary movement), 1:118.

24. Chen, *A Little Raindrop*, 7–9.

25. See Chen, "New Fiction Genres."

26. Leo Ou-fan Lee described these early May Fourth writers as the "romantic generation" in *The Romantic Generation in the May Fourth Period*.

27. Chen, *A Little Raindrop*, 93–94.

28. Lu Yin, Lu Jingqing, and Shi Pingmei, all first-generation May Fourth

women writers, are a well-known literary threesome. Their works are often letters to or imaginary dialogues with each other.

29. Bai Wei, "The Reason I Joined the Literary Circle" (Wo toudao wenxuequan li de chuqong), in *The Best Short Pieces from Chinese Women Writers*, ed. You Lian (Fujian: Haixia, 1994).

30. For more illustrations of May Fourth women's writings, see Dooling and Torgeson's anthology *Writing Women;* and Janet Ng and Janice Wickeri, *May Fourth Women Writers: Memoirs* (Hong Kong: Renditions Paperback, 1996).

31. Chen, "New Fiction Genres."

32. This piece is collected in Shen Congwen, *Xiangxing sanji* (Random notes on travels to west Hunan) (Beijing: Kaiming Chubanshe, 1992).

33. See David Der-Wei Wang, "Shen Congwen and Native Soil Literature," in *Fictional Realism in Twentieth-Century China: Mao Dun, Lao She, Shen Congwen* (New York: Columbia University Press, 1992), 201–45.

34. All these stories are collected in *A Little Raindrop*.

35. The significance of this freeing of women from traditional roles is particularly obvious when one compares Chen's story to Ling Shuhua (1904–1990). Ling excels in depicting the misery, suffocation, and desperation of women trapped in traditional roles. In her autobiographical *Ancient Melodies* (1952), for example, all the women in the household are defined strictly by their household positions. They are only known to Ling and to her readers as her mothers: First mother, third mother, forth mother, etc. These women, confined in a family compound, spent their lives competing with each other for the patriarch's affection. Another writer, Eileen Chang (1921–1995), is also well known for her depiction of the intolerable lives of women confined in traditional social roles. See Janet Ng, "Writing in Her Father's House: The Feminine Autobiographical Strategies of Ling Shuhua," *Prose Studies* 16 (1993): 232–50.

Chapter Two

1. Liu, "Female Body."

2. According to Zhou Zuoren, "The discovery of children only began to germinate as late as the Nineteenth Century.... In China, discussion of this issue has to start from the beginning. There has never been a solution to the problem of individuality, let alone women and children." See Zhou Zuoren, "Rende wenxue" (On human literature), in *Documents of the Literary Movement*, 101.

3. For example, see Lu Yin's "Jinhou funu de chulu" (The future of women), in *Xiandai zuojia xuanji: Lu Yin* (The modern writers series: Lu Yin) (Hong Kong: Joint Publishing, 1983), 95–120. Also see Yuan Changying's

"Lun nuzi liuxue debiyao" (On the necessity of women's studying abroad), in Yuan Changying, *Yuan Changying sanwenji* (The essays of Yuan Changying) (Tianjin: Baihua wenyi, 1991), 13–20.

4. See *New Youth* 1 (1918).

5. Chow, "Virtuous Transactions."

6. Lydia Liu, "Invention and Intervention: The Female Tradition in Modern Chinese Literature," in Barlow, *Gender Politics*, 33–57.

7. Liu, "The Female Body and Nationalist Discourse."

8. Wendy Larson, *Women and Writing in Modern China* (Stanford: Stanford University Press, 1998). See also "The End of *Funu wenxue:* Women's Literature from 1925 to 1935," in Barlow, *Gender Politics*.

9. Tani Barlow, *I Myself a Woman: Selected Writings of Ding Ling* (Boston: Beacon Press, 1989), 41.

10. Miller, *Subject to Change*, 167.

11. Ibid., 164.

12. *Zhang Ailing xiaoshuoji* (The short stories of Eileen Chang) (Taipei: Huangguan, 1984), 263.

13. Chang, *Short Stories*, 462.

14. Quoted in De Lauretis, *Technologies of Gender*, 38.

15. Susan Sontag comments, "Women are taught to see their bodies in *parts*, and to evaluate each part separately. Breasts, feet, hips, waistline, neck, eyes, nose, complexion, hair and so on—each in turn is submitted to an anxious, fretful, often despairing scrutiny. Even if some pass muster, some will always be found wanting. Nothing less than perfect will do. In men, good looks is a whole, something taken in at a glance." "In Plato's Cave," in *On Photography* (New York: Farrar, Straus and Giroux, 1985), 36.

16. According to Brian Finney, "While the traditional male artist uses the mirror for self-portraiture, women find themselves painting their faces in the looking-glass to conform to a male-formulated image of femininity which deprives them of their own sense of Identity." "Sexual Identity in Modern British Autobiography," *Prose Studies* 8, no. 2 (1985): 33.

17. Virginia Woolf, *A Room of One's Own* (New York: Harcourt, Brace and World, 1957), 35.

18. Ling Shuhua. *Ancient Melodies* (London: Hogarth Press, 1953). See my discussion in "Her Father's House."

19. Ling, *Ancient Melodies*, 53.

20. See Ng, "Her Father's House."

21. Jenni Joy Labelle, *Herself Beheld: The Literature of the Looking Glass* (Ithaca: Cornell University Press, 1988), 40.

22. Finney, "Sexual Identity," 33.

23. John Berger, *Ways of Seeing* (New York: Grove Press, 1961), 43.

24. De Lauretis, *Technologies of Gender*, 5.

25. Ibid., 15.

26. Chow, *Woman and the Chinese Modernity: The Politics of Reading between West and East* (Minneapolis: Minnesota University Press, 1991), 3–33.

27. De Lauretis, *Technologies of Gender,* 18.

28. Chow, "Virtuous Transactions."

29. Chang, *Short Stories,* 139.

30. Chang, "Intimate Words," trans. Janet Ng, *Renditions: A Chinese-English Translation Magazine* 45 (1996): 18.

31. Lu Xun, "Mianpu yice" (Some conjectures about theatrical masks), in *Lu Xun zawen chuanji* (Complete collection of the miscellaneous essays of Lu Xun) (Sichuan: Henan renmin, 1994), 744.

32. Qian Xuantong, "Letter to *Chen Duxiu* (1917)," in *Documents of the Literary Movement,* 31.

33. Chen Du Xiu, "Letter to Qian Xuantong (1917)," in *Documents of the Literary Movement,* 22–23.

34. Xie Bingying, *Nübing zizhuan* (Autobiography of a woman soldier) (Beijing: Zhongguo huaqiao, 1994), 156.

35. Ibid., 158.

36. Ibid., 13.

37. Chang, *Short Stories,* 211–12; emphasis added.

38. Chang, "Intimate Words," 33.

39. Eileen Chang, *Liuyan* (Flow of words) (Taibei: Huangguan, 1984), 14–15.

40. See Yang Yi, *Qinuzi Zhang Ailing* (The extraordinary woman Eileen Chang) (Hong Kong: Binma, 1984), 16.

41. The Taiwan publisher Huangguan, which specializes in popular "female" romances, has republished all her works.

42. She is also particularly tainted because of her liaison with Hu Lancheng, an official of the puppet government in Japanese-occupied China between 1944 and 1947.

43. Chang, "A Child's Words," in *Flow of Words,* 8.

44. Ibid., 7.

45. See Nivison, "Traditional Chinese Biography," 458.

46. Chang, "A Child's Words," 9.

47. See Su Qing, *Jiehun shinian* (Ten years of marriage) (Shanghai: Shanghai shudian, 1989).

48. Chang, "A Child's Words," 9.

49. Chang, *Flow of Words,* 131.

50. I am referring to Lu Xun's "A Madman's Diary," in which he creates the famous metaphor of cannibalism in describing the ruthless social usurpation of individual desire.

51. Liu, "Female Body."

52. Huters, *Modern Chinese Short Story,* 3–21.

53. See for example, Rey Chow's theory of "Virtuous Transactions" in her reading of Ling Shuhua.

54. Ji Ji, "Woyu Zhang Ailing de laji" (Eileen Chang's rubbish and me), *Jiushi niandai* (The Nineties), 311 (December 1995), 90–95.

55. Shui Jing, *Zhang Ailing de Xiaoshuo yishu* (The art of Eileen Chang's fiction) (Taibei: Dadi chubanshe, 1973).

Chapter Three

1. Yu Dafu, "Riji wenxue" (Diary literature), in *Yu Dafu Wenji* (Essays of Yu Dafu), vol. 7 (Hong Kong: Sanlian shudian, 1982), 261.

2. Much scholarship on the rise of individualism, on Yu's specifically, and the Creation Society's literary romanticism in general, falls under the category of influence studies. Foreign literary influences on the May Fourth society are easy to detect and are doubtless an important aspect of the literary development of this period. This kind of "impact" approach accounts for the wide variety of literary styles available for use for modern Chinese writers, but does little to explain the reason for the acceptance of particular forms and the career of these forms once adopted. By examining this issue of individualism from a different angle, my discussion completes what is left unanswered in most influence studies by investigating a new form in connection to its usage by a particular writer for a specific agenda. Readers interested in the issues of influence studies and its problematics should consult the introduction to this volume.

3. Michael Egan, "Yu Dafu and the Transition to Modern Chinese Literature," in *Modern Chinese Literature in the May Fourth Era*, ed. Merle Goldman (Cambridge: Harvard University Press, 1977), 312.

4. C. T. Hsia, for example, charges that Yu's writing reflects an adolescent angst. *A History of Modern Chinese Fiction, 1917–1949* (New Haven: Yale University Press, 1961).

5. Egan, "Yu Dafu."

6. Kirk Denton, "The Distant Shore: Nationalism in Yu Dafu's 'Sinking,'" *Chinese Literature, Essays, and Articles* 14 (1992): 107–25. Although I am in agreement with Denton's emphasis on the nationalistic sentiment in Yu's writing, his tracing of an immediate lineage between May Fourth thought with Song and Ming neo-Confucian ideas of "holism" as a counterbalance to May Fourth iconoclasm is problematic. It assumes a single lineage in modern thought that is spurious. This notion of a single tradition of Confucian thought that travels down to modern times as a unity is an assumption now rigorously challenged by Lionel Jensen, in *Manufacturing Confucianism: Chinese Traditions and Universal Civilization* (Durham: Duke University Press, 1997).

7. According to Roland Barthes: "Text means Tissue; but whereas hith-

erto we have always seen this tissue as a product, a ready-made veil behind which lies, more or less hidden, meaning (truth), we are now emphasizing, in the tissue, the generative idea that this text is made, is worked out in a perpetual interweaving; lost in this tissue—this textum—the subject unmakes himself, like a spider dissolving in the constructive secretions of his web. Were we fond of neologisms, we might define the theory of the text as an *hyphology* (*hyphos* is the tissue and the spider's web)." Roland Barthes, *The Pleasure of the Text*, trans. Richard Miller (New York: Noonday Press, 1990), 64.

  8. Lejeune, "The Autobiographical Contract," thus insists that one needs to be already a public personality in order to write an autobiography. See chapter 1 for a discussion of Lejeune's concept of the autobiographical contract.

  9. Zhao and Zheng, *Modern Chinese Fiction*, 463–75.

  10. Fujii, *Complicit Fictions*, 116.

  11. C. T. Hsia and Leo Ou-fan Lee, in their respective studies, honored Yu with this designation. See Hsia, *History of Modern Chinese Fiction;* Lee, *The Romantic Generation of Modern Chinese Writers* (Cambridge: Harvard University Press, 1973).

  12. Zhou Zuoren, "Rende wenxue" (On human literature), in *Documents of the Literary Movement*, 16.

  13. Yu Dafu, "Huanxiangji" (Returning home), in *Yu Dafu zuopin xuan* (Selected works of Yu Dafu) (Hong Kong: Sanbianshe, 1989), 20.

  14. Peter Brooks, *The Melodramatic Imagination: Balzac, Henry James, Melodrama, and the Mode of Excess* (New Haven: Yale University Press, 1995).

  15. Ibid., xii.

  16. Ibid., 72.

  17. For this reason, Brooks argues that melodrama is a particularly modern form. Both melodrama and psychoanalysis arose during the same period. And though the fundamental impulses of each are markedly different, melodrama's use of gesture is similar to Freud's dream rhetoric; both are an outward expression of what is unexpressed on the level of speech or consciousness. However, Brooks is careful to point out that despite the seeming similarity to psychoanalysis, melodrama is strictly about surfaces. It is therefore a mistake to look for neurosis as an explanation for the protagonist's actions in a melodramatic text. Brooks argues that despite the similarity to Freud's dream rhetoric in "gapping" the conscious and unconscious, the surface actuality and the unspeakable, it is a mistake to treat the occult in melodramatic texts as psychological depth. The second level of reality in melodrama is not about unconscious desires. The desire is totally conscious. It is just inexpressible (ibid., 18).

  18. Ibid., 35.

  19. Yu, *Selected Works*, 19–20.

  20. Yu, *The Nine Diaries*, 109; the last sentence is in English in the original.

  21. Yu, *Selected Works*, 96.

  22. Zheng Boqi, general introduction to *Zhongguo xin wenxue daxi* (The

great compendium of new Chinese literature), ed. Zhao Jiabi, vol. 5 (Hong Kong: Xianggang wenxue yanjiushe, 1962), 214.

23. Guo Moro, "Wode tongnian" (My childhood), in *Guo Moro xuanji* (Selected works of Guo Moro), vol. 1 (Chengdu: Sichuan Renmin, 1979), 1.

24. Yu Dafu, "Guanyu xiaoshuo de hua" (About fiction), in *Yu Dafu Chuanji* (The complete works of Yu Dafu), vol. 3 (Shanghai: Beixin shuju, 1930), 19.

25. Yu Dafu, "Zaitan riji" (More about diaries), in *Essays of Yu Dafu*, 7:266.

26. Yu, *The Nine Diaries*, 179–80.

27. Yu, "Diary as Literature," 262.

28. James Fujii calls this a "dialogic text" in his discussion of Tokuda Shusei in *Complicit Fictions: The Subject in the Modern Japanese Prose Narrative* (Berkeley: University of California Press, 1993), 189–90.

29. Zhao and Zheng, *Modern Chinese Fiction*, 489.

30. Shen Congwen, "Lun zhongguo chuangzuo xiaoshuo" (On Chinese creative fiction), in *Shen Congwen wenji* (Writings of Shen Congwen) (Hong Kong: Sanlian shudian, 1983), 1:248.

31. Yu Dafu, *Dafu Zizhuan* (Autobiography of Yu Dafu), in *Collected Diaries*, 335–58.

32. Though not directly related to the issue at hand, the implicit connotation of a regicide and patricide in Yu's telling of the death of the emperor and his father is worth noting. Yu severs all filial ties by these metaphorical "murders." His disconnectedness to any filiation and his self-exile are textualizations of the condition of the alienated modern individual that I discussed earlier.

33. Yu, *The Nine Diaries*, 358.

34. Ibid., 417.

35. Ibid., 366.

36. Ibid., 390.

37. Liu, "Female Body," 43–44.

38. Yu, *The Nine Diaries*, 413.

39. Denton, "The Distant Shore," 116.

40. Ibid., 117.

41. Ibid., 115.

42. Yu, *The Nine Diaries*, 413–14.

Chapter Four

1. Lejeune, "The Autobiographical Contract," 211.

2. Ibid., 203.

3. I draw from Gunn's three moments of autobiography in my discussion of the autobiographical impulse: pretextual level; autobiographical perspec-

tive—self-situation in the world; and autobiographical responses (readers' as well as the autobiographer's). These three steps embody the roles of the originating subject, the textual subject and the paradigmatic reader. Janet Varner Gunn, *Autobiography: Toward a Poetics of Experience* (Philadelphia: University of Pennsylvania Press, 1982).

4. Lejeune, "The Autobiographical Contract," 209.

5. Eileen Chang, "Biye zhengmingfu" (One should also rectify one's name), in *Flow of Words*, 35–41.

6. Ibid., 35.

7. Ibid.

8. It is a well-known fact that the second character of Xiao Hong's name, when paired with the second character of her lover's name, Xiao Jun, forms the compound *Hong Jun* (Red Army), an obvious indication of political sympathy.

9. For the facts of Xiao Hong's life, see Howard Goldblatt and Ellen Yeung, trans., *The Field of Life and Death* and *Tales of Hulan River* (Bloomington: Indiana University Press, 1979). Also see Xiao Hong, "Yongjiu de tongjing he zhuiqiu" (Eternal dreams and pursuits), in *Zhongguo nu zuojia sanwen xuancui* (Selected essays of Chinese women writers), ed. You Kang (Fujian: Haixia wenyi, 1994), 281–382.

10. Hu Shi, *Self-Narration at Forty*, 1.

11. Hu Shi mentions in his autobiography his indebtedness to Liang Qichao for his intellectual growth. (See chapter 3, "In Shanghai.") Hu Shi's writing of *Sishi zishu* might also have been directly inspired by Liang's *Sanshi zishu* (Autobiography at thirty), in *Lidai zixushuan* (Self-narrative through the ages), ed. Guo Dongfang (Shanghai: Shanghai shangwu yinshuguan, 1937), 91–101.

Liang discusses five types of "specialized history" *(zhuan shi)*, of which biography is one. Among the various kinds of biographies, Liang singles out "special biographic narrative" *(zhuan zhuan)* as the most important. Liang emphasizes the equal attention paid on both the biographical subject and his historical milieu, as opposed to the traditional biographical narratives of dynastic history *(lie zhuan)*, which delineate only the events directly relevant to the subject's life. Liang Qichao, *Lishi yanjiu fa bupian* (Supplement to the methods of the study of Chinese history) (Shanghai: Shanghai shudian, 1989), 58–73.

Liang's emphasis on the special biography *zhuan zhuan* is a result of his notion of history writing, which is shared by Hu Shi. Liang believes that the history of a particular period can be presented through recording lives of several representative figures of the period. He thus proposes writing the biographies of significant personages who represent the intellectual, political, and artistic areas of the period. The composite picture derived from these biographies will capture the characteristics of the era. Like Hu Shi, Liang devices a list of eminent men for each period in history, proposing a biography for each.

(For a discussion of Liang's notion of biography, see Richard Howard, "Modern Chinese Biography," *Journal of Asian Studies (JAS)* 21, no. 4 [1962]: 465–75.)

For Hu Shi and Liang, biography is seen as a venue for understanding a particular period in history.

12. Liang, *Supplement to Methods of Study*, 59.

13. According to Howard, Liang's most important biographies were written in the early 1900s and showed obvious influence from the West, in particular Carlyle's notion of the actions of individuals as having historical consequences of vast proportions (Howard, "Modern Chinese Biography," 470).

14. Liang, *Supplement to Methods of Study*, 73.

15. See Lydia Liu's discussion of Hu Shi's interpretation of the dialectic of the two selves, which "echoes that of Gao Yuhan's *xiaoji* and *daji*." "Translingual Practice: The Discourse of Individualism between China and the West," in *Narrative of Agency: Self-Making in China, India and Japan*, ed. Wimal Dissanayake (Minneapolis: University of Minnesota Press, 1996), 24.

16. Hu, *Self-Narration at Forty*, 6.

17. According to Grieder, "Within a few years of its publication, *Evolution and Ethics* gained widespread popularity throughout the country, and even became reading matter for middle-school students. Very few who read the book could understand [the significance of] Huxley's contribution to scientific and intellectual history. What they did understand was the significance of such phrases as "the strong are victorious and the weak perish" as they applied to international politics.... Within a few years these ideas spread like a prairie fire, setting ablaze the hearts and blood of many young people. Technical terms like 'evolution' and 'natural selection' became common in journalistic prose, and slogans on the lips of patriotic young heroes." Jerome Grieder, *Hu Shih and the Chinese Renaissance: Liberalism in the Chinese Revolution, 1917–1937* (Cambridge: Harvard University Press, 1970), 26–27.

18. Hu, *Self-Narration at Forty*, 179.

19. See the discussion in chapter 3.

20. "An author is not just a person, he is a person who writes and publishes. With one foot in the text, and one outside, he is the point of contact between the two. The author is defined as being simultaneously a socially responsible real person, and the producer of a discourse.... Perhaps one really becomes an author only with one's second book, when the name written on the cover is the common denominator for at least two different texts, and thus gives the idea of a person who is not reducible to any particular one of his texts, and who, being capable of producing others, goes beyond all of them.... [T]his is very important for the reading of autobiographies: if the autobiography is the author's first book, he is an unknown—even if he is telling his own story in the book, he lacks, in the eyes of the reader, that sign of reality constituted by the prior production of *other texts* (non-autobiographical ones), which is indispensable to

what we will call 'the autobiographical space'" (Lejeune, "The Autobiographical Contract," 200).

21. According to Lydia Liu, this concept, long believed to be a Chinese national characteristic, was coined only in the 1920s as a result of the writings of Arthur Smith. See Liu, "Translating National Character: Lu Xun and Arthur Smith," in *Translingual Practice: Literature, National Culture, and Translated Modernity; China, 1900–1937* (Stanford: Stanford University Press, 1995), 45–76.

22. De Man, "Autobiography as De-Facement." De Man puts forth a theory that the study of autobiography as a literary genre is futile and inconclusive because it is dependent on the assumption that the autobiographical self is necessarily referential to the author's life and not vice versa and that the identity of the author is a stable entity. De Man believes autobiography, or "the specular moment[,] is not primarily a situation or an event that can be located in a history, but . . . the manifestation, on the level of the referent, of a linguistic structure" (922). He proposes the reading of autobiographies as a trope: "Prosopopeia is the trope of autobiography, by which one's name . . . is made as intelligible and memorable as a face. Our topic deals with the giving and taking away of faces, with face and efface, figure and figuration and disfiguration" (926).

23. See Hu Shi, preface to *Chronological Biography of Master Zhang*, 2.

24. This translation is adapted from Howard, "Modern Chinese Biography," 474.

25. Hu Shi, *Self-Narrative at Forty*, 29.

26. Ibid., 30.

27. Ibid., 34.

28. Ibid., 55.

29. Larson, *Literary Authority*, 12.

30. Ibid.

31. According to Larson, "the allusion to ancestry, history, actual time and social event which is characteristic of the circumstantial text more readily corresponds to the socially engaged, nationally aware position of the modern intellectual who is unwilling to permit textual work to become the primary indicator of his social function." Larson thus claims writers of "impressionistic autobiography" are more conservative politically (*Literary Authority*, 51). In my discussion of Hu Shi, this point does not seem to bear out. I show that Hu Shi, despite of his rhetoric of change, is interested in preserving traditional institutions of power.

32. See Yu Dafu's autobiography, *Dafu zizhuan*, for example. He opens his writing by claiming that his birth not only corresponded to, and hence is implicated with, the fall of the last dynasty of China, but also the death of his father.

33. Lu Xun, *Zhaohua xishi* (Morning blossoms picked at dusk) (Hong Kong: Xinyi, 1979).

34. *Morning Blossoms Picked at Dusk* (*Zhaohua xishi*) is a collection of ten essays, written over a period of nine months between February and November 1926 and published separately in *Mangyuan* (*Wilderness*) biweekly under the title *Retelling Old Things* (Jiushi chongtan). They were renamed *Zhaohua xishi* when published as a collection in 1927. For a detailed investigation of the circumstances of the writing and publication of Lu Xun's work, consult Bao Ziyan, "Zhaohua xishi suoji" (Miscellaneous notes on *Morning Blossoms Picked at Dusk*), in *Lu Xun riji Zhaji* (Reading notes on Lu Xun's diaries) (Hunan renmin chubanshe, 1980), 50–58. In this study, Bao investigates the events of Lu Xun's writing and publication of the essays through the records in his diaries.

35. This is Paul Ricoeur's definition in *Interpretation Theory: Discourse and the Surplus of Meaning* (Fort Worth: Texas Christian University Press, 1976), 51.

36. Edward Said, *Beginnings* (New York: Columbia University Press, 1985), 143.

37. In 1935, Tiyi chubanshe of Shanghai published a special series of autobiographies that included the works of Lu Yin, Ba Jin, Shen Congwen, Chang Zhiping, Yu Dafu, etc., in *Zizhuan Congshu* (Series on autobiography) (Shanghai: Tiyi Chubanshe, 1935).

38. Hsia Chih-tsing, *Twentieth-Century Chinese Stories: 1919–1949* (New York: Columbia University Press, 1971), 154.

39. Lu Xun, *Dawn Blossoms Plucked at Dusk,* trans. Yang Hsin Yi and Gladys Yang (Beijing: Foreign Language Press, 1976), 1–2.

40. Lu Xun comments in reference to the myth recorded in the *Shuo Tang:* "Let the awakened man burden himself with the weight of tradition and shoulder up the gate of darkness." Quoted in T. A. Hsia, *The Gate of Darkness* (Seattle: University of Washington Press, 1968).

41. Georges May, "Autobiography and the Eighteenth Century," in *The Author in His Work,* ed. Louis L. Martz and Aubrey Williams (New Haven: Yale University Press, 1978), 323.

42. In *The Culture of Redemption,* Leo Bersani demonstrates this complex autobiographical process in his study of Proust's *La Recherche de Temps Perdu*. He argues that Proust "had first of all abstracted his experience into general laws then deduced another version of the particular from those laws, a kind of second-degree particularity of experience disengaged from existence." One of his arguments is that experience translated into art is a form of "departicularization." Through the act of repetition that is artistic representation, there is a move from the particular events and people represented into truth or essences. As Bersani argues through a reading of Proust, art is "truth liberated from phenomena." Leo Bersani, *The Culture of Redemption* (Cambridge: Harvard University Press, 1990), 13. Not wishing to engage in the philosophical discussion of the redemptive powers of art as a result of this transformative aspect, I am

using Bersani's concept loosely to point to the relationship between individual experiences and general or universal truth.

43. Anderson suggests that Lu Xun's writings are equally motivated by the impulse to reflect social ills and by self-reflexive examination of his own ethical responsibility as an intellectual (*The Limits of Realism*, 77).

44. Anderson points out an intrinsic contradiction in Lu Xun's writing. While Lu Xun's intention is to portray the oppressed, to present a moral lesson, there is always a great danger that the victims will inadvertently become objects of curiosity, while the reader's emotional response is transferred to the narrator instead of being directed toward the victim of the story. Anderson suggests that Lu Xun tries to remedy such danger through his use of *qubi* (distortions) (ibid., 86).

45. *Selected Short Stories of Lu Hsun*, trans. Yang Hsien Yi and Gladys Yang (Beijing: Foreign Languages Press, 1978), 128–29.

46. Zhong Jingwen concurs on this point. Describing characters such as Mr. Fujino, Fan Ainong, and Changma, Zhong points out that "although they all have models in real people . . . through Lu Xun's literary manipulation, they all embody an archetype." See Zhong Jingwen, "Tan Zhaohua xishi" (On *Morning Blossoms Picked at Dusk*), in *Guanyu Lu Xun, Lunkao yu huixiang* (On Lu Xun's essay and reminiscences) (Shanxi: Renmin Chubanshe, 1982), 103.

47. In his study of the *Story of Ah Q*, Anderson comes to a similar conclusion about the interchangeability of the positions between the narrating subject and the object of the text: "The narrator complains of being 'possessed' by his subject and observes that his own fate as an author is intimately entwined with Ah Q's: the subject of a biography 'becomes known to posterity through the writing and the writing known to posterity through the subject—until finally it is not clear who is making whom known'" (*The Limits of Realism*, 84).

48. Lu Xun, *Zhaohua xishi*, 52.

49. Ibid., 50.

50. Ibid., 54.

51. Maire Jaanus Kurrik, *Literature and Negation* (New York: Columbia University Press, 1979), 3.

52. Lu Xun, *Zhaohua xishi*, 57.

53. This is the premise of Hu Shi's argument in "Preliminary Proposal for the Reform of Literature," in *Documents of the Literary Movement*, 12–21.

54. Lu Xun, *Zhaohua xishi*, 26.

55. Ibid., 50.

56. Ibid.

57. For example, Hu Shi's "Shenme jiaozuo duanpian xiaoshuo?" (What is a short story?), in *Hu Shi Wencun*, 93:175–93.

58. Said, *Beginnings*, 143.

Chapter Five

1. Shen Congwen, *Congwen zizhuan* (Autobiography of Shen Congwen) (Taibei: Fuxin chubanshe, 1978), and *Travels to West Hunan*.

2. For example, see Leo Ou-fan Lee, "The Solitary Traveler: Images of Self in Modern Chinese Literature," in *Expressions of Self in Chinese Literature*, ed. Robert E. Hegel and Richard C. Hessney (New York: Columbia University Press, 1985), 282–307; Peng Xiaoyan, *Chaoyue Xieshi* (Taibei: Lianjing, 1993).

3. This point has been argued most famously by Edward Said in *Orientalism* (New York: Vintage, 1979), and again reiterated in his later work, *Culture and Imperialism* (New York: Vintage, 1994), in which he asserts that bringing certain land into representation is "to better see it, to master it and above all, to hold it" (99). The written representation of land is a mapping of it in preparation for colonization, both political and cultural. In a similar vein, Mary Louise Pratt's study *Imperial Eyes* makes the connection between travel writing and imperialism. Pratt makes several refinements on the general idea of seeing as knowledge and power. Also importantly, she points out the interaction and mutual inferences among the different fields of knowledge in the construction of a particular way of seeing the world. In this way, she deconstructs ideology—the political as well as the intellectual genealogy of a particular vision, and in this case, an imperialist vision.

4. Franco Moretti, *The Atlas of the European Novel, 1800–1900* (London: Verso, 1998).

5. In "Solitary Traveler," Lee begins his discussion on "the most famous professional traveller of traditional China," Xu Xiake. He points out that Xu is often considered China's first modern geographer because of his spirit of objectivity and attitude of "scientific inquiry" in his travels (82–307). What is not pointed out about Xu's travels to south China is that they coincided with a long episode of violence between the Ming court and the tribal peoples of the south—mostly due to the Ming expansionist policy in the region. In Guangxi, Hunan, Yunnan, and Guizhou, there were officially recorded a total of 327 tribal uprisings of significance between 1368 and 1644, involving several thousand troops. The number of conflicts gives us some sense of the force of Ming extension in this region. See Harold Wiens, *China's March toward the Tropics* (Hamden, Conn.: Shoe String Press, 1954), 187, and Robert Darrah Jenks, *Insurgency and Social Disorder in Guizhou: The "Miao" Rebellion, 1854–1873* (Honolulu: University of Hawaii Press, 1994). According to Richard Strassburg, Xu made his most extensive travels to these regions during 1636–40. See *Inscribed Landscape: Travel Writings from Imperial China* (Berkeley and Los Angeles: University of California Press, 1994), 326–34.

6. Rosemary Haddon, "Chinese Nativist Literature of the 1920s: The Sojourner-Narrator," *Modern Chinese Literature* 8 (1994): 97–125.

7. Zhu Xiaojin, "Sanshi niandai xiangtu xiaoshuo de wenhua yiwen," reprinted in *Zhongguo xiandai, dangdai wenxue yanjiu* 10 (1994): 66–80.

8. Zhu refers to Lu Xun's "Luelun Zhongguo ren de lian" (A casual discussion of Chinese people's faces), in *Lu Xun zawen quanji* (Henan: Henan renmin chubanshe, 1994), 262–63.

9. See Peng, *Chaoyue Xieshi;* and Lee, "Solitary Traveler."

10. Wang, *Fictional Realism,* 201–45.

11. See Zhu Xiaojin, "Sanshi niandai xiangtu xiaoshuo de wenhua yiwen."

12. See Chang-tai Hung, *Going to the People: Chinese Intellectuals and Folk Literature, 1918–1937* (Cambridge: Harvard University Press, 1985). Hung points out that the intellectuals involved in these movements tended to have romanticized views of the countryside and of their roles as reformers. They wished to sweep away all the backwardness of the interior and become one with the people. In "Linear History and the Nation State," Prasenjit Duara also relates Shen Congwen's writing as part of this movement of "going to the people." See his *Rescuing History from the Nation* (Chicago: University of Chicago Press, 1995), 42.

13. See Hung, *Going to the People.*

14. James Clifford, *The Predicament of Culture: Twentieth Century Ethnography, Literature, and Art* (Cambridge: Harvard University Press, 1988).

15. Renato Rosaldo, *Culture and Truth: The Remaking of Social Analysis* (Boston: Beacon Press, 1989), 34. According to Rosaldo: "Imperialist nostalgia revolves around a paradox: A person kills somebody, and then mourns the victim. In more attenuated form, somebody deliberately alters a form of life, and then regrets that things have not remained as they were prior to the intervention. At one more remove, people destroy their environment, and then they worship nature. In any of its versions, imperialist nostalgia uses a pose of 'innocent yearning' both to capture people's imaginations and to conceal its complicity with often brutal domination."

16. A large part of northwestern Hunan became the Miao western Hunan autonomous region in 1951 under the Communist government. See Jenks, *Insurgency and Social Disorder,* 283–84.

17. Jenks, *Insurgency and Social Disorder,* points out that despite the nomenclature, the rebels also consisted of discontented Han and other minority ethnic groups. At different points, the Qing authorities used the rival tribes against each other. In effect, it was a complex affair in which the object of the rebellion was not necessarily in opposition to the central government.

18. Shen, *Autobiography,* 7.

19. Ibid., 3.

20. Ibid.

21. The symbolic power of sight as an assertion of ideological control has been argued by many different scholars. Rey Chow has demonstrated how Western fetishistic attitudes toward China are a result of a kind of scopophilia

(*Women and Chinese Modernity*, esp. chap. 1). Jonathan Crary *(Techniques of the Observer)* points out that throughout history, technological advances in the instruments of sight often directly or indirectly led to new ways of controlling individuals, while Edward Said relates seeing with knowing and conquest. In the late 1980s Nancy Miller's *(Subject to Change)* and Teresa De Lauretis's *(Technologies of Gender)* works on perspectives on women opened important grounds for the discussion of the ideology of sight, especially in gender politics.

22. Shen, *Autobiography*, 6.
23. Said, *Culture and Imperialism* (New York: Knopf, 1994).
24. Shen, *Autobiography*, 20.
25. The issues of the political and cultural dominance of the countryside are complicated. The nature of dominance is manifested in terms of class, ethnic, and gender oppressions. Since this book is focused on the issues of the literary representation and expression of such dominance, I will not go into the specificities of the problem. By using the notion of dominance loosely here, I mean to articulate the unequal balance of power between those who wield the strong cultural capital of writing and learning, whom I associate with city dwellers and intellectuals in general, and those who do not have such privileges—the general categories of peasants or tribal peoples represent this group. Of course in actuality the division is not so simple. The city has its own underclass and the country its own oppressive gentry. However, taking a cue from Zhu's and Haddon's analyses of native-soil literature, I see this division between city and country, between intellectuals and peasants in Shen's writing as mainly metaphorical.
26. Shen, *Travels to West Hunan*, 2–3.
27. Shen, *Autobiography*, 6.
28. Ibid., 30.
29. "Secularize" in this context has the sense that Said defines in "Secular Criticism" as acknowledging the fact that texts are worldly—a part of the social world and historical moments in which they are located. And thus, Shen's usage of Peach Blossom Spring in his writing refocuses this ancient utopia into his contemporary world, thus also making this text relevant to his own milieu and historical circumstances. See Edward Said, "Secular Criticism," in *The World, the Text, and the Critic* (Cambridge: Harvard University Press, 1983), 1–30.
30. See Lee, "Solitary Traveler."
31. *Writings of Shen Congwen*, 2:362.
32. Kinkley, *Odyssey of Shen Congwen*, 20.
33. Instead of seeing Shen's affiliation with both worlds, Zhu argues that Shen's writings illustrate the paradox between city and country in native-soil literature: they "offered a pastoral tale of rural virtues in remote western Hunan as a 'medicine' for the diseased mind of his urban readers." See Zhu, 73.

34. In *Fictional Resolutions in Three Victorian Novels* (New York: Columbia University Press, 1981), Deirdre David argues that the fictional resolutions of Victorian novels in marriage, ownership of property, or reintegration into society express an acceptance of the status quo of the times if not a consolidation of the existing authority.

35. Shen, *Autobiography*, 98.

36. Wendy Larson in *Literary Authority* argues that Shen, like most May Fourth intellectuals, slowly lost faith in his intellectual endeavors. Shen's writings glorify the life of country folk and his own experience as a man of action in the army, as an alternative to the lack of vigor of most intellectuals. They also illustrate a gradual loss of faith in the authority of literature. Shen's works, as I read them, are precisely a rejection of a life of senseless bravado in military adventures, especially in the spell of political purges and suppressions in that period. My reading thus is in contradiction to Wendy Larson's.

37. David Wang does deal at length with this issue of violence in Shen's works. Wang argues that Shen challenges the limits of both lyrical and realist writing. The result of Shen's lyrical strategies to narrate historical disasters and human travesties is an exploration of the pathos and passions in terms of rationality. Shen's lyrical discourse is thus "a move that fills in those human territories still mapped as *terra incognita* on the charts of realism and rationality" (245). While agreeing with Wang's assessment of the power of Shen's lyrical strategies, I will offer an alternative way of reading that places less emphasis on the exploration of the "heart of darkness" than on the moral effects of his writing on readers.

38. Shen's apparent willful abstention from making a value judgment was certainly a cause for his criticism after 1947 by the Communist Party intellectuals, especially Guo Moruo (1892–1978).

39. Shen, *Autobiography*, 26.

40. Ibid., 65.

41. Hans Kellner, in *Language and Historical Representation: Getting the Story Crooked* (Madison: University of Wisconsin Press, 1989), discusses the kind of history practiced by nineteenth-century British and French historians such as Prosper de Barante and Augustin Thierry. In the face of the new technique in realistic representation in literature, these historians insert "chunks of reality" through extensive quotation, or add "local color" to contribute to the multiple perspective in the texts. Kellner refers to this practice as "showing but not presenting the past" (6). Contrary to this method is that of "emplotment," which is based on a narrative understanding that is "controlled and guided by the basic armature of narrative, what Aristotle called mythos or plot. This emphasis on historical emplotment is an enormous advance over previous ways of reading history because it spotlights the innumerable choices that must be made at every turn" (9). This emplotment is a result of what Kellner understands as the desire to organize chaotic human fragments.

42. This term is coined by David Wang, who deals at length with the theme of decapitation, comparing Shen's usage to Lu Xun's familiar trope. He points out that Lu Xun's use of beheading is to represent a world fallen apart, of lost sentience. Shen, however, is concerned less with what beheading means than "how it can be written about so as to let us remember and re-member the rest of the world" (218). Wang argues that the two writers' depictions of decapitation represent their respective adherence to realism and lyricism as the literary ideology in their writing (*Fictional Realism*, 218).

43. Georges May identifies the crucial textual movement of autobiography as "one long backward glance" ("Autobiography and the Eighteenth Century," in Martz and Williams, *Author in His Work*, 320).

44. Shen, *Autobiography*, 68.

45. Ibid., 28.

46. Shen, *Autobiography*, 67.

47. I am referring to Lu Xun's influential story of 1918, "Madman's Diary" (Kuangren riji), in which the "madman" perceives the moral guardians of society as wanting to devour him. Since this story, cannibalism has become an important trope in modern Chinese literature.

48. See Marston Anderson's discussion of Lu Xun in "The Morality of Form: Lu Xun and the Modern Chinese Short Story," in *Lu Xun and His Legacy*, ed. Leo Ou-fan Lee (Berkeley and Los Angelesn: University of California Press, 1985), 34–62.

49. Shen, *Autobiography*, 64.

50. See Said, *Culture and Imperialism*.

Bibliography

Abbot, H. Porter. "Autobiography, Autography, Fiction." *New Literary History* 19, no. 3 (1988): 1–9.

Adorno, Theodore. "Introduction to Benjamin's *Schriften*." In *On Walter Benjamin: Critical Essays and Recollections*, ed. Gary Smith. Cambridge: MIT Press, 1993.

Anderson, Marston. *The Limits of Realism: Chinese Fiction in the Revolutionary Period*. Berkeley and Los Angeles: University of California Press, 1990.

Azim, Firdous. *The Colonial Rise of the Novel*. New York: Routledge, 1993.

Ba Jin. "Guanyu *Jia*" (About *Family*). In *Tan ziji de chuangzuo* (About my writings). Hong Kong: Nanguo chubanshe.

Bai Wei. "Wo toudao wenxuequan li de chuchong" (The original reason I joined the literary circle). In *Zhongguo nu zuojia sanwen xuancui* (Selected essays from Chinese women writers), ed. You Kangxuan. Fujian: Haixia wenyi, 1994.

Ban Chao and Ban Gu. *Han Shu* (History of Han). 12 vols. Beijing: Zhonghuan shuju, 1990.

Bao Zhiyu. "Zhaohua xishi suoji" (Miscellaneous records of *Morning Blossoms Picked at Dusk*). In *Lu Xun riji zaji* (Lu Xun's miscellaneous essays and diaries). Sichuan: Hunan Renmin chubanshe, 1980.

Barlow, Tani, ed. *Gender Politics in Modern China: Writing and Feminism*. Durham: Duke University Press, 1993.

———. *I Myself a Woman: Selected Writings of Ding Ling*. Boston: Beacon Press, 1989.

Barthes, Roland. *The Pleasure of the Text*, trans. Richard Miller. New York: Noonday Press, 1990.

———. *S/Z*, trans. Richard Miller. New York: Noonday Press, 1990.

Benstock, Shari. *The Private Self*. Chapel Hill: University of Carolina Press, 1984.

Berger, John. *Ways of Seeing*. New York: Grove Press, 1961.

Bernstein, Susan David. *Confessional Subjects: Revelations of Gender and Power in Victorian Literature and Culture*. Chapel Hill: University of North Carolina Press, 1997.

Bersani, Leo. *The Culture of Redemption*. Cambridge: Harvard University Press, 1990.

Birch, Cyril. *Anthology of Chinese Literature from Early Times to the Fourteenth Century*. New York: Grove Press, 1965.

Bloch, Ernst. *The Utopian Function of Art and Literature: Selected Essays*. Trans. Jack Zipes and Frank Mecklenburg. Cambridge: MIT Press, 1993.

Boorman, Howard, ed. "The Biographical Approach to Chinese History: A Symposium." Special issue of *Journal of Asian Studies (JAS)* 31, no. 4 (1962).

Brooks, Peter. *The Melodramatic Imagination: Balzac, Henry James, Melodrama, and the Mode of Excess*. New Haven: Yale University Press, 1995.

Butler, Judith. *The Psychic Life of Power: Theories in Subjection*. Stanford: Stanford University Press, 1997.

Cavaliero, Glen. "Autobiography and Fiction." *Prose Studies* 8 (1985): 156–71.

Chan, Ming K., and Arif Dirlik, eds. *Schools into Fields and Factories: Anarchists, the Guomindang, and the National Labor University in Shanghai, 1927–1932*. Durham: Duke University Press, 1991.

Chandler, James. *England in 1819*. Chicago: University of Chicago Press, 1998.

Chang, Eileen. *Liuyan* (Flow of words). Taipei: Huangguan, 1984.

———. *Zhang Ailing xiaoshuoji* (The short stories of Eileen Chang). Taipei: Huangguan, 1984.

———. "Intimate Words." Trans. Janet Ng. *Renditions: A Chinese-English Translation Magazine* 45 (1996), 33–46.

Chang Tai-hung. *Going to the People: Chinese Intellectuals and Folk Literature, 1918–1937*. Cambridge: Harvard University Press, 1985.

Chen Duxiu. "Wenxue geminglun" (On the literary revolution). In *Wenxue yundongshiliao xuan* (Selections from the documents of the literary movement), vol. 1. Shanghai: Shanghai jiaoyu, 1982.

———. "Letter to Qian Xuantong" (1917). In *Wenxue yundongshiliao xuan* (Selections from the documents of the literary movement), vol. 1. Shanghai: Shanghai jiaoyu, 1982.

Chen Hengzhe. *Xiao yudian* (A little raindrop). Shanghai: Shanghai shudian, 1985.

———. *Chen Hengzhe Sanwen xuanji* (The essays of Chen Hengzhe). Tianjin: Baihua wenyi, 1991.

Chen Pingyuan. "Lun xin xiaoshuo leixing lilun" (On the theory of the new fiction genres). *Zhongguo xiandai wenxue piping congkan* 2 (1991): 114–25.

———. *Zhongguo xiaoshuo shushi moshi de zhuanbian* (Changes in the modes of Chinese fiction). Taipei: Taida wenhua, 1990.

Chow, Rey. *Primitive Passion*. New York: Columbia University Press, 1995.

———. "Virtuous Transactions: A Reading of Three Short Stories by Ling

Shuhua." In *Gender Politics in Modern China: Writing and Feminism*, ed. Tani Barlow. Durham: Duke University Press, 1993.

———. *Woman and the Chinese Modernity: The Politics of Reading between West and East*. Minneapolis: University of Minnesota Press, 1991.

Clifford, James. *The Predicament of Culture: Twentieth Century Ethnography, Literature, and Art*. Cambridge: Harvard University Press, 1988.

Cohen, Margaret, and Christopher Pendergast, eds. *Spectacles of Realism: Gender, Body, Genre*. Minneapolis: University of Minnesota Press, 1995.

Crary, Jonathan. *Techniques of the Observer: On Vision and Modernity in the Nineteenth Century*. Cambridge: MIT Press, 1996.

David, Deirdre. *Fictional Resolutions in Three Victorian Novels*. New York: Columbia University Press, 1981.

de Certeau, Michel. *The Practice of Everyday Life*. Trans. Steven E. Rendall. Berkeley and Los Angeles: University of California Press, 1984.

———. *The Writing of History*. Trans. Tom Conley. New York: Columbia University Press, 1988.

Denton, Kirk. "The Distant Shore: Nationalism in Yu Dafu's 'Sinking.'" *Chinese Literature, Essays, and Articles* 14 (1992): 107–25.

Dissanayake, Wimal, ed. *Narrative of Agency: Self-Making in China, India, and Japan*. Minnesota: University of Minnesota Press, 1996.

Dooling, Amy, and Kristine Torgeson, eds. *Writing Women in Modern China: An Anthology of Women's Literature from the Early Twentieth Century*. New York: Columbia University Press, 1998.

Duara, Prasenjit. *Rescuing History from the Nation*. Chicago: University of Chicago Press, 1995.

DuPlessis, Rachel Blau. *Writing beyond the Ending: Narrative Strategies of Twentieth-Century Women Writers*. Bloomington: Indiana University Press, 1985.

Durrant, Stephen. "Self as the Intersection of Traditions: The Autobiographical Writings of Ssu-ma Ch'ien." *Journal of the American Oriental Society* 106, no. 1 (1986): 33–40.

Eakin, Paul. *Fictions in Autobiography: Studies in the Art of Self-Invention*. Princeton: Princeton University Press, 1985.

Egan, Michael. "Yu Dafu and the Transition to Modern Chinese Literature." In *Modern Chinese Literature in the May Fourth Era*, ed. Merle Goldman. Cambridge: Harvard University Press, 1977.

Finney, Brian. "Sexual Identity in Modern British Autobiography." *Prose Studies* 8, no. 2 (1985): 29–43.

Foucault, Michel. *The Order of Things: An Archeology of the Human Sciences*. New York: Vintage, 1994.

Fu Sinian. "Zhenyang zuo baihuawen" (How to write in the vernacular). In *Wenxue yundongshiliao xuan* (Selections from the documents of the literary movement), vol. 1. Shanghai: Shanghai jiaoyu, 1982.

Fujii, James. *Complicit Fictions: The Subject in the Modern Japanese Prose Narrative*. Berkeley and Los Angeles: University of California Press, 1993.
Goldman, Merle, ed. *Modern Chinese Literature in the May Fourth Era*. Cambridge: Harvard University Press, 1977.
Gordon, David. "Character and Self in Autobiography." *Journal of Narrative Technique* 18, no. 3 (1988): 105–19.
Grewal, Inderpal, and Caren Kaplan, eds. *Scattered Hegemonies: Postmodernity and Transnational Feminist Practices*. Minneapolis: University of Minnesota Press, 1997.
Grieder, Jerome. *Hu Shih and the Chinese Renaissance: Liberalism in the Chinese Revolution, 1917–1937*. Cambridge: Harvard University Press, 1970.
Gu Yisheng and Wang Yunxi, eds. *Zhongguo wenxue pipingshi* (History of Chinese literature and criticism). 4 vols. Shanghai: Shanghai guji, 1991.
Guo Dongfang, ed. *Lidai Zishuxuan* (Self-narrative through the ages). Shanghai: Shanghai yinshuguan, 1937.
———. "Wode tongnian" (My childhood). In *Guo Moro xuanji* (Selected works of Guo Moro), vol. 1. Chengdu: Sichuan Renmin, 1979.
Guo Moro. "Wenxue geming zhihuigu" (A reflection on the literary revolution). In *Wenxue yundongshiliao xuan* (Selections from the documents of the literary movement), vol. 2. Shanghai: Shanghai jiaoyu, 1982.
Guo Shaoyu, ed. *Zhongguo lidai wenlunxuan* (Selection of essays on Chinese literature throughout the ages). 4 vols. Shanghai: Shanghai guji, 1980.
Gunn, Janet Varner. *Autobiography: Towards a Poetics of Experience*. Philadelphia: University of Pennsylvania Press, 1982.
Gusdorf, Georges. "Conditions and Limits of Autobiography." In *Autobiography: Essays Theoretical and Critical*, ed. James Olney. Princeton: Princeton University Press, 1980.
Hacking, Ian. "Making up People." In *Reconstructing Individualism: Autonomy, Individuality, and the Self in Western Thought*, ed. Thomas C. Heller, Morton Sosna, and David E. Wellbery. Stanford: Stanford University Press, 1986.
———. *The Social Construction of What?* Cambridge: Harvard University Press, 1999.
Haddon, Rosemary. "Chinese Nativist Literature of the 1920s: The Sojourner-Narrator." *Modern Chinese Literature* 8 (1994): 97–125.
Heilbrun, Carolyn. "Women's Autobiographical Writings: New Forms." *Prose Studies* 8, no. 2 (1985): 14–28.
———. *Writing a Woman's Life*. New York: Ballantine, 1989.
Heller, Thomas, Sosna Morton, and David E. Wellbery, eds. *Reconstructing Individualism: Autonomy, Individuality, and the Self in Western Thought*. Stanford: Stanford University Press, 1986.
Hsia, C. T. *History of Modern Chinese Fiction, 1917–1957*. New Haven: Yale University Press, 1961.

Hsia, T. A. *The Gate of Darkness*. Seattle: University of Washington Press, 1968.
"Hongshui fuhuo xuanyan" (A declaration on the occasion of the reissue of *Deluge*). In *Wenxue yundongshiliao xuan* (Selections from the documents of the literary movement), vol. 1. Shanghai: Shanghai jiaoyu, 1982.
Howard, Richard. "Modern Chinese Biographical Writing." *Journal of Asian Studies (JAS)* 21, no. 4 (1962): 465–75.
Hu Shi. "Jianshe de wenxue geming lun" (A constructive literary revolution). In *Wenxue yundongshiliao xuan* (Selections from the documents of the literary movement), vol. 1. Shanghai: Shanghai jiaoyu, 1982. Originally printed in *New Youth* (1918).

———. Preface to *A Little Raindrop*, by Chen Hengzhe. Shanghai: Shanghai shudian, 1985.

———. "Wenxue gailiangchuyi." (A preliminary proposal for the reform of literature). In *Wenxue yundongshiliao xuan* (Selections from the documents of the literary movement), vol. 1. Shanghai: Shanghai jiaoyu, 1982. Originally printed in *New Youth* (1917).

———. "Shenme jiaozuo duanpian xiaoshuo" (What is a short story?). In *Hu Shi wencun* (Collected works of Hu Shi), vol. 93. Shanghai: Minguo Congshu, 1953.

———. *Sishi zishu* (Self-narration at forty). Shanghai: Dongya Tushu, 1939.

———. "Zhang Shizai xiansheng nianpu xu" (Preface to the *Chronological Biography of Master Zhang Shizai*). In *Hu Shi wencun* (Collected works of Hu Shi), vol. 93. Shanghai: Minguo Congshu, 1953.

Huang, Martin Weizong. "Dehistoricization and Intertextualization: The Anxiety of Precedents in the Evolution of the Traditional Chinese Novel." *Chinese Literature, Essays, and Articles* 12 (1990): 45–59.
Huters, Theodore, ed. *Reading the Modern Chinese Short Story*. New York: Eastgate, 1990.
Jameson, Frederic. *Nationalism, Colonialism, and Literature: Modernism and Imperialism*. Field Day Pamphlet, no. 14. Derry: Field Day Theatre Co., 1988.
Jenks, Robert Darrah. *Insurgency and Social Disorder in Guishou: The "Miao" Rebellion, 1854–1873*. Honolulu: University of Hawaii Press, 1994.
Jensen, Lionel. *Manufacturing Confucianism: Chinese Traditions and Universal Civilization*. Durham: Duke University Press, 1997.
Ji Ji. "Woyu Zhang Ailing de Laji" (Eileen Chang's rubbish and me). *Jiushi niandai* (The nineties) 311, no. 12 (1995): 90–95.
Kang Yongqiu. "Xin wenxue de diyiwei nuzuojia Chen Hengzhe" (The first woman writer of the new literature, Chen Hengzhe). *Zhongguo xiandai, dangdai wenxue yanjiu* 6 (1990): 77–82.
Kaplan, Caren, and Inderpal Grewal, eds. *Scattered Hegemonies: Postmodernity and Transnational Feminist Practices*. Minneapolis: University of Minnesota Press, 1997.

Karatani, Koojin. *The Origins of Modern Japanese Literature*. Durham: Duke University Press, 1993.
Kellner, Hans. *Language and Historical Representation: Getting the Story Crooked*. Madison: University of Wisconsin, 1989.
Kinkley, Jeffrey. *The Odyssey of Shen Congwen*. Stanford: Stanford University Press, 1987.
Kurrik, Maire Jaanus. *Literature and Negation*. New York: Columbia University Press, 1979.
Labelle, Jenni Joy. *Herself Beheld: The Literature of the Looking Glass*. Ithaca: Cornell University Press, 1988.
Lacan, Jacques. "The Mirror Stage as Formative of the Function of the I as Revealed in Psychoanalytic Experience." In *Ecrits*, trans. Alan Sheridan. New York: W. W. Norton, 1977.
Larson, Wendy. "The End of *Funu wenxue:* Women's Literature from 1925 to 1935." In *Gender Politics in Modern China: Writing and Feminism*, ed. Tani Barlow. Durham: Duke University Press, 1993.
———. *Literary Authority and the Modern Chinese Writer*. Durham: Duke University Press, 1991.
———. *Women and Writing in Modern China*. Stanford: Stanford University Press, 1998.
Lau, Joseph, C. T. Hsia, and Y. L. Ma, eds. *Modern Chinese Stories and Novellas*. New York: Columbia University Press, 1981.
De Lauretis, Teresa. *Alice Doesn't: Feminism, Semiotics, Cinema*. Bloomington: Indiana University Press, 1982.
———. *Technologies of Gender: Essays on Theory, Film, and Fiction*. Bloomington: Indiana University Press, 1987.
Layoun, Mary. *Travels of a Genre: The Modern Novel and Ideology*. Princeton: Princeton University Press, 1990.
Lee, Leo Ou-fan. "In Search of Modernity: Some Reflections on a New Mode of Consciousness in Twentieth-Century Chinese History and Literature." In *Ideas across Cultures: Essays on Chinese Thought in Honor of Benjamin I. Schwartz*, ed. Paul A. Cohen and Merle Goldman. Cambridge: Harvard University Press, 1990.
———. *The Romantic Generation in the May Fourth Period*. Cambridge: Harvard University Press, 1973.
———. "The Solitary Traveler: Images of Self in Modern Chinese Literature." In *Expressions of Self in Chinese Literature*, ed. Robert E. Hegel and Richard C. Hessney. New York: Columbia University Press, 1985.
Lejeune, Philippe. "The Autobiographical Contract." In *French Literary Theory Today*, ed. Tzvetan Todorov. Cambridge: Cambridge University Press, 1982.
———. "Autobiography in the Third Person." *New Literary History* 9 (1977): 27–50.

Lian Zi. "Lun wusi nuxing wenxue de gexing juyi tese" (On the characteristic of individualism of the May Fourth women's literature). *Zhongguo xiandai dangdai wenxue yanjiu* 4 (1990): 95–99.

Liang Qichao. *Sanshi zishu* (Self-narration at thirty). In *Lidai zishuxuan* (Self-narrative through the ages), ed. Guo Dongfang. Shanghai: Shanghai shangwu yinshuguan, 1937.

———. "Xiaoshuo xiaohua" (A short discussion on fiction). In *Zhongguo lidai wenlun xuan*, ed. Guo Shaoyu. Shanghai: Shanghai guji, 1980.

———. "Xiaoshuo yu chunzhi zhi guanxi" (The relationship between fiction and the ruling of the masses). In *Zhongguo wenxue pipingshi* (History of Chinese literary criticism), ed. Wang Yunxi and Gu Yisheng, vol. 3. Shanghai: Shanghai guji, 1991.

———. *Zhongguo lishi yanjiufa bupian* (Supplement to the methods of the study of Chinese history). Minguo Congshu Series. Vol. 73. Shanghai: Shanghai shudian, 1989.

Ling Shuhua. *Ancient Melodies*. London: Hogarth Press, 1953.

———. *Ling Shuhua xuanji* (Selected works of Ling Shuhua). Singapore: Shijie Shuju, 1960.

Liu, Lydia. "The Female Body and Nationalist Discourse: The *Field of Life and Death* Revisited." In *Scattered Hegemonies: Postmodernity and Transnational Feminist Practices*, ed. Inderpal Grewal and Caren Kaplan. Minneapolis: University of Minnesota Press, 1997.

———. "Invention and Intervention: The Female Tradition in Modern Chinese Literature." In *Gender Politics in Modern China: Writing and Feminism*, ed. Tani Barlow. Durham: Duke University Press, 1993.

———. *Translingual Practice: Literature, National Culture, and Translated Modernity; China, 1900–1937*. Stanford: Stanford University Press, 1995.

———. "Translingual Practice: The Discourse of Individualism between China and the West." In *Narrative of Agency: Self-Making in China, India, and Japan*, ed. Wimal Dissanayake. Minneapolis: University of Minnesota Press, 1996.

Liu Zhiji. "Xu zhuan" (Biographical Preface). In *Shitong xinjiaozhu* (New annotation of the *Shitong*). Annotated by Yue Lubu. Chongqing: Chongqing chubanshe, 1990.

Lu Ji. "Wenfu" (Essay on literature). In *Zhongguo Lidai wenlunxuan* (Selection of essays on Chinese literature through the ages), ed. Guo Shaoyu, vol. 1. Shanghai: Shanghai guji, 1980. Trans. Cyril Birch in *Anthology of Chinese Literature* (New York: Grove Press, 1965).

Lu Jingqing. "Liu Langji" (Drifting—excerpt). In *May Fourth Women Writers: Memoirs*, ed. Janet Ng and Janice Wickeri. Hong Kong: Renditions Paperbacks, Chinese University of Hong Kong, 1996.

Lu Xun. *Dawn Blossoms Picked at Dusk*. Trans. Yang Hsin Yi and Gladys Yang. Beijing: Foreign Language Press.

———. *Lu Xun Chuanji* (Complete works of Lu Xun). 16 vols. Beijing: Renmin Chubanshe, 1981.

———. "Luelun zhongguo ren de lian" (About the faces of Chinese people). In *Lu Xun zawen chuanji* (The complete collection of the miscellaneous essays of Lu Xun). Sichuan: Henan renmin, 1994.

———. "Mahsang Riji" (Immediate diaries). In *Lu Xun Chuanji* (Complete works of Lu Xun). Beijing: Renmin Chubanshe, 1981.

———. "Mianpu yice" (Some conjectures about theatrical masks). In *Lu Xun zawen chuanji* (Complete collection of the miscellaneous essays of Lu Xun). Sichuan: Henan renmin, 1994.

———. *Selected Short Stories of Lu Hsun*. Trans. Yang Hsin Yi and Gladys Yang. Beijing: Foreign Languages Press, 1978.

———. *Zhaohua xishi* (Morning blossoms picked at dusk). Hong Kong: Xinyi, 1979.

Lu Yin. "Jinhou funnu de qulu" (The future of women). In *Xiandai zuojia xuanji: Lu Yin* (The modern writers series: Lu Yin). Hong Kong: Joint Publishing, 1983.

———. *Lu Yin Zizhuan* (Autobiography of Lu Yin). Translated excerpts in *May Fourth Women Writers: Memoirs*, ed. Janet Ng and Wickeri. Hong Kong: Renditions Paperback, Chinese University of Hong Kong, 1996.

———. *Xiangya Jiezhi* (Ivory rings). Shaanxi: Remin chubanshe, 1986.

de Man, Paul. "Autobiography as De-Facement." *Modern Language Notes (MLN)* 94 (1979): 919–30.

———. *Resistance to Theory II*. Minneapolis: University of Minnesota Press, 1993.

Mao Dun. "Lun Lu Yin" (On Lu Yin). In *Xiandai zuojia xuanji: Lu Yin* (Modern writers series: Lu Yin). Hong Kong: Joint Publishing, 1983.

———. "Zhuanji wenxue" (Literature of biographies). In *Mao Dun chuanji* (Complete works of Mao Dun), vol. 19. Beijing: Renmin wenxue, 1991.

May, Georges. "Autobiography and the Eighteenth Century." In *The Author in His Work: Essays on a Problem in Criticism*, ed. Louis L. Martz and Aubrey Williams. New Haven: Yale University Press, 1978.

McDougall, Bonnie. *The Introduction of Western Literary Theories into Modern China, 1919–1925*. Tokyo: Centre for East Asian Culture Studies, 1971.

Miller, J. Hillis. *Fiction and Repetition*. Cambridge: Harvard University Press, 1982.

———. *Topographies*. Stanford: Stanford University Press, 1995.

Miller, Nancy. *Subject to Change: Reading Feminist Writing*. New York: Columbia University Press, 1988.

Moretti, Franco. *Atlas of the European Novel, 1800–1900*. New York: Verso, 1998.

———. *Signs Taken for Wonders*. New York: Verso, 1997.

Ng, Janet. "Writing in Her Father's House: The Feminine Autobiographical Strategies of Ling ShuHua." *Prose Studies* 16, no. 3 (1993): 235–50.

Ng, Janet, and Janice Wickeri, eds. and trans. *May Fourth Women Writers: Memoirs*. Hong Kong: Renditions Paperback, Chinese University of Hong Kong, 1996.

Ng, Mau-sang. *The Russian Hero in Modern Chinese Fiction*. Hong Kong: Chinese University Press, 1988.

Nieh, Hua-ling. *Shen Ts'ung-Wen*. New York: Twayne, 1972.

Nivison, David. "Aspects of Traditional Chinese Biography." *Journal of Asian Studies (JAS)* 21, no. 4 (1962): 457–64.

Olney, James. *Autobiography: Essay Theoretical and Critical*. Princeton: Princeton University Press, 1980.

———. *Metaphors of the Self: The Meaning in Autobiography*. Princeton: Princeton University Press, 1981.

———, ed. *Studies in Autobiography*. New York: Oxford University Press, 1988.

Owen, Stephen. *The End of the Chinese "Middle Ages": Essays in Mid-Tang Literary Culture*. Stanford: Stanford University Press, 1996.

———. *Readings in Chinese Literary Thought*. Cambridge: Harvard University Press, 1992.

Pan Liudai. *Tuizhi furen zizhuan* (The autobiography of a wife who quit). Shanghai: Shanghai shudian, 1989.

Peng Xiaoyan. *Chaoyue Xieshi* (Beyond realism). Taibei: Lianjing, 1993.

Pratt, Mary Louise. *Imperial Eyes: Travel Writing and Transculturation*. New York: Routledge, 1992.

Qi Zhiheng. "Biaoxian juyi yu Zhongguo wusi xin wenxue" (Expressionism and the new literature of the Chinese May Fourth period). *Zhongguo xiandaidangdai wenxue yanjiu* 7 (1991): 13–19.

Qian Xuantong. "To Chen Duxiu (1917)." In *Wenxue yundongshiliao xuan* (Selections from the documents of the literary movement), vol. 1. Shanghai: Shanghai jiaoyu, 1982.

Qiao Yigang. "Chen Hengzhe jiqi Chuangzuo" (The writings of Chen Hengzhe). *Nankai xuebao* 3, no. 33 (1993): 33–38.

———. "Chen Hengzhe jiqi chuangzuo: Lun Zhongguo xiandai wentan di yi wei nu zuojia" (Chen Hengzhe and her writings: On the first women writer of the Chinese modern literary scene). *Zhongguo xiandai dangdai wenxue yanjiu* 3 (1993): 196–201.

Ricoeur, Paul. *Interpretation Theory: Discourse and the Surplus of Meaning*. Fort Worth: Texas Christian University Press, 1976.

Rolston, David, ed. *How to Read the Chinese Novel*. Princeton: Princeton University Press, 1990.

Rosaldo, Renato. *Culture and Truth: The Remaking of Social Analysis*. Boston: Beacon Press, 1989.

Said, Edward. *Beginnings*. New York: Columbia University Press, 1985.
———. *Culture and Imperialism*. New York: Vintage, 1994.
———. *Orientalism*. New York: Vintage, 1979.
———. *The World, the Text, and the Critic*. Cambridge: Harvard University Press, 1983.
Schwartz, Vera. *The Chinese Enlightenment: Intellectuals and the Legacy of the May Fourth Movement of 1919*. Berkeley and Los Angeles: University of California Press, 1986.
Shapiro, Stephen A. "The Dark Continent of Literature: Autobiography." *Comparative Literary Studies* 5 (1968): 421–54.
Shen Congwen. *Congwen zizhuan* (The autobiographies of Shen Congwen). Zhongghuo Mingjia Series. Taibei: Fuxin Chubanshe, 1978.
———. "Lun Zhongguo chuangzuo xiaoshuo" (On Chinese creative fiction). In *Shen Congwen wenji* (Writings of Shen Congwen), vol. 1. Hong Kong: Sanlian shudian, 1983.
———. *Shen Congwen wenji*. 12 vols. Hong Kong: Sanlian shudian, 1983.
———. *Shen Congwen xiaoshuo xuan* (Selected stories of Shen Congwen). Ed. Ling Yu. Beijing: Renmin wenxue chubanshe, 1982.
———. *Xiangxing sanji* (Random records of the travels to west Hunan). Beijing: Kaiming Chubanshe, 1992.
Shi Pingmei. *Shi Pingmei Zuopinji (Xiju, youji, shuxin)* (Collected works of Shi Pingmei [drama, travelogue, and letters]). Beijing: Shumuwenxian chubanshe, 1985.
Shih, Shu-mei. *The Lure of the Modern: Writing Modernism in Semicolonial China, 1917–1937*. Berkeley and Los Angeles: University of California Press, 2001.
Shui Jing. *Zhang Ailing de Xiaoshuo yishu*. Taibei: Dadi chubanshe, 1973.
Sima Qian. *Shiji* (The records of the great historian). Taibei: Tiangong shuju.
Smith, Sidonie. *Poetics of Women's Autobiography*. Bloomington: Indiana University Press, 1989.
Sontag, Susan. "In Plato's Cave." In *On Photography*. New York: Farrar, Straus and Giroux, 1985.
Spengeman, William. *The Forms of Autobiography: Episodes in the History of a Literary Genre*. New Haven: Yale University Press, 1980.
Spivak, Gayatri Chakravorty. *The Postcolonial Critic: Interviews, Strategies, Dialogues*. Ed. Sarah Harasym. New York: Routledge, 1990.
Strassburg, Richard. *Inscribed Landscape: Travel Writings from Imperial China*. Berkeley and Los Angeles: University of California Press, 1994.
Sturrock, John. "The New Model Autobiography." *New Literary History* 9 (1977): 57–63.
Su Qing. *Huanjinji* (The washing brocade collection). Shanghai: Tiandi tushu, 1944.

———. *Jiehun shinian* (Ten years of marriage). Shanghai: Shanghai shudian, 1989.
———. *Su Qing Sanwen jingpian* (The best essays of Su Qing). Ed. Zhang Deqiang. Zhejiang: Zhejiang wenyi, 1985.
Su Xuelin. *Ersanshinian dai de zuojia yu zuopin* (The writers of the twenties and thirties and their works). Tabei: Guanglai, 1979.
Tan Shicun. "Lun cangzao she yu biaoxianjuyi" (On the Creation Society and expressionism). *Zhongguo xiandai wenxue piping congkan* 2 (1991): 152–66.
Tao Qian. "Tao Huan Yuanji" (Peach Blossom Spring). In *Weijin nambeichao jujia sanwenxuan* (The selected prose of various writers of the six dynasties), ed. Wei Fengjuan. Hong Kong: Sanlian, 1988.
———. "Wuliao xiansheng zhuan" (Master Five Willows). In *Weijin nambeichao jujia sanwenxuan* (The selected prose of various writers of the six dynasties), ed. Wei Fengjuan. Hong Kong: Sanlian, 1988.
Todorov, Tzvetan. *Genres in Discourse*. Cambridge University Press, 1990.
Waley, Arthur, trans. *The Analects of Confucius*. New York: Vintage, 1989.
Wang Chefu. *Zhongguo xinwensue yundong shi* (1933). Reprint, Shanghai: Shanghai Shudian, 1986.
Wang, David Der-wei. *Fictional Realism in Twentieth-Century China: Mao Dun, Lao She, Shen Congwen*. New York: Columbia University Press, 1992.
———. *Zhongsheng xuanhua* (Caccophony). Taibei: Yuanliu Chubanshe, 1988.
Wang Jinyuan. *Wusi wenxue yu waiguo wenxue* (May Fourth literature and foreign literatures). Chengdu: Sichuan Daxue, 1989.
Wei Fengjuan, ed. *Weijin nanbeichao zhujia sanwenxuan* (Selection of essays from the various writers of the six dynasties). Hong Kong: Sanlian, 1991.
Wenxue yundongshiliao xuan (Selections from the documents of the literary movement). 4 vols. Shanghai: Shanghai jiaoyu, 1982.
Wiens, Harold. *China's March towards the Tropics*. Hamden, Conn.: Shoe String Press, 1954.
Wolfe, Alan. *Suicidal Narrative in Modern Japan: The Case of Dasai Osamu*. Princeton: Princeton University Press, 1990.
Woolf, Virginia. *A Room of One's Own*. New York: Harcourt, Brace and World, 1957.
Wu Pei-yi. *The Confucian's Progress: Autobiographical Writings in Traditional China*. Princeton: Princeton University Press, 1990.
———. "Self-Examination and Confession of Sins in Traditional China." *Harvard Journal of Asian Studies (HJAS)* 39, no. 1 (1979): 5–38.
Wu Woyao. "Liang Jin Yanyi zixu" (Preface to the *Romance of the Two Jin Dynasties*). In *Zhongguo lidai Wenlunxuan* (Essays on Chinese literature through the ages), ed. Guo Shaoyu, vol. 4. Shanghai: Shanghai guji, 1980.
———. "Yueyue xiaoshuo xu" (Preface to *Fiction Monthly*). In *Zhongguo*

lidai Wenlunxuan (Essays on Chinese literature through the ages), ed. Guo Shaoyu, vol. 4. Shanghai: Shanghai guji, 1980.

Xiao Hong. *Market Street*. Trans. Howard Goldblatt. Seattle: University of Washington Press, 1986.

———. *Shangshi jie* (Market Street). Taipei: Linbai Chubanshe, 1987.

———. *The Field of Life and Death* and *Tales of Hulan River*. Trans. Howard Goldblatt and Ellen Yeung. Bloomington: Indiana University Press, 1979.

———. *Sheng si chang* (The field of life and death). Shanghai: Xinwenyi chubanshe, 1935.

———. "Yongjiu de tongjing he zhuiqiu" (Eternal dreams and pursuits). In *Zhongguo nu zuojia sanwen xuancui* (Selected essays of Chinese women writers), ed. You Kang. Fujian: Haixia wenyi, 1994.

Xie Bingying. *Nübing zizhuan*. Beijing: Zhongguo huaqiao, 1994.

Yang Yi. *Qinuzi Zhang Ailing* (The extraordinary woman Eileen Chang). Hong Kong: Binma, 1984.

Yen Min. "Shishi wusi wentan jeishuo Nicai xueshuo de yuanyin" (An attempt to analyze the acceptance of Nietzsche's thoughts by the May Fourth literary coterie). *Zhongguo xiandai dangdai wenxue yanjiu* 7 (1991): 7–10.

You Kang, ed. *Zhongguo nu zuojia sanwen xuancui* (Selected essays of Chinese women writers). Fujian: Haixia wenyi, 1994.

You Lian, ed. *The Best Short Pieces from Chinese Women Writers*. Fujian: Haixia, 1994.

Yu Dafu. *Yu Dafu Chuanji* (The complete works of Yu Dafu). 4 vols. Shanghai: Beixin shuju, 1930.

———. "Guanyu xiaoshuo de hua" (About fiction). In *Yu Dafu chuanji* (The complete works of Yu Dafu), vol. 3 (Shanghai: Beixin shuju, 1930).

———. *Yu Dafu zuopin xuan* (Selected works of Yu Dafu). Hong Kong: Sanbianshe, 1989.

———. *Riji jiuzhong* (The Nine Diaries). In *Yu Dafu rijiji* (Collected diaries of Yu Dafu). Shanxi: Renmin Chubanshe, 1984.

———. *Dafu Zizhuan* (Autobiography of Yu Dafu). In *Yu Dafu rijiji* (Collected diaries of Yu Dafu). Shanxi: Renmin Chubanshe, 1984.

———. "*Riji wenxue* (Diary literature)." In *Yu Dafu Wenji* (Essays of Yu Dafu), vol. 7. Hong Kong: Sanlian shudian, 1982.

———. "*Zaitan riji* (More about diaries)." In *Yu Dafu Wenji* (Essays of Yu Dafu), vol. 7. Hong Kong: Sanlian shudian, 1982.

Yu, Pauline. *The Reading of Imagery in the Chinese Poetic Tradition*. Princeton: Princeton University Press, 1987.

Yuan Changying. "Lun nuzi liuxue de biyao" (On the necessity of women's studying abroad). In *Yuan Changying sanwenji* (The essays of Yuan Changying). Tianjin: Baihuawenyi, 1991.

Zhang, Jingyuan. *Psychoanalysis in China: Literary Transformations, 1919–1949*. Cornell East Asia Series. Ithaca: Cornell University Press, 1992.

Zhao Jiabi, ed. *Zhongguo xin wenxue daxi* (Great compendium of new Chinese literature). 10 vols. Hong Kong: Xianggang wenxue yanjiushe, 1962.
Zhao Xiaqiu and Zheng Qingrui. *Zhongguo xiandai xiaoshuo shi* (History of modern Chinese fiction. Beijing: Zhongguo renmin, 1984.
Zheng Boqi. General introduction to *Zhongguo xin wenxue daxi* (Great compendium of new Chinese literature), ed. Zhao Jiabi, vol. 5. Hong Kong: Xianggang wenxue yanjiushe, 1962.
Zhong Jingwen. "Tan Zhaohua xishi" (On *Morning Blossoms Picked at Dusk*). In *Guanyu Lu Xun, Lunkao yu huixiang* (On Lu Xun's essays and reminiscences). Shaanxi: Renmin Chubanshe, 1982.
Zhou Zuoren. "Rende wenxue" (On humane literature). In *Wenxue yundong shiliaoxuan* (Documents of the literary movement), vol. 1. Shanghai: Shanghai jiaoyu, 1982.
Zhu Defa. *Ershishiji zhongguo wenxue liupai lungang* (A general outline of literary schools in twentieth-century Chinese literature). Shandong: Shandong jiaoyu, 1992.
Zhu Xiaojin. "Sanshi niandai xiangtu xiaoshuo de wenhua yiwen" (The cultural implication of native-soil fiction in the 1930s.) Reprinted in *Zhongguo xiandai dangdai wenxue yanjiu* 10 (1994): 66–80.

Index

"About Fiction" (Yu Dafu), 163n. 24
"After Victory" (Lu Yin), 35
Ancient Melodies (Ling Shuhua), 46–47, 158n. 35, 159n. 19
Anderson, Marston, 27–28, 155n. 5, 157nn. 19, 22, 168nn. 43, 44, 47, 173n. 48
The Art of Eileen Chang's Fiction (Shui Jing), 66, 161n. 55
"The Autobiographical Contract" (Philippe Lejeune), 10, 11, 72, 91–92, 99, 153nn. 30, 32, 161n. 8, 163nn. 1, 2, 4, 165–66n. 20
Autobiography at Thirty (Liang Qichao), 164n. 11
Autobiography of a Woman Soldier (Xie Bingying), 54–57, 61, 94, 102, 149, 160nn. 34–36
Autobiography of Shen Congwen (Shen Congwen), 18, 36, 119–50, 158n. 32, 169n. 1, 170nn. 18–20, 171nn. 22, 26–28, 172nn. 35, 39, 40, 173nn. 44, 45, 49
Azim, Firdous, 26, 154n. 41, 156nn. 12, 14

Bai Wei, 35, 148, 158n. 29
Ba Jin, 43, 148
Bao Ziyan, 167n. 34
Barlow, Tani, 44, 155n. 3, 159n. 9
Barthes, Roland, 38, 157n. 15; *textum*, 71, 105, 161nn. 7–8
Beijing school (*jingpai*), 127, 132, 133
Berger, John, 47, 159n. 23
Bersani, Leo, 167–68n. 42
Biography of Lofty Recluses (Huang Fumi), 6
"Biography of Master Five Willows" (Tao Qian), 6, 102, 152n. 21
Bizarre Happenings Eyewitnessed in Two Decades (Wu Woyao), 32
"Blood and Tears" (Yu Dafu), 83

"Bo-er" (Chen Hengzhe), 36
Book of Songs, "Great Preface," 157n. 22
Book of Twenty-four Filial Pieties, 105, 107
"A Brief Discussion of Fiction" (Liang Qichao), 27
Brooks, Peter, 16, 75, 76–77, 162nn. 14–17
Butler, Judith, 11–12, 153nn. 35, 36

Cai Yuanpei, 95, 99
Call to Arms (Lu Xun), 109
"The Canal and the Yangzi River" (Chen Hengzhe), 36–37
Cao Ming, 62
Ceng Qingrui, 25
Chandler, James, 151n. 5
Chang, Eileen, 9, 41–67, 92–93, 107, 150, 158n. 35; "A Child's Words are without Inhibition," 60–61, 65, 160nn. 43, 46, 48; *Flow of Words*, 65, 92, 169nn. 39, 43, 44, 49; "Intimate Words," 59–60, 65, 160nn. 30, 38; "Jasmine Tea," 45; "Love in a Fallen City," 57–58; "One should also rectify one's name," 164nn. 5–7; "Poetry and Nonsense," 64; "Records of Changing Clothes," 61; *The Short Stories of Eileen Chang*, 159nn. 12, 13, 160nn. 29, 37; "Withering Flower," 45
Chang Tai-Hung, 170nn. 12, 13
Chen Duxiu, 54, 95, 99, 160n. 33
Chen Hengzhe, 21–39, 73–75; "Bo-er," 36; "The Canal and the Yangzi River," 36; "The Dilemma of Louise," 36; *A Little Raindrop*, 36; "A Little Raindrop," 36, 157n. 27; "One Day," 2, 9, 21–39; "Westerly Wind," 36; "The Woman in the Wu Gorges," 36

INDEX

Chen Pingyuan, 7, 36, 152n. 24, 156n. 6, 157n. 25, 158n. 31
"A Child's Words are without Inhibition" (Eileen Chang), 60–61, 65, 160nn. 43, 46, 48
Chow, Rey, 43, 48, 153n. 33, 155n. 3, 159n. 5, 160nn. 26, 28, 161n. 53, 170–71n. 21
Chronological Biography of Zhang Xuecheng (Hu Shi), 100, 152n. 17, 166n. 23
Circumstantial autobiography, 6, 102, 106, 117
Classic of Mountains and Oceans, 107
Clifford, James, 170n. 14
Confucianism, 116–17
Crary, Jonathan, 27, 157n. 16, 171n. 21
Creation Society, Creationists, 14–15, 21, 69, 72, 81–82

Dafu's Autobiography (Yu Dafu), 71, 84–86, 89, 163n. 31, 166n. 32
La Dame Aux Camélias (Dumas *fils*, translation by Lin Shu), 7
David, Deirdre, 133, 172n. 34
Dawo, xiaowo (great "I" and small "I"), 82
De Certeau, Michel, 152n. 14
De Lauretis, Teresa, 26, 47, 50, 59, 156n. 13, 159nn. 14, 24, 25, 160n. 27
De Man, Paul, 11, 100, 153nn. 31, 34, 166n. 22
Deng Zhongxia, 122
Denton, Kirk, 70, 88, 161n. 6, 163n. 39
"Diary as Literature" (Yu Dafu), 8, 161n. 6, 163n. 27
"The Dilemma of Louise" (Chen Hengzhe), 36
Ding Ling, *Diary of Miss Sophie*, 43, 62
Dooling, Amy, 156n. 7, 158n. 30
Duara, Prasenjit, 170n. 12
Dumas *fils*, *La Dame Aux Camélias*, 7
Durrant, Stephen, 5, 152nn. 11, 12, 16

Egan, Michael, 70, 78, 161nn. 3, 5
Encountering Sorrow (Qu Yuan, 55–67), 5
"An Evening in the Intoxicating Spring Breeze" (Yu Dafu), 80
Evolution and Ethics (T. X. Huxley), 97
The Extraordinary Woman Eileen Chang (Yang Yi), 66, 160n. 40

Feng Yuanjun, "Separation," 35
Field of Life and Death (Xiao Hong), 94, 164n. 9
Finney, Brian, 47, 159nn. 16, 22
Flow of Words (Eileen Chang), 65, 92, 169nn. 39, 43, 44, 49
Freud, Sigmund, 22
Fujii, James, 72, 153n. 38, 162n. 10, 163n. 28
Fu Sinian, "How to Write in the Vernacular?" 30–31, 157n. 22
"The future of women" (Lu Yin), 158n. 3

Generalities on History (Liu Zhiji), 5
Going to the People movement, 122
Great "I" and small "I" (*dawo, xiaowo*), 82, 96, 106
Grieder, Jerome, 165n. 17
Gu Jeigang, 122
Gunn, Janet Varner, 163–64n. 3
Guo Moro, 13, 69, 148, 163n. 23, 172n. 38; *My Childhood*, 82

Haddon, Rosemary, 121, 133, 135, 169n. 6, 171n. 25
Heilbrun, Carolyn, 60, 157n. 15
Hong Xiling, 95, 99
Howard, Richard, 100, 165n. 13, 166n. 24
"How to Write in the Vernacular?" (Fu Sinian), 30–31, 157n. 22
Hsia, C. T., 161n. 4, 167n. 38
Hsia, T. A., 167n. 40

Huang Fumi, *Biography of Lofty Recluses*, 6
Hu Shi, 4, 18, 19, 21, 31, 104, 106, 117–18, 164nn. 11–12, 16, 18; *Chronological Biography of Zhang Xuecheng*, 100, 152n. 17, 166n. 23; "On Constructive Literary Revolution," 30; "Preliminary Proposal for the Reform of Literature," 2, 29–30, 168n. 53; *Self-Narration at Forty*, 5, 9, 12, 91–118, 151n. 8, 152n. 18, 164n. 10, 165nn. 16, 18, 166nn. 25–28; "What is a short story?" 168n. 57
Huters, Theodore, 66, 154n. 47, 160n. 52
Huxley, T. X., *Evolution and Ethics*, 97

Impressionistic autobiography, 6, 102, 166n. 31
Individualism, 69–70, 71
I-novels, 22, 72
"In the Wine Shop" (Lu Xun), 108, 110
"Intimate Words" (Eileen Chang), 59–60, 65, 160nn. 30, 38
Ivory Rings (Lu Yin), 35

Jameson, Frederic, 4, 151n. 5
"Jasmine Tea" (Eileen Chang), 45
Jenks, Robert Darrah, 169n. 5, 170nn. 17, 18
Jensen, Lionel, 161n. 6
Ji Ji, 161n. 54
"Jinhou funu de chulu" (The future of women) (Lu Yin), 158n. 3

Kang Yongqiu, 25
Kang Yuwei, 42
Kellner, Hans, 136–37, 172n. 41
Kinkley, Jeffrey, 153n. 29, 171n. 32
Kurrik, Maire, 113, 168n. 51

Labelle, Jenni Joy, 47, 159n. 21

Larson, Wendy, 16, 44, 153n. 29, 166nn. 29, 30, 172n. 36; circumstantial autobiography, 6, 102, 152n. 22, 159n. 8; impressionistic autobiography, 6, 166n. 31
Layoun, Mary, 14, 153n. 39, 154n. 42
Lee, Leo Ou-fan, 121, 127, 153n. 29, 155n. 4, 157n. 26, 169nn. 2, 5, 171n. 30
Lejeune, Philippe, 19, 72; "The Autobiographical Contract," 10, 11, 72, 91–92, 99, 153nn. 30, 32, 161n. 8, 163nn. 1, 2, 4, 165–66n. 20
"Letter to Ren An" (Sima Qian), 4
Liang Qichao, 23, 25–27, 29, 34, 38, 42, 95–96, 156n. 6, 164n. 11; *Autobiography at Thirty*, 164n. 11; "A Brief Discussion of Fiction," 27; *New People's Miscellany*, 97; "The Relationship between Fiction and the Governing of the Masses," 25, 156n. 9; *Supplement to Methods of Study*, 165nn. 12–14
Ling Shuhua, *Ancient Melodies*, 46–47, 158n. 35, 159n. 19
Lin Shu (1852–1924), translation of *La Dame Aux Camélias*, 7
"Lipsticks and Fountain Pens," 61
A Little Raindrop (Chen Hengzhe), 36
"A Little Raindrop" (Chen Hengzhe), 36, 157n. 27
Liu, Lydia: "The Female Body and Nationalist Discourse," 43, 65, 87, 154n. 48, 158n. 1, 159n. 7, 160n. 51, 163n. 37; "Translingual Practice," 15–16, 154nn. 42, 44, 45, 165n. 15, 166n. 21
Liu Zhiji (661–721), *Generalities on History*, 5
"Love in a Fallen City" (Eileen Chang), 57–58
Lu Jingqing, 35; circle of friends with Lu Yin and Shi Pingmei, 157–58n. 28
Lukács, Georg, 1, 151nn. 2–4

Lu Xun, 9, 18, 64, 94, 102, 121, 140, 141; *Call to Arms,* 109; "In the Wine Shop," 108, 110; "The Madman's Diary," 2, 21, 32, 160n. 50, 173n. 47; *Morning Blossoms Picked at Dusk,* 103–18, 166n. 33, 167nn. 34, 39, 168nn. 48–50, 52, 54–56; "My Old Home," 110; "The New Year's Sacrifice," 110; *Selected Short Stories,* 168n. 45; "Some Conjectures about Theatrical Masks," 52–54, 160n. 31; *Story of Ah Q,* 168n. 47

Lu Yin, 13, 43, 62, 110, 148, 155n. 3; "After Victory," 35; circle of friends with Lu Jingqing and Shi Pingmei, 35, 157–58n. 28; "The future of women,"158n. 3; *Ivory Rings,* 35

"The Madman's Diary" (Lu Xun), 2, 21, 32, 160n. 50, 173n. 47
Mao Dun, 4, 43, 151n. 7, 155n. 3
Market Street (Xiao Hong), 50, 94
May, Georges, 109, 167n. 41, 173n. 43
May Fourth, viii, x, 3, 4, 9, 17, 21, 23, 25–29, 33, 41, 54, 69, 116, 145
May Fourth Incident of 1919, 2, 3, 7–8
McDougall, Bonnie, 155n. 4
Miaofang beilan (A manual for the defense against the Miao), 124
Miller, Nancy, 26, 28, 44, 156n. 13, 159nn. 10, 11
"More about Diaries" (Yu Dafu), 163n. 25
Moretti, Franco, 1, 2, 120, 169n. 4
Morning Blossoms Picked at Dusk (Lu Xun), 103–18, 166n. 33, 167nn. 34, 39, 168nn. 48–50, 52, 54–56
Mulvey, Laura, 46
"My Old Home" (Lu Xun), 110
"My Own Room" (Su Qing), 63–64, 65

Native-soil literature, 119–44
New Fiction, 25
New People's Miscellany (Liang Qichao), 97
"The New Year's Sacrifice" (Lu Xun), 110
New Youth Magazine, 2, 21, 32, 43, 54, 74, 95, 159n. 4
Ng, Janet, 158nn. 30, 35, 159nn. 18, 20
Nine Diaries (Yu Dafu), 71, 79–80, 152n. 26, 162n. 20, 163nn. 26, 33–36, 38, 42
Nivison, David, 151nn. 6, 9, 152nn. 13, 15, 160n. 45

Old Testament, 113
Olney, James, 5, 152n. 14
"On Constructive Literary Revolution" (Hu Shi), 30
"One Day" (Chen Hengzhe), 2, 9, 21–39
"One should also rectify one's name" (Eileen Chang), 164nn. 5–7
"On Humane Literature" (Zhou Zuoren), 42, 74, 122, 158n. 2, 161n. 12
Onomatology/onomastic power, 92, 99–100
Owen, Stephen, 152n. 19, 153n. 27

Pan Liudai, 61
"Peach Blossom Spring" (Tao Qian), 36, 130, 139, 143
Peng Xiaoyan, 121–22, 127, 133, 169n. 2, 170n. 9
"Poetry and Nonsense" (Eileen Chang), 64
Pratt, Mary Louise, 26, 28, 120, 156n. 12, 169n. 3
"Preliminary Proposal for the Reform of Literature" (Hu Shi), 2, 29–30, 168n. 53
Psychological fiction, 69, 74
Pygmalion, 46, 59, 62

Qian Xuantong, description of traditional opera, 54, 160n. 32
Qiao Yigang, 154n. 1

Quanbu (whole), *jubu* (part), 95

Random Sketches on Travels to Western Hunan (Shen Congwen), 18, 36, 119–50, 158n. 32, 169n. 1, 170nn. 18–20, 171nn. 22, 26–28, 172nn. 35, 39, 40, 173nn. 44, 45, 49
"Records of Changing Clothes" (Eileen Chang), 61
Records of the Historian (Sima Qian, 145–85 B.C.), 4
"The Relationship between Fiction and Governing of the Masses" (Liang Qichao), 25, 156n. 9
"Returning Home" (Yu Dafu), 78–79, 161n. 13
Ricoeur, Paul, 167n. 35
Romanticism, ix, 10, 13, 22, 69, 145
"A Room of One's Own" (Virginia Woolf), 63, 159n. 17
Rosaldo, Renato, "Imperialistic Nostalgia," 123, 170n. 15

Said, Edward, 105–6, 120, 127, 154n. 46, 167n. 36, 168n. 58, 169n. 3, 171nn. 23, 29, 173n. 50
Selected Short Stories (Lu Xun), 168n. 45
Selected Works (Yu Dafu), 162nn. 19, 21
Self-Narration at Forty (Hu Shi), 5, 9, 12, 91–118, 151n. 8, 152n. 18, 164n. 10, 165nn. 16, 18, 166nn. 25–28
"Separation" (Feng Yuanjun), 35
Shapiro, Stephen, 1, 151n. 1
Shen Congwen, *The Autobiography of Shen Congwen*, 18, 36, 119–50, 158n. 32, 169n. 1, 170nn. 18–20, 171nn. 22, 26–28, 172nn. 35, 39, 40, 173nn. 44, 45, 49; "On Chinese creative fiction," 163n. 30; *Random Sketches on Travels to Western Hunan*, 18, 36, 119–50, 158n. 32, 169n. 1, 170nn. 18–20, 171nn. 22, 26–28, 172nn. 35, 39, 40, 173nn. 44, 45, 49; *Writings of Shen Congwen*, 171n. 31; on Yu Dafu, 83, 150

Shi, Shu-mei, 152n. 25
Shi Pingmei, 35; circle of friends with Lu Yin and Lu Jingqing, 157–58n. 28
The Short Stories of Eileen Chang, 159nn. 12, 13, 160nn. 29, 37
Shui Jing, *The Art of Eileen Chang's Fiction*, 66, 161n. 55
Sima Qian: "Letter to Ren An," 4; *Records of the Historian*, 4, 151–52n. 10
"Sinking" (Yu Dafu), 79, 88
"Some Conjectures about Theatrical Masks" (Lu Xun), 52–54, 160n. 31
Sontag, Susan, 46, 65, 159n. 15
The Sorrowful History of the Snow Swan (Xu Chenya), 7
The Spirit of the Jade Pear (Xu Chenya), 7
Standard Histories, 4
Story of Ah Q (Lu Xun), 168n. 47
Strassburg, Richard, 169n. 5
Supplement to Methods of Study (Liang Qichao), 165nn. 12–14
Su Qing, 61, 64; "My Own Room," 63–64, 65

Tales of Hulan River (Xiao Hong), 94, 164n. 9
Tang Zhengxu, 155n. 4
Tao Qian: "Biography of Master Five Willows," 6, 102, 152n. 21; "Peach Blossom Spring," 36, 130, 139, 143
textum (Roland Barthes), 71, 105
Tian Han, 69
Torgeson, Kristina M., 156n. 7, 158n. 30

Wang, David Der-Wei, 16, 122, 136–37, 158n. 33, 172n. 37, 173n. 42
Wen Yiduo, 148
"Westerly Wind" (Chen Hengzhe), 36

"What is a short story?" (Hu Shi), 168n. 57
Wiens, Harold, 169n. 5
"Withering Flower" (Eileen Chang), 45
Wolfe, Alan, 13, 153–54n. 39
"The Woman in the Wu Gorges" (Chen Hengzhe), 36
Woolf, Virginia, 46; "A Room of One's Own," 63, 159n. 17
Writings of Shen Congwen (Shen Congwen), 171n. 31
Wu, Pei-yi, 6, 151n. 10, 152nn. 19–21
Wu Woyao, *Bizarre Happenings Eyewitnessed in Two Decades*, 32

Xiao Hong, 43–44, 61, 149, 164n. 9; *Field of Life and Death*, 94, 164n. 9; *Market Street*, 50, 94; *Tales of Hulan River*, 94, 164n. 9
Xie Bingying, *Autobiography of a Woman Soldier*, 54–57, 61, 94, 102, 149, 160nn. 34–36
Xu Chenya: *The Sorrowful History of the Snow Swan*, 7; *The Spirit of the Jade Pear*, 7
Xu Xiake, 121, 169n. 5

Yan Fu, translation of T. X. Huxley, 97
Yang Yi, *The Extraordinary Woman Eileen Chang*, 66, 160n. 40
Yan Min, 155n. 4
Ye Shaojun, 157n. 22
Yuan Changying, 43, 158–59n. 3
Yu Dafu, 12, 18, 69–90, 94, 102, 110, 120, 148–49, 163n. 32; "About Fiction," 163n. 24; "Blood and Tears," 83; *Dafu's Autobiography*, 71, 84–86, 89, 163n. 31, 166n. 32; "Diary as Literature," 8, 161n. 1, 163n. 27; "An Evening in the Intoxicating Spring Breeze," 80; "More about Diaries," 163n. 25; *Nine Diaries*, 71, 79–80, 152n. 26, 162n. 20, 163nn. 26, 33–36, 38, 42; "Returning Home," 78–79, 161n. 13; *Selected Works*, 162nn. 19, 21; "Sinking," 79, 88

Zhao Xiaqiu, 25, 153n. 37, 156n. 8, 161n. 9, 163n. 29
Zheng Boqi, 14–15, 69, 81, 154nn. 40, 43, 162n. 22
Zheng Qingrui, 25, 153n. 37, 156n. 8, 161n. 9, 163n. 29
Zheng Zhenduo, 157n. 22
Zhong Jingwen, 168n. 46
Zhou Zuoren, "On Humane Literature," 42, 74, 122, 158n. 2, 161n. 12
Zhu Defa, 156n. 6
Zhu Xi, 116
Zhu Xiaojin, 121–23, 128, 133, 135, 170nn. 7, 8, 11, 171–72nn. 25, 31
Zizhuan congshu (Series on autobiography), 167n. 37